1161-

D1134972

FOUR PLAYS

—

BERNARD KOPS

BERNARD KOPS

Four Plays

—

THE HAMLET OF STEPNEY GREEN

ENTER SOLLY GOLD

HOME SWEET HONEYCOMB

THE LEMMINGS

LONDON
MACGIBBON & KEE
MCMLXIV

First published in this edition 1964
by MacGibbon & Kee Limited
Copyright © Bernard Kops 1964
Printed in Great Britain by
Bristol Typesetting Co. Ltd.
Bristol

CONTENTS

For

ERICA

PREFACE

All my plays are concerned with family relationships. These are the themes that obsess me.

My first play, *The Hamlet of Stepney Green*, is about the dying Jewish community of the East End of London. It is a comedy yet it laments a world that has passed away. There are songs in the play and these are an integral part of it; no character steps forward out of the action. When I wrote this play in 1956 I was told that I had written it in the form of traditional Yiddish Theatre. These songs came about because I remembered how my mother would suddenly burst out singing. How when words or emotions got too much for her she expressed herself in song. In quite a few of my plays, songs are placed throughout the action; underlining or summing up a certain point. The play possibly tends to be too optimistic in tone, but I was seriously concerned with getting over the idea that one had to live while one was alive, that one had to affirm while one had breath, that every day was a holiday from the dark. In the words of Sam Levy " Life slipped through my fingers and as it was slipping, that was life."

If Sam Levy had been a bit shrewder and made more money he might have moved to Hampstead Garden Suburb where *Enter Solly Gold* is set. But living there wouldn't have made him any happier. In fact he would have been less happy there than in Stepney. For despite the affluence of the Swartz family there is no happiness. There is no feeling of community at all in this expensive suburb. They all live in their own private worlds. It is Solly Gold, a petty con-man who inadvertently changes their lives a little. *Enter Solly Gold* is a comedy touching upon a serious theme, concerned with the possibility of change.

Home Sweet Honeycomb and *The Lemmings* were written

A*

after having travelled to Eastern Europe. These are both pessimistic plays.

Home Sweet Honeycomb could be called a cautionary tale. It is also a play of possibility. It is an extension of a personal nightmare; about a world devoid of love and feeling. A world where people talk in slogans and get executed for trivial offences. Every flat has a firing squad and every person about to be shot accepts the inevitable with a shrug. The hero, Danny Todd, rejects the slogans and yearns for the destruction of this soulless world; he rejects the emotionless family and the zombie community. He is in love with the bomb. But he is caught up in the family he loathes, he is trapped by the horror of inevitable relationships and he is finally destroyed. But his destruction is not before the firing squad. He willingly capitulates, returns to the bosom of the family, trots out slogans, conforms with the community and joins the firing squad. All this after he shouted the loudest. In this play I wanted to get closer to the darker side of human nature, to try and understand it more fully.

The Lemmings goes one step further. It is the ultimate in pessimism; the ultimate in absurdity. The play begins where everyone is walking into the sea and ends when everyone has walked into the sea. The death wish of man has finally come out on top, has finally destroyed the dream, destroyed all possibility.

Instead of a dying community it has now become the dying of the human race. Perhaps my first play was too naïve, perhaps my last play is too pessimistic, it is I believe, in the two middle plays, in *Enter Solly Gold* and in *Home Sweet Honeycomb* that I have struck the correct balance; and it is somewhere between these two that I see the most possibility.

BERNARD KOPS, June 1964

The
Hamlet of Stepney Green

A SAD COMEDY WITH SOME SONGS

CHARACTERS OF THE PLAY

SAM LEVY: 65, *small and agile, a pickled-herring seller of Wentworth Street*

BESSIE LEVY: 52, *his wife. Plump and wears cheap jewellery*

DAVID LEVY: 22, *their son; tall and intelligent. Wants to be a singer*

SOLLY SEGAL: 60, *retired. A friend of the family*

HAVA SEGAL: 18, *beautiful, and sure of herself. Has just returned from Israel*

MR STONE: *Fat and jovial; foolish and about fifty years old*

MRS STONE: *Fat and foolish; jovial and about fifty years old*

MR WHITE: *About 32, looks older. Insurance agent, over-positive and smug*

MR BLACK: 27, *well dressed. A tombstone salesman. Small and thin*

MR GREEN: 27, *well dressed. A tombstone salesman. Small and fat*

THREE CHILDREN

The action of the play is centred around the house of MR *and*
MRS LEVY
Time: *The present.*
Place: *Stepney Green in the East End of London.*

*The setting is constant throughout and the stage is in two
sections; one half is part of the house, showing a cross section
of the living-room and the corridor. The living-room has the
various pieces of furniture that one would expect in a Jewish
lower middle-class family, not too much bad taste is apparent;
the furnishing should be sparse and straightforward.*
The other half should be the garden of the LEVYS. *There are
flowers in rich profusion but this garden is surrounded by a
great area of bomb damage; it gives the hint of almost being
an oasis; there is a fence around the garden, and a gate leading
off L: there should be a certain warmth about the set, as if
Van Gogh and Chagall had collaborated on this urban scene.
Curtain goes up revealing an empty stage. It is a very hot July
afternoon; nearby some* CHILDREN *are heard skipping and
singing:*

CHILDREN [*off*] : On the hill there stands a lady, who she
is I do not know; all she wants is gold and silver, all she
wants is a fine young man.
[*A ball comes over the fence and the* CHILDREN *run
on stage after it; they explore the garden and sniff the
flowers and then they begin to sing again.*]
On the hill there stands a lady, who she is I do not know—
[*They are dancing round in a ring when they are inter-
rupted by* HAVA *who comes into the garden from the
house.*]
HAVA: Here, go on and buy some ice cream; play in the park.
[*She hands one of the children a sixpence; they just stare at*

her.] Please run away and play; Mr Levy isn't feeling too
well.

[*The* CHILDREN *run off and sing as they exit.*]

CHILDREN: All she wants is gold and silver, all she wants
is a fine young man.

[*They exit.*]

HAVA: Don't we all. [*She sits down and reads a woman's
magazine.*]

BESSIE [*off*]: I said no! ... N ... O ... NO, no, no, NO.

SAM [*off*]: I tell you yes: YE-YES. All my life I worked
in the open air and you bet your life, I'm going to die
there ...

Come on, Mr Segal, push me into the garden.

BESSIE [*off*]: All right, I should worry! It's your funeral!

SAM [*off*]: You said it.

[*A small man is seen trying to push a bed into the garden
from the back room;* HAVA *immediately gets up and
helps her father, and both of them manage to push the
bed into the centre of the garden;* MR SEGAL *is immacu-
lately dressed and smokes a cigar.*]

MR SEGAL: Is this spot all right? Just here, Sam?

[*A frail old man levers himself up from his lying position
in the bed; it is* SAM *and he wears pyjamas; he looks
around.*]

SAM: This'll do fine. Just here. Thank you, Mr Segal. What
a lovely day! What a lovely daughter you have! She's a
credit to you; what's the matter, Hava? Why did you come
back home? Didn't you like it out in Israel?

HAVA: It wasn't bad, but I was lonely; the life was different
out there. I couldn't seem to settle down. England's where
I belong. At least I've learned that much.

SAM: Still, you're looking very well. I was telling my Davey
to go there; he wouldn't listen.

HAVA: I am looking forward to meeting David again. How
is he, Mr Levy?

MR SEGAL: A lot of good that boy will be to you, anywhere
in the world. Excuse me, Sam, but you must agree; he's
good for nothing.

SAM: There I disagree with you, Mr Segal, he'll find his

feet; he's going through a difficult phase, he's not so bad.

MR SEGAL: He's been going through this difficult phase for fifteen years; it's about time he settled down; it's your fault, you're not strict enough.

HAVA: I think David is a lovely boy; he's got such a wonderful voice, he'll go a long way.

MR SEGAL: The longer the way, the better. What a voice! Sam, she drives me mad talking about him. It wouldn't have been such a bad idea for your son and my daughter to—well—if he had a nice job with prospects, but a singer? Hava, you've got a screw loose.

SAM: Hava, do you like my boy? Do you? Maybe you can help him. Help him to see sense; persuade him to give up his crazy ideas; does he like you?

HAVA: Like me? He never even sees me. He looks straight through me. The other day I passed him by near Brick Lane; he was just staring at the sky: I said 'Hello, Davey'. He didn't even bother to look my way! Oh well, what can you do?

SAM: It isn't natural. He's ambitious. I said: 'Look, Davey, all right I'll help you; go and study music, learn all about notes', but he refused.

HAVA: He's got a wonderful voice. He was always such a gentle boy.

SAM: If that is a wonderful voice then I'm Gregory Peck.

HAVA: He's got a lovely voice. He'll go a long way. You'll see.

SAM: What did you miss out there?

HAVA: I missed the cinemas and the dance halls; all my friends. I missed my own room and my own bed. I was homesick.

SAM: Are you going back?

HAVA: No. I don't think so; it's unwise to go back. I'm not fooling myself. I'm no pioneer.

SAM: I suppose you're right; anyway, everything turns out for the best. You'll meet a nice respectable boy, you'll settle down, get a nice flat and you'll get everything you want and deserve. You're attractive, you'll have no trouble.

HAVA: I hope so. Where's Davey now?

SAM: How should I know? Who knows where that boy is, even when he's here?

MR SEGAL: Forget about him! Do you know, Sam, she drives me mad, all day she's talking about him! What's he got, I wonder? What's he got that others ain't?

SAM: By the way it sounds, it seems he has a wonderful voice. What can you do with them?

HAVA: Here you go again! The younger generation! Good-bye, Daddy. [*She kisses* MR SEGAL.] I promised Miriam that I'd go over this afternoon. Don't come home too late. Good-bye, Mr. Levy, take care of yourself. [*They shake hands.*] Good-bye. [*She exits.*]

SAM: What a nice girl! Do you know, Mr Segal, that for many years I thought about today. I wondered what it would be like when I died; I wondered what the weather would be like and if I would be nervous. It's funny, for years I've worried that I wouldn't have the chance to die naturally. I thought that it would be the A-Bomb or the H-Bomb or the Z-Bomb or bacteria, rockets, or gas, yet here I am on a fine summer's day going to die quietly in my garden; why, I never even retired, never even moved to Golders Green.

MR SEGAL: I know what you mean. Mr Miller was killed the other day by a van; he was worried about the world situation and was reading a newspaper as he crossed the road; you remember Mr Miller?

SAM: Not off-hand.

[*The* CHILDREN *have returned to the outside of the garden again; once more they start singing.*]

CHILDREN [*singing off*]: Julius Caesar, such a silly geezer, caught his head in a lemon squeezer.

MR SEGAL: I'll go and stop that noise; they should be ashamed of themselves. I tell you, Sam, the children of today—

[*He is about to go when* SAM *catches hold of his sleeve.*]

SAM: No, no, Mr Segal, let them sing; let them sing. Let everybody sing. Music makes the world go round. Mr Segal, you should never stop a child from singing. You should be ashamed of yourself, a man of your age. Tomorrow I'd give my right arm for the slightest sound from the tiniest throat.

MR SEGAL: What do you mean, Sam? You talk in riddles.

SAM: I mean that I shan't be here tomorrow. I won't have a right arm to give away. [*He is looking at his right arm and is shaking it.*] It's all over, Mr Segal. Life slipped through my fingers and as it was slipping, that was life.

MR SEGAL: Of course. What do you mean?

SAM: I mean, life was no other time, no other place; it is here and now and gone. I came in at Odessa sixty-five years ago and today I'm going to die in Stepney Green, that's what I mean.

MR SEGAL: Don't be silly, Sam. You're not going to die, you're a bit delirious. If I died every time I thought like that I would have had forty or fifty coffins. Don't talk silly, you make me feel miserable.

SAM: I'm sorry. No, this is it, believe me. I've got more than a cold, I can tell you. I've been frightened recently; I've lain awake nearly all night and broke out into a terrible cold sweat when I realized that I was getting older and older and that I was getting nearer and nearer to—nothing! You can't run away from death, Mr Segal, there's no escaping it, it catches you in the end; my end is here and now, and now I'm resigned to it.

MR SEGAL: You've got a very vivid imagination, Sam; that's always been your trouble; now I know who your David takes after.

SAM: He takes after my grandfather's brother, according to what I heard about him, Manny Levy, got in with a bad crowd; but had a heart of gold. He ran away with an actress and everyone talked about it. [*pause*] Mr Segal, now I realize that I never lived; all my life I've been asleep. Been dead! My physical death will prove for ever that there was never anyone called Samuel Levy, pickled herring seller of Wentworth Street; two children and a widow; you'll read all about it in the *Jewish Chronicle* next week; they'll make up a little rhyme and then someone will come and sell my wife a stone.

MR SEGAL: Sam, what's come over you? You make me sad talking like this.

SAM: Don't upset yourself on my account. It hasn't been a bad life. Have the boys missed me in the market? Have any of them asked after me?

MR SEGAL: Yes. Moishe Newman told me to remind you that you still owe him thirty shillings.

SAM: Yes, I remember, for the chickens; tell Bessie, would you? She'll take care of everything. Thank God I've got myself insured, tomorrow she's got two hundred and fifty pounds coming to her.

MR SEGAL: Such money she can do without. What is going to matter if you die, anyway? Don't make me laugh; you're not going to die.

SAM: We're all going to die; you don't have to be a prophet to know that. I'm worried about my herring stall. I shall have to talk to Davey and make him see sense; he's got to get rid of these bright ideas; he's no longer a kid.

MR SEGAL: Why don't you try to rest now, Sam? Try and sleep.

SAM [*he sits right up in bed and leans forward*]: Try to sleep? Rest? Do me a favour. I've got a lot of rest coming to me, I can tell you. No—I must keep awake and take everything in; I want to be more observant today than I have ever been. Smoking cigars, eh. You bloody miser, how can you afford them on the old age pension? I always suspected that you had a tidy sum stuck away. Come on, own up, I'm a dying man.

MR SEGAL: My boy sends them to me from New York; he sends me fifty dollars a month, also; he's a good boy. I spoke to him on the telephone two months ago. He's got a proper Yank accent. He's married there to a girl.

SAM: I didn't think that he married a boy; what does he do for a living?

MR SEGAL: He travels; business, you know.

[SAM *nods*.]

I tell you, my children are as good as gold. Hava even came back to look after me when her mother died; she's just like a little mother, what would I have done without them?

SAM: Children, oy vay, don't talk to me about children. All your life you sweat your kishkers out to give them a good education and everything they want and what happens? Davey turns around and tells me that two and two don't add up to four, and Lottie joins the Communist Party. The Communist Party I can stand, but to add insult to injury she runs away with a goy; I've pushed it all inside me and I've swallowed it, so please don't talk about children.

MR SEGAL: Still, David isn't as bad as all that.

SAM: He was all right until he started going up west when he was 17; soon as his pimples went so do he, drifting from job to job, more out than in, getting a craze over one thing after another; but for years now he's been singing and when he's not singing he's listening to records of singers; I wish he'd even go out sometimes but now he's got a new habit. He sits in the house every evening, mooching around and sighing. Who knows where it will end? Come on, give us a cigar, you stingy old sod.

[SAM *gets out of bed, to* MR SEGAL'S *horror. He walks over to* MR SEGAL *and* MR SEGAL *gravely hands him a cigar and lights it for him.* SAM *paces around the stage puffing at the cigar.* DAVID *comes on. He hovers in the background. He is dressed in a well-made suit.*]

SAM: Beggars can't be choosers,
    So pass the word around,
    No matter what you do,
    You'll end up underground.

[MR SEGAL *tries to steer him back to bed but* SAM *refuses to go and walks around the stage looking at imaginary fruit and groceries.* DAVID *follows them, unseen. He sings.*]

DAVID [*sings*]: Silver trout are sleeping in heaps upon the
                    slabs,
                With mackerel and lobsters and lethargic
                    crabs.
                The dead are busy sleeping eternity away,
                They cannot go out shopping on this fair
                    summer's day.

SEGAL ⎫
SAM   ⎬ [*sing*]: Beggars can't be choosers, the executioner
               said,

And if you beg for life, you're bound to lose
your head.

DAVID [*sings*] : They do not smell the flowers that take the
breath away,

Mimosa and Rose, Carnation and Lily;

The dead are busy sleeping in the eternal
dark,

They do not go out shopping or walk in the
park.

SEGAL ⎫
       ⎬ [*sing*] :   No matter how you climb, you'll end up in
SAM   ⎭   the clay.

Beggars can't be choosers, so pass the world
away.

DAVID [*sings*] : They do not buy the warm bread, the wine
and watercress,

Or give a copper coin to a bronze accord-
ionist,

The dead are busy sleeping eternity away,

They come not to the market, on this fair
summer's day.

SEGAL ⎫
        ⎬ [*sing*] :   Beggars can't be choosers, no matter what
SAM   ⎭   you're worth,

The best of us, the worst of us,

Will burst beneath the earth.

[*They are both standing now arm in arm, breathless and
happy.* DAVID *retires to the background.*]

SAM : Yes, Mr Segal, in the market now there is a glut of
cherries, big, ripe, and red, red-currants and black-currants
and golden goosegogs as large as Chinese lanterns; grapes,
figs, olives, dates, melons, lemons. I tell you, Mr Segal,
that's what I've missed.

MR SEGAL : What? Fruit?

SAM [*in the course of this speech music is playing.* SAM
*almost breaks out into song but never quite makes it. He
speaks slowly*] : Oh, don't be such a bloody fool, of course
not. I mean going places and seeing people. After all, that is
all that there is in life, going places and seeing people, different places, different people. I promised myself a world trip
before I died, to see for myself how people in other countries

lived. It never transpired. Working in the market makes you curious; it does that for you ... You see the coloured labels stuck upon the boxes, and you think of the man who packed those boxes, and of the girl who stuck that label on. You think of the sun beating down on the wharves and the boat being loaded by sweating men, gently swaying in the golden waves; but—it's too late for the holiday you planned and you never left the market where you stand.

MR SEGAL: A vivid imagination, Sam, that's your trouble.

SAM: Beggars can't be choosers, Mr Segal, and my only regret is not travelling, not having seen California and the Caucasus, Haifa and Helsinki. I never even saw Odessa again; not that I ever saw it really. I came on an onion boat to Tilbury when I was 14. Boxes and boxes of onions on that boat, all with labels stuck on saying ONIONS, MADE IN RUSSIA. I was also made in Russia, so I came to Tilbury, and then I came here and I have been here ever since.

BOTH [*sing slowly*]: Beggars can't be choosers,
So pass the word around,
You do not need a passport when you
travel to the ground.

[*The mood changes and* SAM *seems very tired again.*]

SAM: Would you please help me back into bed, Mr Segal?

[MR SEGAL *does so and* SAM *settles down.* DAVID *comes forward. He speaks very slowly as if every word were a jewel to be weighed and valued.*]

SAM: Where have you been all day, Davey boy?

DAVID: Whitechapel Art Gallery and the Public Library next door, that is to say if one should call them that. The Art Gallery contained no art and the Public Library contained no public, just one or two down-and-outs reading the long newspapers in the racks.

[MR SEGAL *whispers to* DAVID.]

MR SEGAL: David, listen to me, try and be a good boy for a change, your father is dying.

DAVID: So are we all, all the time.

SAM: Stop whispering, Mr Segal. It's not good manners.

DAVID: Anyway, he looks perfectly all right to me.

SAM: Mr Segal, do me a favour, leave me here with my boy for a moment; I want to talk to him.

[MR SEGAL *is looking over the wall and is shouting at the children who have been making a little noise.*]

MR SEGAL: Go on—do us a favour—play somewhere else, little ruffians. [*He goes off in their direction.*]

CHILDREN [*off*]: Silly Solly Segal—nose like an eagle— eyes like two jelly-fish—teeth like a weasel . . . [*Their voices disappear in the distance.*]

[DAVID *walks round the stage: he stretches his arms exuberantly but he is nervous.*]

SAM: Na Davey, what can I say to you? All these years I wanted you to work in the market with me, then I told myself—'Don't worry, Sam, he's looking for something better'—well—what are you going to do? No more pie in the sky. You've got to support your mother now.

DAVID: Oh, what can I do?

SAM: You'll have to work.

DAVID: Why should I work when I've got my health and strength? The thought of having to spend the rest of my life looking at the heads of herrings and the heads of hungry people makes me sick.

SAM: What do you think singers see? Stop dreaming and settle down.

DAVID [*swings around the stage*]: I want to be a singer— I want to be a king—to be looked at—to be looked up to. I want people to nudge each other as they pass and say 'Look! there goes David Levy—the most famous—fabulous singer in the world'. I want to hear my voice blaring from the record shops as I whizz by in my Jaguar—I want to switch on the radio—any time—and any day and hear my voice on records.

SAM: Why, Davey? Why have you got these crazy ideas? Who do you take after?

DAVID: I feel good when I'm singing.

SAM: But I'm going to die—who'll look after you?

DAVID: Don't worry about me—I'll be all right, and don't keep on saying you're dying. Whatever happens, though—

I won't work down the lane—I refuse—I won't—I'll . . .

SAM: It's not natural—already you're 22—other boys grow out of these mad ideas already. Other people have only joy from their children—I have a pain in my heart—just my luck. You have no trade—no profession—you're not interested in politics and you drift from job to job—All this has got to stop—I'm a dying man—don't argue.

DAVID: I'm fed up round here. I'm bored. Nothing happens except to other people in the papers. It was bad enough before we got television—now it's worse—everyone sleeps all the time—no one's got any life—now if they gave me a chance on the tele I'd wake them all up—I'd stun them— I'd be the greatest thing—don't ya see—I want to make people happy—I'VE GOT TO MAKE them listen—they'd love me.

SAM: And they call me delirious. What do you want? Look! Tell me—between you and me—I told you the facts of life, didn't I?—Well, you owe me something in exchange—I helped to make you—well, don't make any more nonsense— tell me.

DAVID: You made me all right—you made me what I am. Aren't you proud of me? I know you are deep down—What do you want me to do?—be honest.

SAM: To settle down—take over the business—marry a nice girl.

DAVID: What, and then have a complicated son like me? Something's wrong and you know it. You haven't really been a success because you don't really want me to end up in the market like you—come on, own up.

SAM: Naturally—I expect you to improve—big business man with a wonderful education.

DAVID: You admit, then, you don't want me to have the same life as yourself?

[SAM *cannot reply.*]

It didn't turn out too well, so surely you don't want me to fail—do you? [SAM *cannot reply.*] Well, do you? See— you don't know what to say.

SAM: All I can say is that I don't know where you come from.

DAVID: Singing makes me feel safe—it'll give me a place in the world.

SAM: What a complicated boy I have to turn out!

DAVID: When I sing I feel free.

SAM: Davey—all this nonsense has got to stop.

DAVID: Pipe down—you're dying, remember—we've been through this so many times.

SAM: What a way to treat a father; especially on his death-bed. [*He almost cries.*]

DAVID: Sorry, Dad—but you've been on this death-bed so many times before—don't blackmail me—anyway—why do you want to bequeath me the things you hated—and I know you hated—you told me you hated—as often as you said you were going to kick the bucket—tell me that?

SAM: I shall die a very confused man—now I don't know what I mean.

DAVID: Say that again and anyway even if you were dying how do you do—I'm dying also—dying to be famous and express myself—you'll be all right—It's me I'm worried about—but just give me a chance—Give me time and I'll make you proud of me—So long—I'll be seeing you. I've got some mirror exercises to do. See you soon.

SAM: I wonder.

[DAVID *goes off.* SAM *laughs ironically.* HAVA *enters from the garden and* BESSIE *enters from the house.*]

BESSIE: Sam, Sam. What's the matter with you? Have you been lecturing my Davey again? You'll upset him.

[*Her hair is dyed blonde; she is trying to look ten years younger, and uses cosmetics profusely.*]

SAM: Bessie, please believe me; I tell you I'm very ill, please believe me.

BESSIE: If you say so who am I to argue. You were very ill last year and the year before that and the year before that; it's funny but every time it becomes July, you become ill as regular as clockwork. Just when everyone starts to think about holidays, he gets ill. What's the matter? Why don't you say that you don't want to take me to the seaside? And if you're so ill why won't you let me call for a doctor?

SAM: Oh, leave me alone, what do you care? You'll be able

to play on your little spirit board and talk to me next
week.

BESSIE: Look, Sammy, please be a good boy; it's so hot and
I'm expecting Mr and Mrs Stone to tea.

SAM: How is the new Jewish Spiritualist Synagogue doing?
Are you playing to full houses? Who ever heard of it?
Yiddisher Spiritualism! Is there anyone there? Is it you up
there Moishe: send me down a dozen pairs of nylons and
five pounds of smoked salmon; I should like to see you all
tapping the table for a change, instead of each other.

BESSIE: You disgust me, you old fool; and if you're going
to die, please do it before tea-time because I've got a sponge-
cake in the oven. [*She exits into the house.*]

   [HAVA *comes forward.*]

SAM [*does not see her*]: Eh? Sammy? So this is what you
made of your life; well, maybe it's just as well; think how
difficult it would be to part for ever if you loved each other.

HAVA: Don't worry, Mr Levy, try and go to sleep.

SAM: Who's that? [*He sits up.*] Oh, it's you, Hava. Looking
for your Dad?

HAVA: No, I just looked in. Miriam wasn't in.

SAM: Oh, God, life was a mistake; it shouldn't have been
given to us, we didn't deserve it. The cockroaches deserve
life more than human beings.

HAVA: Don't you love each other any more?

SAM: No, no more.

HAVA: Did you ever love each other?

SAM: Yes; I tell you this as a warning. I was on a steamer
going to Southend for the day; she was sitting on the top
deck in a white calico dress and her lovely black eyes smiled
down at me, oh, so expressive. Two years later we got
married, and moved to this house and after Davey was born
we went shopping and bought twin beds. What went
wrong? I shall never know! There is too much in life, too
much to learn, not enough time. Too many problems to be
solved. It's too late, now.

   [DAVID *comes back into the garden; his mood has
   changed.*]

HAVA: Look, there's David.

[DAVID *ignores her completely as if she doesn't exist.*
SAM *continues talking.*]

SAM: I used to think that the top of my head would blow off
trying to answer these questions; then one day I thought
that I'd grow a new head where these problems would seem
like simple sums, nice pieces of cake that you could digest
and get rid of easily. Hello, Davey, you met Hava, didn't
you?

DAVID: I'm sorry, Dad, but a person can't help being himself. Oh? Yes, I've seen her around. [*He ignores her.*]

SAM: Hava, come here, you've met my boy, Davey, haven't
you?

HAVA: Well, we never quite—

[HAVA *offers* DAVID *her hand and he shakes it limply
and then continues to ignore her. She just does not exist
in* DAVID'S *eyes.*

SAM *pulls* DAVID *close and ruffles his hair.* HAVA
*walks around the garden sometimes looking at them and
sometimes looking at and sniffing the flowers.*]

Don't mind me.

SAM: We shouldn't argue, you and I. I've always loved
you. You were all I really ever lived for; part of that lovely
dream that slipped through my fingers. I'm sure you'll find
yourself, one day, and when you do remember me and
all the others who never got anywhere.

[DAVID *is sad.*]

Come on, Davey, pull yourself together; liven up, sing. Say
all those crazy things I used to chastise you for saying.
Spout all the things you read from books and heard from
your strange friends. I want to change everything. I want
something new to happen. I want to lose all sense of order,
so that I'll be prepared for my new existence if there is one!
Everyone where I'm going may be like you; I want my
son to vouch for me in the unaccustomed darkness. Come
on, Davey, '*Hurrah, Hurrah*'; come on, darling, spout
poetry, sing, shout, come on, Davey. [*He claps his hands
and so does* HAVA. SAM *has got out of bed again.*]

DAVID [*shouting*]: Listen, everyone; listen, folks. This is
David Levy speaking, your master of ceremonies, your own

prince of song, a prisoner of seasons, a disciple of dust. I fell out of the sky and a name fell upon me, and I was called Levy and now for a time I answer to that. My old man is going to die and so are we all before your very eyes.

HAVA: Come on, Davey, sing. I like hearing your voice.

SAM: Come on, Davey, sing.

DAVID: No! Not now. I want to speak. Tonight, friends, I'm going to launch my father into space.

SAM: Halleluia, I'm a bum; Halleluia, bum again; halleluia, give us a handout to revive us again.

[*There is a general commotion in the neighbourhood; irate voices are heard and the* CHILDREN *have come on the stage and are standing around happy and delighted.*]

DAVID: This is David Levy speaking to you; I'm consigning my father to you, oh mighty dead, he is a king if ever there was one, first because he is my father, and then he is king of the herrings; to you, oh mighty dead, to you, all you billions and billions of dead who have passed this way over the earth, since it shot off from the sun, accept my father, a humble novice in this game of chance, in this maze of existence, look after him for my sake.

[MR SEGAL *enters.*]

SEGAL: What on earth are you doing? Sam, get back into bed at once, do you want to catch your death of cold?

HAVA: Daddy, please; don't interfere.

SAM: I'll die from what I choose. I'll die from playing blind man's buff if I feel like it; it's a free country; come on, kiddies, come and play with me.

SEGAL [*to* HAVA]: You shouldn't have let him, anyway what are you doing now? [*He sees* DAVID.] Don't you get mixed up with him, that's all I ask. Haven't I been a good father? Don't the things that I tell you count?

HAVA: Oh, Daddy, shut up, shush . . .

[*The* CHILDREN *are reluctantly approaching* SAM, *who is beckoning them.*]

SAM: Go on, sing and dance, show me how to do it.

[*The* CHILDREN *move around in a circle.*]

What games shall we play? What songs do you know?

[*The* CHILDREN *move around in a circle.*]

CHILDREN: There were three crows sat on a stone.
               Fal, la, la, la, lal, de.
               Two flew away and then there was one.
               Fal, la, la, la, lal, de.
               The other crow finding himself alone,
               Fal, la, la, la, lal, de.
               He flew away and then there was none,
               Fal, la, la, la, lal, de.

[*They continue dancing around like this and* SAM *and* HAVA *join in with them. They become quieter and dance on like this whilst* DAVID *looks at them and sings simultaneously.*]

DAVID: Sky, sky, the children cry,
          Where do we go to when we die?
          What are we doing in this dream?
          Sky, sky, the children scream,
          Sky, sky, the children scream,
          Life is nothing but a dream,
          A game of dancing in a ring,
          Sky, sky, the children sing.
          Sky, sky, the children sing,
          Who'll be beggar? Who'll be king?
          Let's dance for joy, let's sing and leap,
          And comfort everyone who weeps.
          Sky, sky, the children weep,
          Why are we falling fast asleep?
          We'll play this game until we die.
          Sky, sky, the children cry.

CHILDREN: He flew away and then there was none;
               Fal, la, la, la, lal, de.

[*The* CHILDREN *clap and* SAM *is encouraging them.* SEGAL *is still trying to get him back into bed, without success.*]

HAVA [*to* DAVID]: That was very nice, you can really sing.

DAVID: Who are you? Oh, yes! Thanks. [*He smiles and moves away, disinterested before she can reply.*]

HAVA: My—I'm—Hava . . . You've got a lovely—voi . . .
Oh, dear, what a life!

SAM: Come on, now, ring-a-ring-a-roses. [*He and* DAVID *now form a circle with the* CHILDREN.]

[HAVA *stands sadly near her father, watching.*]

Ring-a-ring-a-roses, a pocket full of posies,

Usher, usher, we . . . all fall . . . DOWN.

[*They all fall on the grass, and* DAVID *and the* CHILDREN *manage to get up, but* SAM *can't manage it.*]

DAVID: Come on, Dad, come back to bed.

[SAM *pushes him away with a silent gesture of his hands, crawls over to a rose-bush. He plucks enough and then he staggers to his feet; he stoops and gives a flower to each child, one to* DAVID, *which he puts into his lapel, and one to* HAVA.]

SAM: Go on now, kiddies, hide-and-seek, now we are playing hide-and-seek; run away and hide; run away, quickly get away, hide-and-seek. [*He is shouting at them and the* CHILDREN *quickly run from the garden.*]

[DAVID *and* HAVA *help* SAM *back into bed.* SAM *settles back and is calm again.*]

Now, seriously, let's face facts, what's going to happen to you, Davey?

SEGAL: What do you mean? God forbid if anything happens to you, he'll take over the stall; he's bound to.

DAVID: Here we go again. Oh well, I know—I've had it— I'm caught—What do you want of me? Bang go my dreams, my lovely dreams, my prospects.

SEGAL: Now he's beginning to see sense. By the way, Davey, have you met my daughter . . . ?

DAVID: Yes. We met.

SAM: Mr Segal, would you mind not interfering in my business; you've done so long enough.

[SEGAL *is offended and sits back and reads a newspaper, and through the next scene he is very interested, though every time* DAVID *or* SAM *looks his way he quickly reverts to the paper.*]

HAVA: Well, I'll go now. Good-bye, Mr Levy. Good-bye, Davey. Don't worry, everything will be all right.

SAM: Good-bye, darling . . . What a lovely g . . .

DAVID: Oh? Oh, good-bye . . . I'm sure it will.

[HAVA *kisses her father on the cheek and goes sadly off.*]

SAM: You are covered, Davey boy, I hope you realize that; I've got a special endowment for you. When I die you will get two hundred pounds. Well? You don't seem very eager, don't you want the money?

DAVID: I don't want that sort of money. Anyway, what can you do with two hundred pounds?

SAM: You can build up the business into a really posh lay-out; or you can take a world trip before you begin.

DAVID: Don't make me laugh, a world trip? You're living in the past. All I could do is buy a motor-scooter or eight new suits.

[*The stage is slowly getting darker, slightly.*]

Look, Dad, no one thinks for one moment that you're going to die. Nobody takes you seriously; everybody believes that you'll outlive the lot of us.

SAM: Believe it or not, I want to tell you something and I want you to make me one promise. Listen, Davey; today boys and girls go out with each other, they press against each other in doorways, under the moon, they experience a thrill and they call it love. They get married. All right for a time, this new experience waking up in the morning and finding a warm, naked girl beside you in bed; but soon the only time they meet is in bed and they meet there less and less. About this time the child usually comes and the woman has something to keep her occupied and the man drinks and returns to his dreams. It is too late. Time passes; they decide to make the most of a bad job. Don't settle for second best like your mother and I did. Marry a girl who shares your interests, so that when the love of passion cools down, the love of admiration and real friendship flares up and compensates; and then you have the deep ties that can never be broken, not by anything. Do you understand what I mean?

DAVID: Of course.

SAM: Then promise me you'll try your best.

DAVID: Oh, Dad, why do you think . . .? Oh, never mind —I'll try.

SAM: Will you stay here when I'm dead?

DAVID: I don't know—I suppose so.

SAM: Good boy, but are you sure? I mean, be careful of your mother—She'll kill you with her love for you.

DAVID: Make up your mind—now I decide to stay you start getting cold feet.

SAM: I've got more than cold feet—I've got the screaming willies and the heeby-jeebies multiplied together. There's a great wail leaving my soul as if my body was the great wailing wall.

[*Enter* BESSIE *with* MR *and* MRS STONE.]

MR STONE: How are you, Sam?

SAM: Not so bad. How are you?

MR STONE: Mustn't grumble.

SAM: Why not? [*There is a shaking of hands all round and the guests sit down.*] How are you Mrs Stone?

MRS STONE: All right, thank you. How are you, Bessie?

BESSIE: Don't ask me; what with one thing and another I don't know if I'm coming or going. [*She exits into the house.* MRS STONE *nods continuously like a Chinese mandarin.*]

MRS STONE: Well, Sam, how are you feeling? Bessie tells me you have a chill.

SAM: The chill is gone, thank God; I'm going to follow it.

MRS STONE: Good, good. How are you, David? Working?

DAVID: I'm fine. I've got a job circumsizing yiddisher mice.

MRS STONE: Sounds an interesting job.

MR STONE: He's having you on.

[BESSIE *returns with a tray of tea-things.*]

BESSIE: Take no notice of him, Mrs Stone—what a life I have with that boy, no tongue can tell; there's no house like this, not another house in the world like this; all we do is argue. Oh—come on, let's all have a nice cup of tea. [*They are all seated around the small garden table that has a striped coloured umbrella above it. They sip tea and talk.*]

MR STONE: What do you think of the political situation, Sam?

SAM: What about it? [*He shrugs.*]

MRS STONE: How's Lottie, Mrs Levy?

BESSIE: She's very well, when I heard last; she's living in Leeds—of course you know. He's a school teacher up there; so I mustn't grumble. He looks after her even if he isn't a yiddisher feller. Beautiful weather we are having. How's business, Mr Stone?

MR STONE: Mustn't grumble.

SAM: Why not?

MR STONE: The taxi game never changes; too many new boys taking it up; they all think it a cushy life; they'll learn soon enough. I also stand down the Lane on Sundays now and again. I'm what you might call a purveyor of bad taste; anything that I can get my hands on I sell; you know, those horrible plaster dogs and boys eating cherries, balloons, little men running up sticks, nonsense. Give the British public something to waste money on and they cry for the opportunity. Alabaster saints and plaster ducks, oh, horrible. Mustn't grumble. Did you hear that fight the other night, Sam? Gerry Freed, the yiddisher boy from Brooklyn, got knocked out in the first round by the coloured boy. I told you so.

SAM: I don't listen to boxing any more.

SEGAL: He reads the Bible instead. Nearly all day, nearly all night.

MR STONE: And how are you, Mr Segal?

SEGAL: Why should I complain? I've got such good children: my son sends me fifty dollars a month from the States and my girl looks after me like a little mother. Have a cigar? [*He hands one to* MR STONE *and one to* SAM.] He sends these to me from America; I feel like a millionaire; still, why not? Didn't I slave long enough for them?

MRS STONE: I wish I had some children to appreciate me. I would appreciate that.

　　[*She looks at* MR STONE *and he pinches her cheek.*]

MR STONE [*sings*]: When your hair has turned to silver
　　　　　　　　　　I will love you just the same;
　　　　　　　　　　I will always call you sweetheart.
　　　　　　　　　　It will always be your name . . .

DAVID: Oh, Christ!

MR STONE: What's the matter, David? Don't you like my voice? I had a good voice when I was younger; I once won an amateur competition at the Troxy. Anyway, Sam, what's all this about you reading the Bible in your old age?

SAM: There are a couple of reasons why I started to re-read the Bible; first, I wanted to get what you may call a little spiritual comfort; I wanted to understand life a bit more.

MRS STONE: Anyway, Alf [*to her husband*], what's wrong with the Bible? Intelligent men read it, educated men, I can tell you that; more people should read it; there wouldn't be so many blackguards about.

DAVID: I am a blackguard and I read the Bible.

SEGAL: What's this? What's this? Sam, do you hear that? Your own son said he was a blackshirt. You should be ashamed of yourself.

[BESSIE *hands him some cake.*]

SAM: Shut up, Davey, take no notice of him everyone, he's trying to assert himself. Well, where was I? Oh, yes. I wanted to clear up a few points that worried me since I was a child. Now, Adam and Eve had only two sons: Cain and Abel; as you know Cain killed Abel. Well, how did future generations come about? Who did Cain sleep with, I ask you. Incest, you might think. I looked it up yesterday and found that Cain went out into the land of Nod, and knew his wife.

ALL: Land of Nod?

SAM: Yes, the land of Nod.

[*They all look at* MRS STONE *who has been nodding all the time.*]

MRS STONE: Why are you looking at me? What have I got to do with it?

SAM: You see, it's allegorical.

MR STONE: Sounds like a sweet.

SAM: That's paragorical. Listen, don't interrupt; well, who was this wife that he suddenly started to know, who wasn't even created? Where did she come from? Was she a monkey? So what can you believe? Then there's the Talmud, the Apocrypha, the story of Lilith, Susanna and the Elders; you see, none of you have heard of these things. This is the age of the specialist; you've got to specialize, otherwise where are you? Has anyone here heard of the Tarot cards? The Kaballa?

[*They all shake their heads.*]

MRS STONE: Kaballa, Shmaballa, leave us alone. What's the matter, Bessie? Is he delirious? Bessie, I bought a lovely halibut for tomorrow's dinner—Well, Bessie, how are you keeping?

BESSIE: I've got a bit of fibrositis as usual, the same as yesterday.

MRS STONE: Yes, Sam, the world's in a terrible state.

DAVID: Well—Halibuts are in a terrible state—and the world's suffering from fibrositis—my old man's dying to die—my mother's got a Kaballa in the oven—all right with the world—please nod by you—The world's turning and I'm yearning to sing through the streets about my sadness and joy—Good-bye—so nice to have met you—don't call again. Charming nice son you have—tata—What a world!—What a crazy, beautiful world!

[*He goes off humming and* BESSIE *chases off after him.*]

BESSIE [*off*]: Davey—wrap up warm—it's getting chilly.

[MR *and* MRS STONE *get up and make ready to go.* BESSIE *comes on again.*]

MR STONE: Well, Sam, take it easy; I wish you better.

MRS STONE: So long, Sammy, see you some more. Good-bye, Mr Segal, take care of yourself.

BESSIE: Wheel him back into the house, Mr Segal. Don't listen to him.

[BESSIE *exits with* MR *and* MRS STONE.]

SAM: Good-bye—good-bye. Thank God for that.

[*It is getting very dark now.*]

SEGAL: Shall I wheel it in now; you heard what she said?

SAM: Segal, never be intimidated by a woman; leave me here for another half an hour. I want to see the first star in the sky. Thank you, go on now, go inside, leave me alone; we'll play cards later.

SEGAL: You know what I miss? A good game of chess;

there are no chess players left in the East End. Mr Solomans and me were the champion players; I haven't played since he died last year. Where has Bessie gone?

SAM: To the spiritualist meeting with the others; they want to talk to the dead; they are fed up with the living.

SEGAL [*puffing on his cigar*]: Madame Blavatsky was an intelligent woman; I saw her once.

SAM: So was Ouspensky.

SEGAL: Rasputin was a terrible man; evil and hypnotic.

SAM: So was Ivan.

SEGAL: So was Stalin.

SAM: So they say.

SEGAL: So was Bakunin.

SAM: So was Trotsky.

SEGAL: Oh, no, Trotsky was a wonderful man.

SAM: Lenin was a wonderful man.

SEGAL: Kropotkin was a wonderful man.

SAM: My father was a wonderful man.

SEGAL: Gorki was a wonderful man, my father knew him.

SAM: Tolstoi was a wonderful man, my father never knew him. Mr Segal, do you think that there's going to be a war?

SEGAL: What do you mean? The war never finishes; the independent struggles of the individual to break his chains; the Workers themselves—and the distribution of property. In the words of our greatest comrade, 'Comrades, down with politics'.

SAM: What's the name of this greatest comrade?

SEGAL: Izzy Cohen; you know him. He's a furrier, lives in Commercial Street.

[SEGAL *exits and* HAVA *enters.*]

HAVA: Hello, Mr Levy, have you seen my father?

SAM: He's gone inside for a moment. Is it urgent?

HAVA: No. I've just come to take him home. How are you feeling?

SAM: Not too good, but I'll be better presently.

[*He seems to be in pain.*]

HAVA: You rest. It'll do you the world of good.

SAM: Do me a favour, Hava. Try to get to know my son.

HAVA: I would love to. We used to play together, but since I came back he looks right through me. I think he's a very nice boy and I wish he would speak to me; he probably thinks I'm still a child.

SAM: Maybe it's a natural reaction against women; after all, he hasn't exactly a good impression of married life. Listen, I'm going to die—

HAVA: Going to die? Please, Mr Levy, don't speak that way; you scare me. It's a lovely day, all the flowers are out—

SAM: Listen, be a good, sensible girl—I've had my time and I'm going to die—what's more natural than that? Face facts —you're a woman now.

HAVA: What will happen to David?

SAM: Try to get to know him—he's my big worry.

HAVA: If only he'd let me—I don't want to push myself— he's too busy with worrying about his voice.

SAM: But I thought you liked his voice.

HAVA: I do—I love it—but he doesn't like me. What can I do?

SAM: Take your time—there isn't a woman yet born who let her quarry slip through her fingers—encourage him to sing if you want to—my part—but bring him down to earth— tempt him—you're just the girl he needs.

HAVA: Do you think so?

SAM: Sure—you're such a lovely girl—so attractive and good-natured—ideals are very fine but they don't keep you warm in bed—he'll fall—be patient.

HAVA: Do you really think so? Anyway—I'm not that hard up—plenty more fish in the sea.

SAM: Yes, but not such a lovely red herring like my Davey— anyway—do your best.

HAVA: I'll try.

SAM: Promise? For my sake—his sake—your sake?

HAVA: I promise. You sleep now, Mr Levy—you'll feel much better tomorrow, you'll see. I must go now and find my Dad—Are you comfortable? Can I get you something?

SAM: No, no, no. There's a good girl—Go now—you're an angel.

HAVA: Are you sure you don't need anything?

[SAM *shakes his head.* HAVA *goes off into the house.*]

SAM: Little girls are so lovely—so gentle and kind. Lots of things I need, darling, but it's too late to think about them now.

[*The* CHILDREN *start to sing again: their voices are much slower and slightly off key.*]

CHILDREN [*off*] : On the hill there stands a lady,
　　　　　　　　　Who she is I do not know.
　　　　　　　　　All she wants is gold and silver,
　　　　　　　　　All she wants is a fine young man—

[DAVID *jumps over the garden fence and stands inconspicuously among some flowers.*]

DAVID [*sings*] : On the hill there stands a lady,
　　　　　　　　　Who she is I do not know.
　　　　　　　　　All she wants is gold and silver,
　　　　　　　　　All she wants is a fine young man.
　　　　　　　　　On the hill there stands a lady
　　　　　　　　　Who she is I do not know,
　　　　　　　　　I have seen her often lately,
　　　　　　　　　In the sun and in the snow.
　　　　　　　　　All she wants is golden rings and silver,
　　　　　　　　　So I heard the little children sing,
　　　　　　　　　She must know that I am not a Rockefeller,
　　　　　　　　　I am skint and haven't got a thing.
　　　　　　　　　All she wants are diamonds, and all she
　　　　　　　　　　　wants are sables,
　　　　　　　　　All she wants are all the things that I could
　　　　　　　　　　　never
　　　　　　　　　Hope to give her—
　　　　　　　　　When I stretch my hands to reach her,
　　　　　　　　　Stretch my longing hands to reach her,
　　　　　　　　　The city throws its lonely streets at me.

SAM: It got dark suddenly, as if the sun fell like a stone; I thought I heard someone singing. The world would be very dark if there wasn't any light; that goes without saying. Ah, there it is, the evening star. Starlight. Starbright, first star I've seen tonight, wish I may, wish I might, grant this wish. [*He closes his eyes and makes a wish and then he opens them again and fumbles in the bedclothes for a cigarette; he lights the cigarette, puffs at it for a few moments and then throws it away.* DAVID *picks up the cigarette and smokes it.*] A funny thing has happened to me, I know it. I've been poisoned.

DAVID: Poisoned?

SAM: My heart is jumping, all the bitterness of years I can taste in my throat. I've been poisoned by someone or something. What's the odds? By my life or my wife. But my wife was my life; so my life poisoned me, so my wife poisoned me.

DAVID: She? Poisoned him? My mother?

SAM: What do I care? I don't want to live another day; die quietly, Sam, let no shame come on the name of Levy. Who'll miss me anyway? Caruso is dead and Chaliapin is dead; Melba is dead; Stepney Green is dead; Whitechapel is dead. What am I waiting for? Whatever became of Whitechapel? Teeming with people, so gay, so alive . . . where are they? Where are the old men with the long white beards, where are the women selling beigels? Where are the young fellers following the young ladies along the waste? Everyone I ever loved is dead, everything that was any good is dead, has been murdered.

[DAVID *hurriedly walks across the back of the garden and goes into the house.*]

SAM: Our standards are lowering; everything is dead and being put into tins, smaller and smaller, good-bye cabbages, good-bye oranges, good-bye silver fishes; everything is in tins and compressed, frozen and chopped up. We are being dried and turned inside out and we are watching ourselves in this process on little silver screens; I may as well be dead.

[DAVID *returns to the garden and is about to go over to his father when he decides against this and takes his previous position.*]

Mumma? Yes, I can hear you. Speak louder. How are you? [*He is sitting up and staring at the air.*] I am cold. Oh, rock me, Mumma, I am tired. Oh Mumma, Mumma, hold me. Where are you? Let me see, oh there you are. Come

closer, closer, stand by the candles. You haven't changed.
There is a long river that flows from the Minories, under
Tower Bridge; it flows into the sea, but it doesn't lose itself;
it flows all over the long ocean and I am swimming so easily
along it—to you. To Russia, where you are standing,
smiling at me; oh, Mumma, how lovely you look!

[*He climbs out of bed.*]

What's up with you, Sam? Your mind's wandering. You
should be ashamed of yourself, calling for your mother.

[*He walks about the stage deliriously and by the time the
next speech ends he is slumped across the bed.*]

Oy, Mumma, I remember how you used to swing me, right
up into the sky, and then—down to the ground . . . I
remember you singing . . . [*He sings.*]

[*Note: Song will be sung in Russian or Yiddish.*]

[*singing*] : Go to sleep, mine baby, go to sleep.

> Whilst the stars above begin to peep,
> Through the window of heaven, angels watch
> over you.
> Roshinkes mit mandlen shluf mein kindele,
> shluf . . .

Oh, Mumma, look. I am crying on your apron. Let me sleep
against you. I love the smell of your clothing. Oy, what
can you do when you die alone?

[*He is lying spreadeagled across the bed looking up-
wards. DAVID rushes to him.*]

DAVID: Dad, listen to me; you are not alone.

SAM: If you die alone, wherever you are, what can you do?

DAVID [*shakes him*] : I tell you, Dad, you are not alone.
Oh, can't you hear me?

SAM: Even if fifty people surround your bed, you die alone.

DAVID: Dad, Dad, you are not alone. This is David. I'm
with you.

SAM: For when the eyes close—no one can go into that total
darkness with you.

DAVID: I'm with you. Listen, Dad, I love you.

SAM: So here—goes—Sam—Lev—y poisoned by his life; a
smaltz herring dealer of Wentworth Street—mourned by
his d-ial-ect-ical daughter and by his crazy singing son.

Oy, oy Shema Yisroel—Dear Mother keep me warm.
[*He dies.*]

DAVID [*rushing round the stage*]: Hi, there, everyone;
come out, come out, my father is dead; he is dead; he's
been poisoned; for God's sake let's have some light, lights
—lights . . .

[*All the lights go full on.* SEGAL *and* HAVA *rush on
to the stage.* DAVID *weeps on his father's body.*
SEGAL *rushes to* DAVID *and pulls him away.* HAVA
clutches at DAVID'S *sleeve.*]

DAVID: Who are you? What do you want?

[HAVA *runs off the stage crying.* SEGAL *and* DAVID
stand together looking at SAM'S *body, unable to move.
The* CHILDREN *are heard singing quietly.*]

CHILDREN: Sky, sky the children cry,
Where do we go to when we die?
What are we doing in this dream?
Sky, sky, the children scream.
SKY: SKY: SKY: SKY: SKY: SKY:
SKY: SKY.

[*The word becomes louder and louder until it becomes
metallic and unbearable.*]

SLOW CURTAIN

44

ACT TWO

SCENE I

It is a few days later.
The late evening, stage is almost in darkness. Only a little of the garden is now seen.
When the curtain rises a figure is seen walking slowly into the house from the garden. It walks slowly round the room, looking at things, then sighs audibly and slumps into an armchair.
DAVID enters. He is dressed in a casual dark grey suit. He puts on the light and sings. The figure (SAM) joins in the the chorus but DAVID at first does not notice anything.

DAVID: Quiet and still was the garden of Eden,
   Oh woe—woe is me—
TOGETHER: Oh woe—woe is me—
DAVID: God said I'll start humanity breathing,
   wake my baby son Adam,
   under the tree the serpent lay scheming,
   Oh—woe is me.
   Eve gave Adam the apple of bitterness,
   Oh woe—woe is me—
TOGETHER: Oh woe—woe is me—
DAVID: Guilty and sad they covered their nakedness,
   out of Eden they ran,
   far from that place they fled into nothingness,
   Oh—woe is me.

   Quiet and still is the garden of Eden,
   Oh woe—woe is me—
TOGETHER: Oh woe—woe is me—
DAVID: There sits the Lord alone and grieving,
   weeping over his son—
   Under the tree the serpent lies sleeping—

[DAVID *is choked and stops singing;* SAM *continues.*]

SAM: Oh—woe is me.

[DAVID *turns around and gasps; rushes quickly to the door and switches the light off.*]

SAM: Come on, Davey boy, don't be scared of your own father.

DAVID: I must be going out of my mind. I don't believe it. [*He switches on the light.*] But—b-b-b-but—you're dead . . .

SAM [*looking slightly better in health than he did in the previous Act and still in pyjamas*]: Believe me, I should be as scared as you, after all, it's my funeral you've just come from.

DAVID [*approaches* SAM *slowly and cautiously*]: I must be dreaming all this. That's right, I'm dreaming. I'm dreaming I'm awake. I'm dreaming that we buried you. [*He touches* SAM'S *face, then shakes his head several times.*]

No! I'm not dreaming.

SAM: Who knows who's dreaming?

DAVID: Are you—a ghost?

SAM: What's in a name?

DAVID: But you are dead.

SAM: Yes, I'm dead. It's as if I just walked in from that garden because I was cold; came in to sit down and think.

DAVID: I must be going crazy, of course he's dead. I've just come from the grounds. I threw earth on his coffin. Oh, that terrible sound of earth falling on wood.

SAM: Don't be morbid. Where are the others?

DAVID: They'll be here soon. We washed our hands and strangers filled up the hole. Daimlers brought us back. Those same cars will be fluttering with white ribbons on Sunday, carrying brides instead of corpses.

SAM: Shut up, you give me the willies.

DAVID: The shiva is starting soon. Oh, those seven days of mourning. The weeping and wailing.

SAM: Arh! Weeping will do them good—let them get it all out of their systems. When I came in just now I went to look at myself, and when I saw the mirror was covered I knew definitely that I was dead.

DAVID: Why do we cover mirrors?

SAM: So that we shouldn't see our own grief.

DAVID: Why shouldn't we see our own grief?

SAM: How should I know?
    [*Pause.*]

DAVID: Why did you come back?

SAM: To help you.

DAVID [*annoyed and surprised*]: What do you mean?

SAM: I only mean and know one thing: you need me.

DAVID: Don't make me laugh. [*He laughs.*]

SAM: You're unhappy—that's why I came; you're holding on to me.

DAVID: I'm not doing anything of the kind. Don't give me that—there's another reason—a deeper reason—you're fooling yourself.

SAM: Davey—you're all mixed up—I've come to help you settle down—I'm at your disposal.

DAVID: Help me? How can you? Besides, you can't even help yourself. Everyone knows that ghosts are displaced persons. You made a mess of your life and now you're making a mess of your death—if you want to hang around the house don't use me as an excuse. You came back because you were killed and not because I'm unhappy.

SAM: So—you admit you're unhappy—why?

DAVID: Oh! Well, because—you died too soon.

SAM: But I kept warning you.

DAVID: Yes, but I never listened and I argued with you and never amounted to anything—oh, go away.

SAM: You called me, so I'm here—everything's turning out fine.

DAVID: No, it's not. You died in very strange circumstances.

SAM: Stop depressing me. Listen, Davey—life is a very strange circumstance; for years I told you I was going to die. Well, here I am, or rather, here I am not.

DAVID: You're hedging—poor ghost.

SAM: 'Ere, cut that out. Don't you poor ghost me. And don't sulk. Incidentally you've got a lovely voice.

DAVID: But only the other day you were saying exactly the opposite.

SAM: Only the other day I was exactly the opposite.

DAVID: What's it like being dead?

SAM: I can't answer that question. It's without meaning. You may as well ask a blind man to describe the colour green.

DAVID: It's going to be just fine, I know—apart from all my other worries, I now have a ghost on my hands—another father would have the decency to die and to stay dead—trust you.

SAM: Davey, don't you see—I live only in your mind and heart. No one else will see me; nobody else will want to.

DAVID: Tell me, Dad—do you believe in God?

SAM: Do I believe in God? Davey, do I believe in ghosts? Well, not really, yet I am a ghost. Only certain people see ghosts, only certain people want to see ghosts. You don't look into the gutter for flying birds. Only certain people see God, only certain people want to see Him. I want to find God and I'm still looking for Him, that's why I believe in Him.

DAVID [recites]: I fled Him down the years and down the days—

I fled Him down the arches of the years—

SAM: Come on, Davey—don't mope—you're only young once—let's be gay.

DAVID: Look—how can I? Especially now—don't you see you were killed—we've got to avenge your murder.

[DAVID wanders around the room wrapped in thought.]

SAM: Murder? Oh, what's he on about now? Oh, well—listen—even if I was killed, I don't want revenge for that, whether I was poisoned, gassed, burned, or struck by lightning. I want revenge for the way I lived—for the self-deception, the petty lies and silly quarrels. Anyway, what do you mean, murdered?

DAVID: Come off it—you know perfectly well that you were poisoned.

SAM: Oh, Davey—you've got it all—

DAVID: I heard you on your death-bed.

SAM: Oh—listen—I meant—

[*There is a ring on the bell.* SAM *is about to go to the door when he realizes his ghostly position. He beckons* DAVID *to go.* DAVID *returns with a young man; dressed in the manner of a City gentleman.*]

MAN: So terribly sorry to disturb you, especially at a time like this. Could I speak with Mrs Levy, please?

DAVID: My mother hasn't come back yet. Can I help you?

MAN: I'm Mr. Green of the Jewish Memorial Company. I would like to wish you a long life.

[*They shake hands and* DAVID *finds in his hand a visiting-card.*]

GREEN: Excuse the slight indiscretion of coming so soon, but facts have to be faced. Your poor father will be needing a stone. We have the finest stones in the country.

SAM: He sounds like a kidney doctor.

[GREEN *takes out a book of photos and shows them to* DAVID.]

GREEN: Italian marble. Lovely green with black streaks; Hard as iron. Same as Lyons Corner House.

DAVID: Look, just leave me alone. I don't think we want any today.

SAM: Oh, cheer up, Davey, you're a long time dead.

GREEN: Well, I'll just wait for your mother—she'll be more practical, more down to earth, about your poor father. [*Muses through his catalogue.*] Yes, we've got the lot— here's a nice inexpensive job—contemporary design, you know, all the rage. I've ordered one for my own mother.

SAM [*looking at the catalogue*]: Arh, it's flashy.

DAVID: Did you meet anybody on the other side?

[GREEN *looks at him strangely.*]

SAM: Not a soul—it was even somehow lonelier than my life.

DAVID: How long do you think you're going to stay?

GREEN: Until she comes.

SAM: Until you become a happy boy.

DAVID: Looks as if we're going to have you around until I'm dead also.

[*There is another ring at the door.* DAVID *shrugs and*

goes and returns with another man. He is wearing glasses and dressed similarly to the first man. The new man remembers that he is wearing a carnation in his button-hole. He discards this promptly and SAM *picks it up, smells it, and puts it in a small jug on the mantelpiece. The new man and* GREEN *frown at each other.*]

MAN: May I have a word with Mrs Levy?

DAVID: Are you a door-to-door salesman?

MAN: Indeed not.

SAM: He is, in a way.

DAVID: She's not home just yet. I'm her son.

MAN [*shakes* DAVID'S *hand violently and leaves within it a visiting-card*]: I wish you long life. I'm Mr Black of the Hebrew Remembrance Company. I want to sell your mother a beautiful memorial stone; one that would be worthy of your dear dead father. Such a fine, kind man, wouldn't harm a fly. I knew him well.

SAM: A feller of infinite jest. Never saw him before in my life, and I used to swat flies all day.

BLACK: Forgive me for coming so soon, but in the words of our motto: GET THE STONE SETTLED AND LEARN TO SMILE AGAIN.

[*He sits down near* GREEN. *They ignore each other.*]

DAVID: Look at them, how similar they are.

SAM: And look how much they hate each other.

DAVID: And you wanted me to become something like this. A nice respectable job with prospects.

SAM: God forbid. I must have been mad.

DAVID: That's what you accused me of being.

SAM: All right—don't go on, and stop arguing. That's what I seemed to do all my life. That's how I wasted it away.

DAVID: You admit, then, that I'm on the right track?

SAM: The trouble is you're not on any track—running wildly nowhere.

DAVID: What do I do? What can I do?

[GREEN *nods to* BLACK: *points a finger to his temple, suggesting that* DAVID *is mad.*]

BLACK: Don't upset yourself, have a rest. You've gone through a hard time.

DAVID: Please don't tell me that everyone lives for ever.

GREEN: All right, we won't tell you that.

SAM: I should say that's extremely unlikely. How many people would want to live for ever? Some want only to die. These two, for instance. How tired of life they must be! Already they are connected with the paraphernalia of death. They even smell of death.

[SAM *sniffs at them and* DAVID *follows suit.*]

DAVID: Yes, you're right, they do.

[*The men feel most uncomfortable.*]

SAM: When these two die, they'll swallow their own kishkers and will be dead for ever.

DAVID: Thank God for that.

GREEN: Thank God for everything. Look, son, what's your name?

DAVID: David. Why?

GREEN: Davey, listen, I'm your age, by my life. Here's my birth certificate to prove it. [*He shows* DAVID *the certificate.*] Please, you can help me; I'm not really a tombstone salesman, God forbid. I'm a feller like yourself really.

[SAM *is blowing on* BLACK'S *neck, who moves to the back of the stage and has a quiet smoke.*]

DAVID: How did you find out so soon that there'd been a death in the family?

GREEN: You're a bright boy. That's a very interesting question and I'm glad that you asked me. [*He puts his arm around* DAVID'S *shoulder.*] This is where the job is really interesting. We follow Coroners' reports, tip the porters at hospitals, make friends with mortuary keepers; check casualty lists for yiddisher names, scan obituary columns. Oh, it's a very subtle and interesting profession. Ever thought of trying it? There's a good living to be made if you're bright.

SAM: How sordid!

DAVID: I find all this very distasteful—excuse me, you see I'm not really myself. [*Turns to* SAM.] Well, what are we going to do?

GREEN [*whispers to* BLACK]: He's mad, you know—stone bonkers. I've often see him around the streets talking to himself, everyone knows him. You may as well leave—it's a waste of time.

BLACK [*now approaches* DAVID *and takes him to one side*]: Dave, listen boy, I want to speak to you openly. Now, I don't know what that other geezer told you, but I can guess. He said his prices were more reasonable—well—it's a lie. My stone is the cheapest.

SAM: It's becoming like Hatton Garden. I should have been cremated.

BLACK [*his voice has disintegrated into Cockney*]: Look, give us a break with our unbreakable stone. Do me a favour, by my life—I should drop dead on this spot if our stone ain't the best. By my mother's life, by my father's life, by my life—I need the order—put in a good word with your mother. Look, Dave—[*He takes a photo out of his pocket and kisses it.*] Here's my wife and my baby daughter—her name's Angela—a real angel—help me earn an honest coin—I'm not really a traveller in tombstones—I'm just a yid-disher boy, like yourself, forced by circumstances to take up this vocation.

[*There is another ring at the door and* DAVID *goes. He returns, followed by a third man.*]

DAVID: I know, don't tell me—you're not really selling tombstones.

MAN: That's right—how did you guess? I'm not selling anything; as a matter of fact, I've come to give you something. Two hundred pounds for you and two hundred and fifty pounds for your mother.

DAVID: Well—please sit down.

[SAM *and* DAVID *bow him into a chair near to the other two.*]

DAVID: Well—isn't this marvellous?—I'm really mixed up now. Suddenly I've got two hundred pounds to play with. What shall I do with it?

SAM: Remember if you keep on talking to me, they'll think you're out of your mind.

DAVID: Who cares what they think?

GREEN [*to the new man, whose name is* WHITE]: Don't be afraid of him—he's quite harmless.

BLACK: Just a bit touched in the head. Nice boy; pity.

WHITE: I've been coming to the house long enough. He hasn't changed one bit. That reminds me—[*He consults a little notebook.*] In the case of insanity I don't think we are liable to pay out on an endowment, but I can't see anything here. I'll check back to the office later. Meanwhile, I'll hold on to the money.

DAVID: I'm going to do something to really make them sit up. [*He stands on a table.*] I'll recite and wake up the world.

SAM: Don't be a bloody fool; come down here. You must grow up. You must become yourself.

DAVID: I've got it! At last! There's someone I will become.

SAM: What do you mean?

DAVID [*excited*]: Everything fits together. Why didn't I think of it before? I'm the boy with a ghost of his own. Isn't that terrific? You're my own special ghost. Before, you were only my father—now! Nothing can stop us—we're going to have a marvellous time. I've got it all worked out.

SAM: Davey—Davey—calm down—take it easy. What can I do with him?

DAVID: Don't worry, Dad—I'm doing this for you. To avenge your death—your murder.

SAM: Where do you keep on getting that idea from—I wasn't—

DAVID [*very excited*]: Listen—Shush! No time for argument—you're right—I must become myself—I must become a crazy prince to the bitter end. I can hardly wait for all that murder and chaos at the end.

SAM: Davey—just explain—what you mean.

DAVID: I'll wait until I have all the evidence and I'll strike! When everyone is dead I'll live here all alone—just singing to the cobwebs.

[DAVID *stands in characteristic 'Hamlet' pose and* SAM *nods his head.*]

SAM: Oh—I see—Oy-vay—smir—I'll have to go along with him—otherwise—Please, Davey—I must hand it to you—a wonderful scheme—but please—take your time—and let me arrange the killings—after all, they can't hang a ghost.

DAVID: Oh—all right—but I must decide—who—when and where.

SAM: Besides, if you are the prince then I am the king.

DAVID: That's right—the king of my imagination. One minute—my mind's playing tricks on me—oh—anyway, who cares——as long as there's a way forward into to-morrow—I wish I really knew what you really wanted of me.

SAM [shrugs]: I wish you knew what you wanted of your-self. Anyway, your guess is as good as mine.

[The men are still looking at DAVID with astonish-ment.]

DAVID: All right, my poor father—my condolences, for, for some reason, you can't rest in peace.

SAM: We make a fine pair.

DAVID: What do we do first?

SAM: First we dance and sing.

[They chant and move together to a Jewish melody. They clap hands and dance around the rather terrified salesmen.]

SAM: They are not really themselves,

DAVID: Oy, oy, oy, oy, oy.
           They are doing it for their girls,
           And their little boys.
           Tombstone selling is a job,
           Like anything else to earn a bob;
           They are not selling themselves,
           Oy, oy, oy, oy, oy.

           They don't know who they are,
           Oy, yoy, yoy, yoy, yoy.
           On this mad demented star,
           Oy, yoy, yoy, yoy, yoy.
           A policy will pay the rent,
           Will buy the bread and his wife's scent.
           They are not really bent,
           Oy, oy, oy, oy, oy.

54

SAM: Have a good time—don't worry—well, how do you want to begin?

DAVID: I want to stay and wait for the fireworks. I want to make them and throw them. I know! I'll dress up. I'll be unique. I'll get a great mad gimmick. I'll dye my hair red or maybe light blue.

SAM: Don't be such a silly fool. That would spoil everything.

DAVID: I'll make and break the rules just as I feel like it. I'll shock them out of their lives. There'll be no more rest for anyone from now on.

[DAVID *rushes off in a maniac state and the three men continue with the card game they have been engrossed in.*]

GREEN: Stick!

BLACK: Twist . . . oh, bust!

SAM: Schmeral.

[BESSIE *comes on, dressed in black, followed by* MR *and* MRS STONE, SEGAL, *and* HAVA, *who also are dressed in mourning.*]

SAM [*goes to* HAVA *and forgets that he is a ghost*]: Hello, sad eyes—why are you looking so sad? Oh, I forgot—is it on account of me? Don't worry, I'm all right.

HAVA: My, it's chilly in here. The nights are drawing in. Where's Davey?

SAM: Do have a word with my boy; try to help him. He needs a nice girl like you.

HAVA: Daddy, I'll be glad when we move from Stepney Green. It's only full of memories now. All my friends are gone. It's full of bomb-sites and ghosts. It was the first funeral I ever went to.

WHITE: Mrs Levy, I would like to speak with you for a moment.

[*They go over to one corner of the room, where they whisper.*]

SAM [*goes to* BESSIE]: Suddenly I'm dead—and buried. Why didn't we make a go of it? Where did our love go to? Oh, I'm not blaming you—I'm only asking.

MRS STONE: Are you feeling all right, dear?

HAVA: Yes, not too bad. Wonder where Davey is? I'd like to talk to him. Maybe he'll take me for a walk and everything will be different.

SEGAL: Don't you worry about him. You worry about your poor old father. So, here we are back at the house, everyone here except poor old Sam.

SAM: Don't be too sure.

STONE [*goes to his wife and places his arm around her*]: It's funny how a person you know suddenly just dies— they go into a room, a hospital, and never come out. My own mother, the last time I saw her, was in a narrow bed surrounded by flowers and fast asleep. She looked just like marble. I left the ward and five minutes later she died. She went into that place and never came out again. They wheeled the body out. A shell, a husk that resembled my mother. Where did she go to?

SEGAL: Ask me.

HAVA: I'm sure Mr Levy wouldn't want us to be morbid.

SAM: Oh darling, you're so right.

STONE: Millie, be a good girl, go and make a nice cup of tea. Come on, everyone, we mustn't get the miseries. That's what shivas are for. For friends and relations to come and try to make the family forget.

BESSIE: I'll never forget him. Never. He was such a good man. I tried. Didn't I try? Ask anyone.

SEGAL: When you've finished moaning Bessie, remember this is a house of mourning.

[HAVA *and* MRS STONE *go off to make tea, and* BESSIE *sits on a low chair.*]

SAM: What a bloody hypocrite you are, Mr Segal. You can't wait to get your hands on my Bessie.

STONE: Where's David, Bessie?

BESSIE: Yes, where is he? Where's my Daverler? Am I the only mourner?

SEGAL: Don't upset yourself. He'll be here soon. He's probably very upset.

STONE: And why didn't Lottie come?

BESSIE: Oh, why didn't she come? Am I the only mourner

for my poor dear husband, God rest his soul? Lottie didn't
come. Her own father and not a word.

[HAVA *and* MRS STONE *return with tea, which they
pour and hand round.*]

HAVA: I wonder why she didn't come? He was such a nice,
kind man.

MRS STONE: Don't cry, Bessie. Don't waste your tears.
The younger generation are not worth it. I'm glad I didn't
have any kids. For what? What for? Do they appreciate
you?

SEGAL: I tell you my son shows respect for me; he sends me
fifty dollars a month; is that bad?

BESSIE: What can you expect? Lottie's husband is a school-
teacher and, apart from being Communists, I think they
are also vegetarian.

STONE: That explains it; blood is thicker than water.

BESSIE: Yes, I am the only mourner. No one ever cared
for my poor husband like I did.

SAM: Why didn't you show it now and again? Still, it's
easy to see things when you're not so mixed up in them.
Don't cry, Bessie. Once I didn't know that everything
was wrong, now I know but I don't know how to put things
right.

HAVA [*to* BESSIE]: Don't cry, because your husband is
sleeping now.

SAM: Yes, but dreaming heavy—no rest for the wicked.

HAVA: He is at rest and better off than the lot of us.

SAM: No—one minute of life is better than a million years
of sleep.

HAVA: You're not the only mourner—all Stepney Green
misses him.

SAM: Thank you, Hava, but real grief is very personal—
Stepney Green will carry on as if nothing happened. Yes,
Bessie, you are the only mourner, I think. Let me see.
There was brother Harry who died in Warsaw thirty-five
years ago. Izzy who deserted in the Great War and was
never seen again. Jack who came to England with me and
died of home-sickness and Betty who went to America
and died drinking highballs in a low dive. Lottie is in

Leeds and Davey is upstairs. There you are—Bessie with all
her faults is the only mourner.

[*The* THREE MEN *approach* BESSIE *and surround
her with photos and catalogues.*]

SAM: Like dirty postcards.

SEGAL: Have a heart, gentlemen, this is a house of mourning.

[*Chastised, the* MEN *make ready to go, but* SEGAL
stops them.]

SEGAL: No, no—don't go. We need you here for prayers.

[SAM *stands facing the audience; the stage gets darker;
all the men stand up and face the appropriate way. They
know their lines perfectly and they chant in chorus. The
women sway and weep softly in the background.*]

ALL MEN: We think of those dear to us . . .
Who are no longer with us in the body . . .

[*Their voices get softer and softer, until it is just above a
whisper, and they continue with the Kaddish. Meanwhile* SAM *interpolates his own chant.*]

SAM: Hear this, all you people. Listen, children of the
world, both high and low, rich and poor; I shall speak the
truth.

ALL: Death does not sever the bonds of devotion which
unite loving hearts.

Oh God, we ever accept your goodness and greatness.

[*They all start dovening in unison until they are a swaying wave of bodies; the stage is getting darker and
darker.*]

Praise be His great name for ever and ever.

SAM: God will redeem my soul from the grasp of the grave.

ALL: Let Him be glorified and exalted—

[*All move together, softly and loudly; up and down goes
the chant of voices. The women weep.*]

He will grant peace unto Israel and all mankind.

SAM: For He alone can grant peace.

May He who is the source of strength grant comfort to
those in sorrow and peace to the heart of all His children.

[DAVID *enters. He is dressed in a white shirt, black
tapering trousers, and a bootlace for a tie; he is now*

what is termed a TEDDY BOY *but the similarity to Hamlet* must *be stressed. He jumps upon a sideboard. They all gasp and are shocked.*]

DAVID [*sings*]: Yiddisher father,
          I bet he misses Matzo Bry,
          Cheesecake and Smoked Salmon,
          I hope he finds some in the sky,
          Will you look at them here,
          As they stand and pray.
          When they're all very glad that he's out of
             the way.
          Oh my wonderful yiddisher father—
          Somebody will have to pay.

[*He points dramatically at his mother as* THE LIGHTS FADE.]

CURTAIN

SCENE 2

When the lights come up a week has apparently passed.
All the characters are placed exactly as before, except SAM,
who is lying on the floor. The mirrors are uncovered and the three MEN *are playing cards.*
BESSIE *and* DAVID *get up from their low chairs.* DAVID
is obviously in a very agitated state but is very excited and manic still. Everyone seems completely tired out—as if he had been driving them right out of their wits.

DAVID: Well—I'm glad that ritual's over—now my little drama can begin.

MRS STONE: David—do me a favour—do us all a favour— don't go on any more. I can't stand it. What's the matter? Aren't you happy? Don't you sleep well?

BESSIE: You've been driving us mad for a week; now take

off those ridiculous clothes and put something decent on. What am I going to do with him?

SEGAL: What's he going to do with us?

DAVID: You'll find out. No—I'm sticking to these clothes.

BESSIE: But why?

DAVID: They make me feel good.

MRS STONE: I don't like saying this, Bessie, but your boy is meshuga. Why do you let him go on like this?

BESSIE [sings to tune Tum Balalaika]:

Listen, Davey, listen to me,
What a bad boy you turned out to be,
Driving me crazy, fast to my grave,
Killing me, darling, can't you behave?

Other mothers see joy from their child,
You are thoughtless, hopeless and wild,
Didn't I bring you into this life?
Do me a favour—go get a wife.

Oy-oy-oy-oy—what have I done
To deserve such a terrible son?
Driving me frantic, driving me mad,
Oh my dear Dave—you're just like your dad.

[She slaps him lightly upon the face, and makes a gesture as if she could kill him.]

BESSIE: Davey—you're killing me.

DAVID: Leave me alone.

BESSIE: I'll be dead and you'll be sorry.

DAVID: You talk too much.

BESSIE: You only have one mother—one mother!

DAVID: Thank God for that.

BESSIE: You'll cry—you'll see—when I'm gone—you don't know when you've got it good. Didn't I give you everything you wanted?

DAVID: You gave me everything you thought I wanted.

BESSIE: Tell me what you want now—I'll give it to you— if it's not too dear—don't you love your mother?

DAVID: What's love? How can I recognize it? I never saw any in this house.

BESSIE: There he goes again—clever dick. Didn't I give you enough food? [*She pinches his face.*] Come on, darling—

DAVID [*embarrassed*]: Oh—get away from me.

BESSIE [*she pinches him harder*]: I could kill him. [*She turns to* MRS STONE.] What can I do with him?

MRS STONE: He'll grow out of it—anyway, who cares what he's like as long as he's a nice boy?

[DAVID *sweeps around the stage and booms out; they all look at him.*]

DAVID: To be or not to bloody well be, believe me, that is the question! Whether it is besser to be a bissel meshuga—

WHITE: Twist.

DAVID: Or to take alms for the love of Allah. To kick the bucket or to take forty winks.

[*All look entranced at the boy.* SAM *wakes up.*]

STONE: He should have been an Hector.

BLACK: BUST!

GREEN: Pay twenty-ones—five cards and pontoons only.

WHITE: Pay me, then.

DAVID: To take forty winks no more and by Ali Abracadabra to end the sourous and the hire purchase, please God by you.

[BESSIE *and* SEGAL *are flirting in a corner.*]

DAVID: These are the consumer goods for the frum yids. To kick the bucket, to take a nap at the race-track—ah! there's the snag, for on that slip of paper what names were written—blown away by the wind—blown away, etcetera, you should live so long.

STONE: Davey! I've got it all worked out. You team up with Prince Monologue and together you sell tips and sing your philosophy to the boys down the lane.

DAVID: Oh, pipe down! [*He turns to* SEGAL.] And you watch yourself.

SEGAL: What do you mean?

DAVID: If you must carry on like that with my mother—at least wait until my father is cold.

SEGAL: You must have more respect for older people.

DAVID: Respect! What a dirty word that is. Look, we

haven't even taken the memorial light from the mantel-piece—when's the wedding?

SEGAL: What are you talking about? I was being sympathetic.

BESSIE: Darling! Davey! How could you? Please, shut up. Do me a favour—be a nice boy. LEAVE HOME.

DAVID: Look—you drove him to the grave and there he is!
 [DAVID *points to* SAM, *who laughs, and all the others look incredulously on.*]

DAVID: No, I'm staying—staying here.

BESSIE: As a matter of fact, we were discussing the details of getting rid of your father's business.

DAVID: Getting rid of it? Oh, no you're not. That herring stall is the kingdom I've inherited. I am THE PRINCE OF HERRINGS. I'm starting work there next Monday. The smell of those little silver fishes will follow me wherever I go. I've seen millions of them one way and another and I'll see millions more. I've brushed those sticky scales from my suits a thousand times. I've watched you cut their heads off and gut them—I've seen you souse them and shmaltz them, pickle them and grill them. I've dreamed of them—had nightmares about them. Millions and millions of herrings, all with the same face; kippers, bucklings, brislings—all my loyal subjects.

SAM: Don't work down the market—plenty of time—don't rush into things. Get that two hundred pounds and go to auditions. I've got faith in you. But I must say herrings are delicious—try one, one day. I even used to eat them now and again. They have a very high vitamin yield.

BESSIE: And what's wrong with herrings? Everything in this house has been bought by them. This table—that pack of cards—your bed upstairs—your clothes—the holidays at Cliftonville.

HAVA: David didn't mean—you see, he's got other fish to fry.
 [MR STONE *laughs.*]

DAVID [*to* SAM]: Honestly! If you had your time over again, which way would you choose to earn a living?

STONE: Well—er—let me see.

SAM: I would probably do exactly the same. I make no excuses. A ghost can't afford to.

HAVA: I would like to have married—a great man—a great singer—like someone I know.

STONE: I would have liked to have been a lawyer.

SEGAL: I would have liked to have been the leader of the greatest political party in the world and a diamond merchant in my spare time.

MRS STONE: I would like to have been a ballet dancer.

BESSIE: I would have liked to have married a Rothschild.

WHITE: Stick. I would have liked to be Joe Lyons.

BLACK: I would have liked to have been an Epstein. Bust.

GREEN: Pay pontoons only. I would have liked to be a Rabbi; you see this is not my real work.

ALL [except SAM]: And you? What would you like to be?

DAVID: The same as I am. Prince of the Herrings. Prince Hamlet . . .

[They all laugh.]

HAVA: I would like to go to the cinema. Coming, anyone?
[She quickly kisses her father and hurriedly exits.]

SAM: Listen, Boychick. Hamlet wasn't an important man. Where would he have been if Shakespeare didn't rescue him from obscurity? Now Shakespeare was a different kettle of fish.

DAVID: You know everything! First I must sell herrings and then I mustn't sell herrings—then I had a terrible voice and now I've a lovely voice—make up your mind.

SAM: Why shouldn't I change my mind? Why should ghosts be different from people?

DAVID: Arh, you're not a very successful ghost—you don't bother anyone—except me.

SAM: I'm doing my work properly—if you've any complaints you'd better get in touch with my union.

DAVID: It's all very well for you to be frivolous.

[The telephone rings; they all rush to lift the receiver but BESSIE beats all of them.]

BESSIE: Hello! Yes! Speaking! Who's that? Lottie? Is that you, Lottie? Darling! [She talks now to the room.] Mrs Stone, my Lottie's on the phone—all the way from

Leeds—Hello, Dolly—speak louder—[*to* DAVID *now*] Davey—your sister's on the line—come and say hello.

DAVID: Oh—do me a favour.

BESSIE: He won't even say hello to his own sister—what do you think of that? The trouble I have with that boy— what's that, darling?—no, he hasn't changed.

DAVID: Stop talking about me and carry on talking about nothing—

BESSIE: He's mad—he's mad—his own sister—believe me, Lottie—you're better off in Leeds.

[DAVID *stomps off into the kitchen.*]

BESSIE: He's gone out of the room now—into the kitchen —how do I know? Well, how are you, darling? Good— you should be ashamed of yourself. What? No! Where? Yes—listen. Lottie—you should be ashamed of yourself— your own father—your own flesh and blood and you never came—after all the years he slaved for you—what? I can't hear! You want to speak to Davey? [*Shouts towards kitchen.*] Davey—Lottie wants a word with you.

DAVID [*off*]: I'm busy.

BESSIE [*into phone*]: He's busy—always busy—he's driving us mad—no tongue can tell what I have to put up with there's no other house like this house—you bad girl—Lottie —why didn't you even come to the shiva? What? Going to have another one? When? That husband of yours—oh, such bad news—it always comes together—Mazeltov, darling—kiss the babies for me—wrap up warm—take care —there are the pips—you should be ashamed—good-bye, Dolly teta! Take care—I'm all right—there're the pips—the pips—I'm all right—I'll survive somehow—Teta, Lottie! [*She puts the phone down.*] She's going to have another baby. Davey! You're going to be an uncle again!

DAVID [*off*]: Hurray!

MRS STONE: How many will this make?

BESSIE [*proudly*]: This will be my fifth grandchild.

MRS STONE: Hasn't she heard of them new clinics? Nobody goes in for big families any more.

BESSIE: Her husband is a Catholic.

SEGAL: Not long ago you said he was a Communist.

BESSIE: He is a Communist and a Catholic.

MRS STONE [*sings suddenly*]: To sigh for you—to cry for you—yes—even die for you—that's what God made mothers for—

BESSIE: Believe me—you're right.

[DAVID *comes on, drinking.*]

SAM: What are you drinking?

DAVID: Chocolate.

SAM: Good—it was the magical drink of the Aztec gods— anyway, it won't do you any harm.

DAVID: No more smoozing me—something has got to happen soon—I must get revenge—they killed you and you won't directly admit it. WHY? You're getting cold feet— you can't rely on your own father—not even when he's a ghost. LOOK AT THEM! Just look at them!

BESSIE: We ruined him—he's feeling like this because he's got to face up to reality. He hasn't worked properly for years. He read too many books. We gave him everything he wanted. The boy with the ever-open hand. Money for jazz records—money for clothes—money for jam. He used to bring back stray dogs and mangy cats.

MRS STONE: Mangy cats?

BESSIE: I put up with a lot to stop him being a low-life. He even kept lizards as pets.

MRS STONE: LIZARDS! Oh, Bessie—how you must have suffered!

BESSIE: It was all Sam's fault. He was too soft with him.

SAM: Go on, blame the dead—how convenient a corpse can be! Why did I marry such a woman?

DAVID: But Dad—surely you loved her once.

SAM: Yes—once. [BESSIE *is eating and stuffing herself with chocolates.*]

DAVID [*to* BESSIE]: Why didn't you love Dad? He was such a good man.

[BESSIE *nearly chokes with a chocolate.*]

SAM: SHUT UP, DAVEY! I had my faults. Things happen between husband and wife that no one else can know about.

BESSIE: Listen to who's talking. The pot calls the kettle black. I'm going to tell you a few things about Sam—

SAM: Change the subject quick. Otherwise you'll end up by sympathizing with her.

DAVID: Mind your own business. You're no help to me. I want revenge and I want it NOW!

SAM: Davey—calm down.

DAVID: Calm! Calm, he says. You were murdered by some people in this room—and they're going to pay. I've got to avenge the injustice and the scandal.

SAM: Who in this room? What are you talking about?

DAVID: When you died you said she poisoned you—I heard you—

SAM: Oh, don't be so silly.

DAVID: It's no good backing out of it now—with my own ears I heard your last words.

SAM: Oh! I didn't really mean that she poisoned me— what I meant to say was that my life poisoned me and because once she was my life—well—

DAVID: You just said 'She poisoned me' and that's good enough for me. I know why she did—they planned it to- gether—she and that little Soppy Segal [points at the frightened SOLLY.]

SAM: You only heard what you wanted to. What was in your mind to pick out.

DAVID: You're a liar! You were telling the truth then, but now you're covering up for them—for some reason.

SAM: Davey—don't be dramatic—settle down like a good boy and learn from my mistakes. Listen, before I didn't know just how much of a mess I made of my life—now I know—but how can I get through to you?—please listen to me.

DAVID: There's only one thing I know or want to know— you were poisoned whether you admit it or not and my sole aim is to avenge your murder—I'm going to do this with or without your help—they've got to pay—anyway, before you promised to help me—well—you'd better make up your mind once and for all.

[He goes into the garden.]

SAM [*reluctantly*]: Very well—I have no choice. I'll have to play along with him.

[DAVID *sulks in the garden.*]

BESSIE: I did love Sam. Yes, I did—I know we didn't get on, but he was a good man and I'm going to miss him so much.

SAM: Poor Bessie—argument was the only way we could stay close. She wasn't a bad girl and if I wasn't a ghost I could get quite carried away and forgive her for everything. ALMOST.

[SAM *follows* DAVID *into the garden; he goes through wall.* SOLLY *goes into the garden.*]

CHILDREN: Silly Solly Segal, nose like an eagle,
　　　　　　　Eyes like two jelly-fish, teeth like a weasel.

[SEGAL *sits down near* SAM *and* DAVID. *The lights in the house go dim.*]

SAM: Davey—please, what's the matter with you?

DAVID: To tell you the truth—I'm unhappy.

SOLLY: Oh, cheer up, my boy—growing up is hard.

SAM: Why? I know that most of the past was undesirable, but now we must look forward.

DAVID: I wanted so much to please you.

SOLLY: Well, that's very nice of you.

DAVID: It looks like we have permanent guests.

SEGAL: Yes.

DAVID: I wasn't speaking to you.

SEGAL: I wish you would sometimes. I might be able to give you some advice.

DAVID: I wanted you to be proud of me.

SAM: There's still time.

DAVID [*mood changes*]: Now that my dad's out of the way I suppose you'll marry my mother.

SEGAL: I'm lonely. Don't think too badly of me. You're too young to understand loneliness.

DAVID: Am I? Yes, ever since you died the house has been full of people.

SEGAL [*jumps up*]: Ever since I died? [*Feels his face.*] What do you mean?

SAM: Poor old boy. Don't be too hard on him.

DAVID: Every time you talk I get the feeling that it's myself thinking. My other self.

SEGAL: That's a good thing. I could teach you a lot. Politics and economics. Syndicalism. The theories of capital and labour . . .

DAVID: I was with you when you died.

SEGAL: When I died! Oh, you're driving me mad.

SAM: I'm happy to know I didn't die alone. Was it difficult seeing me die?

DAVID: Yes.

SEGAL: What do you mean? Yes?

SAM: Did I call for Bessie?

DAVID: No.

SEGAL: What do you mean? Yes! No!

DAVID: I told you—you said you'd been poisoned.

SEGAL: Poisoned? [*He staggers for a moment and splutters.*]

DAVID: Not you—not yet. [*to* SAM] I can't get over it: your best friend and your wife, glad to get you out of the way.

SAM: The real motives in people's minds are terrible things to discover; yours for instance. Don't look too deeply.

SEGAL: Poor Sam—what a responsibility being your father —is it worth it?

DAVID: Coming in? I feel cold.

SEGAL: No—I want to think.

SAM: No—I want to stop thinking. When I'm with you I think too much.

[DAVID *goes inside house and sits alone.*]

SAM [*looks at* SOLLY]: Poor Solly.

SEGAL [*looks up*]: Poor Sammy.

SAM: Bloody hypocrite. Still, Solly wasn't a bad man— sometimes.

SEGAL [*a reprise of the duologue in Act I*]: Sammy was a wonderful man; I never really knew him.

SAM: The boy's restless and it's up to me. There must be a solution. Anyway, that's what I'm here for.

SEGAL: He was so kind.

SAM: I can't leave until I help him see straight.

SEGAL: Poor David. His mother will kill him, if they live alone. He needs a man—a great man—someone to look up to—what am I saying? He needs someone like me; I'll be a real father to him.

SAM: Bloody cheek. One minute. You're right. You're right! I hate to say this but you're right. That's the answer.

SEGAL: It's getting windy. Think I'll go in now and maybe talk to Bessie.

[As he moves to go in, the CHILDREN come and call after him again.]

CHILDREN: Soppy Solly Segal, nose like an eagle,
         Eyes like two jelly-fish—
[With a gesture of dismay he chases them and then goes into the house.]

SAM: Mr Segal I could k—iss you. [Pause.] All right, if you and Bessie get married, but I know what will happen: you'll discuss it for years, you'll argue—you'll say not enough time has passed since my burial—I've got to think of some way to get you married as soon as possible—
[He goes through the wall again into the house and the lights go up.]

DAVID [rushing to SAM and pointing to SOLLY and BESSIE, who are now whispering together]: You know, of course, what they're planning.

SAM [joking]: Are they planning more horrible murders?

DAVID: Not yet. Now they're planning to get married.

SAM: Do you think I am blind? This is a wonderful idea; you must encourage their romance if you want revenge.

DAVID: What do you mean?

SAM: Their marriage would prove they wanted me out of the way—it would prove your theories correct.

DAVID: Yeah! You're right. You're dead right.

SAM: You said it.

WHITE [from card table]: Listen, young man—I'm staying round to check your sanity—well, my report won't be very favourable. Our company need not pay your endowment if you're stone bonkers.

DAVID [to SAM]: You signed this policy knowing this clause?

SAM: Who reads policies when they sign them? Who has that much time to waste? Anyway, I signed when you were one year old—I didn't know you'd grow up to be a madman.

[MR STONE *suddenly stands up.*]

MR STONE: Well, isn't that a coincidence? Listen, everybody, their names are not really White, Black and Green! This is really Mr Blackstone, this is really Mr Whitestone, and this is really Mr Greenstone, and I changed my name by deed poll from Goldstone to Stone.

DAVID: They dropped the stone and you picked it up.

[MR STONE *sits down and the three* MEN *stand up.*]

WHITE: In business it's better—

BLACK: It's brief and to the point.

GREEN: It pays to have a simple name.

[*The three* MEN *get into line and sing a smart clipped song; the tune is a variant of the post-horn gallop.*]

MEN: Mr White, Mr Black, Mr Green,
    Our tombstones are simply serene,
    Our companies never look back,
    Mr White, Mr Green, Mr Black.
    Mr Green, Mr Black, Mr White.
    Our companies soon set it right,
    And they're guaranteed not to crack,
    Mr Green, Mr White, Mr Black.
    Mr Black, Mr Green, Mr White,
    Insurance and tombstones are right;
    Buy British and always fight clean,
    Mr Black, Mr White, Mr Green.

[*They sit down again and play cards.*]

MRS STONE [*suddenly sings*]: You die if you worry, you die if you don't—so why worry at all? It's only worry that killed the cat, anybody can tell you that—That's funny—I feel like singing tonight. My mother used to sing that song, and do you know what? She died worrying just the same.

[SEGAL, MRS STONE, *and* BESSIE *are seated around the table.* DAVID *and* SAM *are talking quietly.*]

BESSIE: Shall we begin? Have you got the letters ready?

[MRS STONE *starts arranging letters around the table.*
BESSIE *returns to the table with a tumbler.*]

MRS STONE: Come on Alf, we're ready to begin.

[*She almost has to pull him away from the card game.*]

SEGAL: What's the matter? What's everyone gone quiet
for?

BESSIE: Why, the seance, of course.

SEGAL: Who do you want to talk with?

BESSIE: Anyone who's interested in talking to us!

SEGAL: Sounds like a Summit Conference. I hope you don't
pick up Sam on the high frequency.

SAM: Oh—he's sensitive.

SEGAL: Oy—the spirits—what they say is sacred—leave
them alone.

[SEGAL *is about to place his arm around* BESSIE
when he changes his mind.]

SEGAL [*looking at the ceiling*]: Sam—oy—Sam, forgive me,
my thoughts are not nice—but my intentions are pure.

SAM: At last! I've got it. The answer.

DAVID: Look at that little hypocrite—I could kill him
now.

SAM: Be patient and wait a little while. They'll kill each
other.

DAVID: I want them to die—like you. No, not like you. Oh,
I don't care how they die.

SAM: I'll help you kill them in such a way that they won't
affect you any more. You'll be free and no one will charge
you with anything. Just be patient. It's all clicked into
place—this is how we get them married. [*He whispers to*
DAVID, *who laughs.*]

DAVID: And once they're married, Bob's your uncle.

SEGAL: I'm filled with remorse. He was right—for once
that madman, my stepson-in-law, please God, was right—
my thoughts are not becoming to a citizen of the world.

BESSIE: What are you muttering about, Mr Segal?

SEGAL: Bessie, how many years have you known me?

BESSIE: About thirty or forty years.

SEGAL: Isn't it time you called me Solly?

SAM: Here we go, Davey.

[BESSIE *smiles and places* SEGAL'S *finger on the tumbler, as the others have done.*]

BESSIE [*whispers*]: Solly, boy, are you comfortable?

STONE: Is there anyone there who wants to speak with anyone here?

[SAM *is laughing his head off, nods, and begins to move the tumbler to various letters. Everyone follows with great concentration the journey of the glass. The* MEN *at the table continue playing cards, totally unaware of the things going on.*]

SAM [*saying the word that he is spelling out*]: HITLER.

[*There is great confusion in the room as the women scream and rush as far from the table as possible.*]

MRS STONE: Oy, what do we do now? Send him back? Send him back, Alf.

BESSIE [*creeps back to the table*]: Let's ignore him and try to get someone else.

STONE: You never know what will turn up.

SEGAL: Maybe he just wants to apologize.

DAVID [*who pretends that he didn't see the message*]: What was the message?

STONE: It just said HITLER. Come on, let's try again. Maybe we didn't write the letters clearly enough or they're short-sighted over there.

[*They repeat the process, and* SAM, *who has been reading the sporting page of the newspaper, begins to move the glass again.*]

DAVID: What does it say now?

BESSIE: Hush.

MRS STONE: Shush.

SEGAL: Hush? Shush? What does that mean? It goes too fast. I can't read upside down.

[SAM *spells out the words again.*]

SAM: RED CLOUD . . . TWO-THIRTY . . . TOMORROW . . .

[*They all repeat this as they read the message.*]

SEGAL: Red cloud? Sounds like a Communist pirate.

BESSIE: Look, there it goes again. Red, cloud, tomorrow, two-thirty. It must be the spirit guide. You know what I mean? White cloud! Red cloud! They're always Red Indians.

MRS STONE: Why?

BESSIE: How should I know?

SEGAL [*sings*]: Red cloud in the sunset . . .

DAVID [*sings*]: Mushrooms on the sea . . .

STONE: One moment: did it say Red Cloud? [*he looks at the back page of the newspaper*] Here it is: Red Cloud running in the big race, two-thirty tomorrow: 100 to 1.
   [*He rushes to the phone and dials.*]

MRS STONE: Izzy Posner won't be there at this hour.

STONE: Izzy never leaves the office; that's his motto. Hello? Is that you, Izzy? This is me: Alf Stone. Five pounds each way, Red Cloud, two-thirty—never mind, do what I tell you.
   [*At this moment the three* MEN *quickly leave the card game and rush for the telephone. One snatches it from* MR STONE *and each in turn pulls it from the others; each retains it long enough only to speak his name.*]

MEN: MR WHITE. MR BLACK. MR GREEN. MR BLACK. MR WHITE. GREEN. WHITE. BLACK. WHITE. BLACK. GREEN.
   [*The names coagulate into a jumble of sound. At the telephone the* MEN *continue at the action, only the sound has faded and they play in dumb show.* SAM *starts spelling out again, and they follow the glass with rapt attention.*]

SAM [*spelling out the letters he is moving the glass to*]: This is—Sam—Levy . . . I forgive you, Mr Segal—take care of—my Bessie . . .
   [*Everyone cheers.* SEGAL *is ecstatic and kisses* BESSIE, *and* DAVID *and* SAM *shake hands.* DAVID *looks at* BESSIE *and* SEGAL, *and rubs his hands.*]

CURTAIN

ACT THREE

Eight months later.
It is a fine afternoon in early spring; in the house there is a festive tone, that completely contrasts with the previous scene. There are flowers everywhere. The table is set with a large white tablecloth on which are bottles of wine and dishes of fruit.
D A V I D is sitting on a chair in the garden, looking more like Hamlet and very morose; S A M is lying on the grass looking up at the sky. C H I L D R E N are playing nearby and are singing.

C H I L D R E N: Poor Jenny is a-weeping, a-weeping, a-weeping.
　　　　　　　Poor Jenny is a-weeping on a bright summer's day.
　　　　　　　Stand up, stand up, on your heels,
　　　　　　　Choose the one you like the best, a lady or a gentleman;
　　　　　　　Now you're married we wish you joy,
　　　　　　　First a girl and then a boy.
　　　　　　　Kiss her once, kiss her twice,
　　　　　　　Kiss her three times over.

　　　[S A M *gets up and does some gardening, digging, and the scene fades slightly. The* T H R E E　S'A L E S M E N *enter and immediately go to the table where they start helping themselves to sandwiches.*]

W H I T E: You'll be happy to know that I sold her a stone; clinched the deal just before she got married.

B L A C K: But you're an insurance man.

W H I T E: I was an insurance man; I've now started my own little monumental stone company. By the way, why not work for me, the two of you?

B L A C K: I'm afraid that's impossible. You see, I've been an insurance agent for several months.

74

GREEN: So am I. That's strange. I came here today to sell her an insurance policy for her husband.

BLACK: So did I and at the same time to try and get that son of hers to take out a life insurance.

GREEN: There seems to be a close parallel in our lives.

BLACK: There certainly does. Where were you educated?

GREEN: Jews' Free School. Where were you?

BLACK: Why, at the same school. Who was your teacher?

GREEN: Mr Rosen. Yours?

BLACK: Rosen also. What year?

GREEN: About 1940 I left.

BLACK: So did I. We must have been there at the same time.

GREEN: Do you like football?

BLACK: No. Do you like cricket?

GREEN: Yes.

BLACK: So do I. What a coincidence!

GREEN: Do you like me?

BLACK: No. Do you like me?

GREEN: No. How wonderful! [*They shake hands and are all smiles.*]

GREEN [*to* WHITE]: Could you get your company to settle the David Levy claim? That is to say, your old company?

WHITE: I believe that they're doing it today. I sold Mrs Levy a stone on that understanding. I'll call in there and get the money for him.

BLACK: Tell me, what company do you represent?

GREEN: The Providential Life of Mile End.

BLACK [*excited and thrilled*]: How do you do? So do I. [*They shake hands excitedly.*]

WHITE: Did you say the Providential Life of Mile End? [*They nod.*] Why, that's the company I used to work for; this calls for a drink. [*Opens a bottle and they all have a drink.*]

GREEN: Tell me, aren't you a little off your territory?

BLACK: I don't think so. My zone starts at Silvertown, extends all along Commercial Road, Watney Street, Hessel Street, Cable Street, Jubilee Street, Redmans Road, and all the area of Stepney Green, southern side.

GREEN: Let me see, my area begins at Bishopsgate, Houndsditch, Commercial Street, Brady Street Buildings, Old Montague Street, and Stepney Green, northern side. Bow Road right up to Stratford.

BLACK: There you are, you said northern side. Sorry, old chap, this is the southern side. You're on my territory; David Levy is mine.

GREEN: I'm so terribly sorry, no hard feelings?

BLACK: Certainly not. Let's all have a drink.

[*They all drink and then* WHITE *and* GREEN *make to exit.*]

GREEN: See you at the office one day. So long.

BLACK: Yes, rather. Who knows, we may see each other quite often. Bye-bye.

[GREEN *exits.* WHITE *is about to leave also.*]

Don't forget to bring him the money today.

WHITE: I shan't. So long, old boy. [*He exits.*]

[BLACK *walks smugly around the stage and starts drinking at the table. He sits down and drinks quite a lot.*]

SAM: Oh, I'm so tired; I feel like I could just sleep and sleep.

DAVID: Why don't you? You always said you deserved a rest—well, here it is.

SAM: I'm worried about you. It's about time you made up your mind? Are you going to look after the barrow or not?

DAVID: I've been in for about ten auditions in the past couple of months. You've got to have a gimmick or influence or both. I've borrowed almost the whole of that two hundred pounds from Mum; it's coming today, but I shan't get any of it. What is going to be the outcome of all this? I mean, what are you going to do? You can't stay here all your life.

SAM: All my life?

DAVID: I mean all your death. It's getting to the state where I'm beginning to think that I'm your father. What are you waiting for now?

SAM: There was the question of revenge and your future that brought me here. I think the two are really the same problem. You must really make up your mind. Do you know that ever since I've been dead I haven't seen anyone over there.

DAVID: You know, of course, what happened today? Today is the big day. The day we've been waiting for.

SAM: I haven't been around so much recently.

DAVID: That's right. Where have you been? A fine ghost you turned out to be. Why, I've almost got to like Segal in your absence. And when you're here you sleep all the time. Today is my day. I'm free either way. I'll kill myself along with the rest.

SAM [*who hasn't been listening*]: Oh, I've been wandering here and there. I went down the Lane to see all the boys. Solly Segal was there selling herrings at my stall. Then I took a boat trip to Putney and I went to the Tower of London. I walked through the front entrance of Buckingham Palace and strolled right through the place. I didn't see not one member of the Royal Family. I also went on a conducted tour with some wealthy Yanks. Hampton Court, Kew, Greenwich, Ken Wood. Davey, why didn't you tell me that London was so beautiful? What a wonderful history it has. It's like a wonderful woman you can live with your whole life and miss the entire point. It's not so bad being dead after all. I saw the city in the early morning, before anyone gets up to go to work. I walked along the riverside: it's very lovely with the sun rising with the mist, rising over the office blocks and the warehouses. I saw the swans wake up and preen themselves in the mud.

DAVID: You know, of course, what happened today. You're evading the issue. You don't want to leave here.

SAM: Being dead has great advantages. Why I even got the best seat in the Festival Hall for nothing, but I suppose it's no use; being dead like this is so impermanent. There's no future in it, don't you agree?

DAVID: You do know what happened today?

SAM: Yes, my Bessie got married.

DAVID: Does that let you out?

SAM: I suppose it must do. Segal is my exit visa.

DAVID: You're still going to help me play it out to the end?

SAM: If you're determined, I suppose so. How do you want them to die?

DAVID: The same way that you died. By poison.

SAM: Fine. Presently I'll give you a list of various ingredients needed. I want you to go out and buy them at the chemist and greengrocer. I want you to mix the concoction to my specification and then you administer it in your own time. Oh well, this is it. Everything is resolved today.

DAVID: What is the purpose in life? It seems senseless to me.

SAM: The purpose in life is to be aware that that question exists. What is the purpose in life? I wonder. I was borrowed from the darkness by your desire. I've been allowed to slip away for a few moments. I never had roots anywhere, Davey, and I'm still wandering. I love London so much that I hate leaving it, for ever and ever. If being a ghost means having a real pain in the heart then I am the biggest and most successful ghost that ever was. But I have the even greater desire to look for some other light; a light brighter than earth, a light I heard about in symphonies and poetry. I am dead and buried and live only in the imagination of a neurotic young man; you are fickle you'll forget all about this, then I'll be really dead.

DAVID: Never.

SAM: Yes, you will, and quite right too. I, Samuel Levy, of no fixed abode am being charged with loitering and soon I must leave London for ever.

DAVID: In spite of your words I'm happy. In a strange way you make me feel wonderful. I don't seem to want revenge so much.

SAM: Oh yes, you do. When you get revenge in this house, everything will turn out all right, just as it should be. But don't be too confident; you'll be hurt over and over again, and always about the same things.

DAVID: I feel I can face everything. As if I'd been taken by the ankles and battered against a wall; bashed to pulp and yet I can stand up and sing.

SAM: You still haven't grown out of that?

DAVID: I want to sing. I've got to. When I stop I'll lay down and die.

SAM: Where will you go when all this revenge business is settled?

DAVID: I'm not sure. It's been nice of you to help me.

SAM: I'm glad that I could help you, because now instead of only being your father, we are close friends. It's so easy to make a child and so hard to make a friend. Where will you go?

DAVID: Anywhere—everywhere! A grand tour—New York, Mexico, Peru, New Guinea, Siam, China, India. Come on, Dad, let me have that prescription.

SAM: Don't be in too much of a hurry. I haven't finished talking yet.

DAVID: What do you mean?

SAM: Some people never leave home; even when they put a thousand miles between them and the street door; when you leave, really leave.

DAVID: Don't start lecturing me again. We've been having a wonderful time. Don't start getting stuffy now.

SAM: Forgive me, but I think that my time is drawing near; I'm beginning to feel like a ghost should; restless and forgetful. I feel guilty and uncomfortable like a bird that should migrate somewhere; a bird that lost its memory. Don't mind me, though. I will disappear soon and then all our troubles will be over. I shan't bother you. I might, though, sort of vanish inside you; wouldn't that be nice? [*He has been writing and hands* DAVID *the piece of paper.*] There you are, my son. Here is your revenge.

DAVID [*reads it and has difficulty*]: By the sound of it it should be very effective. Where did you learn about it?

SAM: Picked it up since I was buried. It's effective, don't you worry. Now go on, off with you; they're returning soon.

[DAVID *goes off into the house reading it.*]
He'll drink some, too; so will I. I hate unhappy endings. It'll work but not in the way that he expects.

[DAVID *is about to leave the house when* BLACK *stops him.*]

BLACK: Excuse me, sir, could I interest you in a very good life insurance policy?

DAVID: But I thought you sold tombstones?

BLACK: I used to, but you see I was never really . . . I'm a student of life.

DAVID: We must have a drink when I get back. I'm going to something very special; I'm sure after that you'll never be yourself again. [*Exits.*]

BLACK: Wonderful. What a charming boy! He's really turning out a decent sort.

[*There is a great commotion and the crowd of people come in the door.* BESSIE *and* SEGAL *come in arm in arm and dancing; they are already quite drunk.* MR *and* MRS STONE *follow. Then* HAVA, *who looks sad;* GREEN *and* WHITE *also enter.* MR STONE *starts the gramophone and plays a typical Hebrew melody and when* SAM *comes in it all seems to go a little quieter. There is much eating and drinking.*]

HAVA: It seems brighter here now.

BLACK [*to* WHITE *and* GREEN]: Hello, you two back?

GREEN: Yes, we bumped into them. [*He is quite tipsy and takes hold of* BLACK *and guides him around the stage in a dreamy love attitude, to the music.*]

WHITE [*follows them around*]: I've got the money! [*He is cuddling a brown paper parcel.*]

[BESSIE *is talking seriously to* MRS STONE. *The* MEN *are now drinking around the table;* HAVA *is looking around the house.*]

BESSIE: I still can't help thinking that I got married too soon. I don't know—I feel it wasn't right.

[SAM *is also drinking.*]

MRS STONE: Don't worry yourself. It wasn't too soon. Enjoy yourself while there is still time. You're still a young girl. Years ago it might have been different but this is the age of the jet; everything is getting faster and faster.

HAVA: I don't think I've been in this house for a month.

[SEGAL, *who is very drunk, now stands on a chair.*]

SEGAL: Tonight, everyone, we are going to have a wonderful party. All Stepney Green is invited. A real old-fashioned party; dancing and singing. Forget wars, forget politics, and enjoy yourself.

HAVA [*goes to him*]: I'm so happy for you, Daddy. You've been such a worry to me.

SEGAL: I've got a beautiful wife and a beautiful daughter. [*He kisses both of them.*]

HAVA: I still don't like the idea of moving here.

MRS STONE: What a man he is; how romantic! Why can't you be like that?

STONE: I will be, when I get married again.

HAVA: I wonder where Davey is?

SEGAL: Maybe right now, dear old Sam is getting married to my Sarah; God rest her soul; isn't that a lovely thought? [SAM *looks round uncomfortably as if he is being pursued.*]

SAM: God forgive you, Mr Segal, don't do me any favours. Bessie is an angel compared to your Sarah. If they gave me a choice of everlasting darkness or your Sarah, I would choose the darkness.

SEGAL [*sings*]: The second time is always nicer,
    And this is my second time.
    For many years I've been a miser,
    That has been my crime.
    Oy, oy, wish me joy,
    Tonight I am a lucky boy.
    The second time is so much nicer;
    This is my second time.

BESSIE: They'll say I didn't wait for long
    But a girl must take her chance.
    Solly is so nice and strong
    And Sam led me a dance;
    Well, well, I'm in a spell,
    Tonight I am a lucky girl.
    The second time is so much nicer;
    This is my second time.

THREE MEN: The second hand is whizzing round;
    Soon we'll be on our way.
    Our policies are really sound;
    Sign one with us today.

Dance, sing, love, and laugh,
We'll make up your epitaph.
The second time is so much nicer;
I DIED OF LOVE TODAY.

MRS STONE: Well, well, Bessie girl, Solly's got you in his spell . . .

ALL [*sing*]: The second time is so much nicer;
This is their second time.

[*They all return to little groups;* DAVID *returns and one can see him busy mixing the ingredients over by a side table;* HAVA *stands close to him but he does not see her.*]

SAM: All right, Bessie, I wish you joy. Mr Segal, er—may I call you Solly now? Solly, Bessie, I wish you both joy. Drive each other mad; here's to your good health and please God by you. [*He raises a glass to them and then he turns and looks in a mirror at himself.*]

HAVA [*to* BESSIE]: Please, er—Mrs—what can I call you?

BESSIE: Call me Aunty Bessie.

HAVA: Please Aunty, help me to know Davey. We can't go on like this.

BESSIE: Leave him alone; don't have much to do with him. He'll drive you mad.

SEGAL: That's all right. They're all a little mad where she came from; working out in the hot sun all day for no pay. Who in his right mind would do that?

[HAVA *goes into the garden sadly;* DAVID *is pouring out the drinks. The* MEN *sit down to play cards and it becomes very quiet in the room; everybody seems moody and only* SAM *is happy.* BLACK *suddenly sees* DAVID; *he leaves the game.*]

BLACK: Oh, there you are. Now what about that insurance policy? Our company believe that . . .

[DAVID *snubs him and* BLACK *moodily returns to the card game.*]

BESSIE: There you are. Come on, darling, Davey, come on. Kiss me and shake your Uncle Solly by the hand.

DAVID: *Leave me alone.* [*Turns his back.*]

[SAM *goes over to him and reasons with him.*]

82

SAM: Go on, Davey, play their game. It's nearly over. Wait and see what I've got in store for you.

DAVID: What?

BESSIE: There he goes, talking to himself again.

SAM: Just be patient. Kiss your mother, wish them joy. Give them all a drink [*he winks*] and Bob's your uncle.

[*HAVA has heard DAVID talking and she comes into the doorway and stands there watching.*]

DAVID [*goes over to BESSIE and SEGAL*]: Mother, I wish you joy and happiness. [*Kisses her.*] Mr Segal, I hope that you'll be very happy. I would like you all to have a little drink with me; I would like to toast your health.

[*DAVID hands around the drinks to everyone. He is about to by-pass SAM, but SAM takes one. DAVID shrugs. He does not give HAVA a drink.*]

SEGAL: Thank you, thank you, thank God. Have you decided what you want to do yet?

DAVID: I'll talk to you about it tomorrow.

SEGAL: You mean you'll take over the herring stall? At last? [*to himself*] I can't stand those herrings any longer.

DAVID: No, I'm not. Tomorrow I'm going to leave home.

[*Everyone is despondent and DAVID raises his glass.*] Here's to tomorrow. I wish you both joy. May this be the last of your worries, Lechaim. [*He raises the glass to his lips and is about to drink when he sees HAVA; lowers his glass and does not drink.*]

[*Everyone else drinks and as soon as they do they immediately start singing and dancing like mad. Everyone is in love with everyone else. SAM is trying to dance with DAVID—MR and MRS STONE are cuddling and kissing.*]

SAM [*thinking that DAVID has had a drink*]: Eh, Davey, what do you think of my love potion? Kaballa, Shmaballah, hahahhhah.

[*Everyone is dancing around in a ring and WHITE hands DAVID the parcel of money.*]

DAVID: What's this? Money? I don't want money, I want revenge. Here, take your money—confetti for the wedding.

[*He showers it over the stage and the others dance through it. The* THREE MEN *throw coloured streamers.* DAVID *looks at* HAVA, *who has been standing outside all this.*]

Oh? What's this? Oh, love, love, what a beautiful girl. I never realized how beautiful she is. Why haven't I seen her before? Who does she belong to?

SAM: She's yours.

[HAVA *goes into the garden.* DAVID *is very happy and now dances with* SAM.]

DAVID: Mine? What do you mean? Sam, oh my darling dear dead Sam. Life is a great time. [*sings*]:

> Life is the gayest time, life is the grandest time,
> Life is the greatest time to be together,
> So sing for all your worth, and learn to love your life,
> And dance upon the earth, and be my lover.
> Life is a dream of sight, life is a blessing bright,
> Life is the time of light, that's not for ever,
> It happens only once, so while we have a chance,
> Come on, let's sing and dance and be my lover.

[BESSIE *is collecting the money together. She hands it to* DAVID.]

DAVID: But I owe it to you—almost the whole of it.

BESSIE: I know, but take it with you—I don't need it.

DAVID: Thank you very much.

[*He looks at her for a while, then she returns to* SEGAL. DAVID *leads* SAM *to the garden where* HAVA *is sitting nearby.*]

DAVID [*to* SAM]: Is she really mine?

SAM: Exchange is no robbery.

DAVID: But who is she?

SAM: Solly Segal's daughter.

DAVID: I know, but apart from that? [*Calls into house.*] Hold everything! I've changed my mind about a lot of things. Do nothing until you hear from me.

SAM [*seeing the way* DAVID *is looking at* HAVA]: Well, Davey, did my potion work or didn't it?

DAVID: I didn't drink any of that stuff [*goes right into the garden and approaches* HAVA.]

84

SAM [*to the audience*]: So, exchange is no robbery. A Levy becomes a Segal and a Segal becomes a Levy.

[SAM *now hovers at the back of the garden. All noise and movement in the house stops. The garden scene becomes idyllic.*]

DAVID: There's so much that I want to tell you.

HAVA: There'll be a lot of time.

DAVID: *All our lives.* [*He kisses her.*] Isn't life wonderful? This is the happiest day of my life.

HAVA: Why have you been so nasty . . .? If you knew how long I waited just for a kind word.

DAVID: Sorry, Sweetheart, I've been too busy with myself—a very busy time I've had, but now I'm waking up.

HAVA: We used to play with each other when we were kids—then I went to Israel to get away from you but when I found you weren't there I came back again.

DAVID: I've been so mad—so crazy—how could I have missed someone so lovely as you—you're lovelier than my voice even.

HAVA: I wouldn't go as far as to say that.

DAVID: Why not—it's true—incredibly true.

HAVA: Oh, we'll get married and have lots of children—beautiful children with lovely voices—life will be wonderful . . .

DAVID: Life will be wonderful and life is wonderful—here we are on this little atlas—the world is a tropical island in space—a bit of dust in time—and I own it and I give it to you—it doesn't matter where we are as long as we're happy.

HAVA: Oh, Davey—Davey—come down to earth a moment. How will we live? Your voice might enchant the gods, but we can't live on those kind of notes.

DAVID: But everything is all right—I've had a brainwave— I'll sell herrings and sing at the same time. Later I'll open a shop to be on the safe side—then I'll open another shop on the other side. What a gimmick! I'll be a sensation. I'll be the first singing herring salesman in history—I'll be terrific—I am terrific—A great success—the happiest singer with the heart of gold.

[*sings*] : A singer I must be, for all the world to see,
    There's no one else like me, the whole world over.
    I want to be a king—a great fantastic thing,
    The boy with everything,
    I love you, Hava.

[HAVA *smiles and hugs* DAVID *for joy.*]

DAVID [*to* SAM] : Well, Dad, what did you think of that? Don't you think it's a marvellous idea? Me in the market: you can visit me there. Why didn't I think of it sooner?

[SAM *looks at the audience and shrugs.*]

SAM: Bravo, Davey boy, I'm pleased your coming to your senses.

HAVA: Oh, dear, are you still talking to yourself?

DAVID: Oh, I'm not talking to myself; I'm talking to my father. I hope you don't mind?

HAVA: Will you be speaking to him for long? This father of yours?

DAVID: No, not for long.

HAVA: Oh, Davey, I'm so happy, all my dreams are coming true.

SAM: What a lucky boy you are, Davey. I envy you.

HAVA [*to* DAVID] : I will not share you with anyone else.

DAVID: May I just have a few last words with him?

HAVA: Of course. I loved your father almost as much as my own.

SAM: Well, Davey, it's all over. Hamlet is dead and may flights of angels sing him down the stairs. He died two hours ago, when Mrs Levy became Mrs Segal; and I can go back whence I came.

DAVID: Are you revenged?

SAM: Certainly. You are the only Levy left in the world, but you are facing the right way. Segal is all right, moody and stingy; they will make an ideal couple. How subtle revenge can be! One last word of advice. I think you will be very happy, but try and remember me, commit arson every day in your imagination, burn down the previous day's lies, have a little revolution now and again in your heart; try and help lonely people. People are lonely all over the world; lonely and lovely because they are animals with souls and memories.

HAVA: Come on, Davey, let's get away from here.

DAVID: Are you saying good-bye to your father?

HAVA: No, not now.

[*She cries softly, but everything else is silent.*]

DAVID: Good-bye, father of mine. This, then, is your exorcism. Good-bye—I'll take the memory of you everywhere that I go.

[*He tries to embrace* SAM, *but* HAVA *is tugging at him.*]

SAM: That's what you think!

DAVID: Good-bye, Dad, go in peace. So long.

[DAVID *leans upon the fence, head in his hands.* HAVA *comforts him.* SAM *dances towards the house, he is very gay.*]

SAM: Good-bye, my boy; take care of your lovely girl. I'm going from Stepney Green and so are you. Your mother will move out from here and others will move in; they will cover the walls and floorboards and ceilings and then call it security. There will be nothing left of the places I knew. I will soar away from Whitechapel, and follow all my dear dead friends. Look out for me now and again, even if I am not there. Whitechapel is curling up and going to sleep, and the Thames looks like a little trail of water running along the stones. All the names and faces I know are fading.

[*He is in the house and he dances among the people. As he does so they become animated again and dance round.* SAM *withdraws to the street door and he stands there.* BLACK *rushes to the garden.*]

Hava, David, Solly, Bessie. I'm so glad that there is going to be a happy ending. [*He stands in the open doorway.*]

[BLACK *touches* DAVID *on the shoulder.*]

DAVID: Didn't you see him? Didn't you hear him?

HAVA: Yes, I almost saw him. I think I heard him.

BLACK [*gives card to him*]: David Levy, I think you have an exceptional voice. With your gimmick, you'll go a long way. Come to my office Monday. I have a proposition for you.

DAVID: But you're not an agent?

BLACK: No, but I'm going to be. I'll start with you. We'll work out something. I'm a student of life. If we put our heads together, plus a little money, the world will hear you.

[BLACK *returns into the house.*]

HAVA: Wonderful, marvellous; come, let's go. Where shall we go to?

DAVID: Let's go to a dance.

HAVA: Life is going to be one long dance; you've got two hundred pounds, let's go and find a place to live.

DAVID: Why do you love me?

HAVA: Because I have no choice. Why do you love me?

DAVID: Because I love you.

[*They kiss, laugh heartily and exit ecstatically, laughing and kissing.*]

SAM: They are not really themselves. I'm going now, my children, to regions unknown—enjoy yourselves. Make the most of your youth—because youth is a wreath of roses— make the most of your life—because life is a holiday from the dark—make the most of the world—because it is YOUR WORLD—because the world is a wedding—so— Let the wedding continue—

[*He shrugs and smiles and as the room animates again and the people dance, he holds out his arms to the audience and then turns and quickly goes.*]

[*The* CHILDREN *are heard singing.*]

CHILDREN [*off*]: Now you're married I wish you joy,
First a girl, then a boy,
Kiss her once, kiss her twice,
Kiss her three times over . . .

[*There is a great gust of laughter as the curtain falls.*]

THE END OF THE PLAY

[Optional]
[*After curtain falls the cast line up and sing.*]

88

DAVID: I am the boy who wanted to be king—see me on the tele—please God by me—please God by you.

HAVA: I am the girl who owns the boy—who wanted to be king—does anyone know of a flat in Golders Green—please God by me—please God by you.

SAM: I am the ghost who was haunted by my life, wasn't lucky enough to love someone like this girl—who owns my only son—who wanted to be king—I'll be seeing you all—please God by me—please God by you.

BESSIE: I am the wife who drove her husband mad so he became the ghost who wanted the girl to take my little boy who wanted to be king—God bless him—it's enough to give you heartburn—still—please God by me—please God by you.

SEGAL: I am the friend who jumped into the bed to comfort poor Bessie who drove Sam to his grave—so he became a ghost with designs on my daughter—and now she owns the boy who wanted to be king—my mad step-son—still I wish them joy—Comrades, down with religion—please God by me—please God by you.

MR STONE: I am the cabbie—believe me, business ain't so good—I drove the Prime Minister the other day—he didn't give me a tip—please God by me—please God by you.

MRS STONE: I am his wife—enough has been said—by my life—by your life—the children of today—please God by your daughter—please God by your son—please God by God—please God by me—please God by you.

THREE: We are the salesmen, the backbone of the nation— may we press our stones upon you in our never-never fashion—Hip, Hip, Hooray, we haven't got a clue—please God—for he's a jolly good fellow—please God by you.

Enter Solly Gold

A COMEDY

CHARACTERS IN THE PLAY

A Prostitute
Solly Gold
A Policeman
Tailor's Wife
Tailor
An Old Woman
Morry Swartz
Millie Swartz
Romaine
Sarah
Melvin
Herbert Fink
Sadie Fink
Alan Fink

SCENE ONE

Street scene. Dark stage and simple setting. A row of small
houses near Aldgate in London's East End. The set is in a
stylized manner and the interior can be seen as well as the
exterior. When action takes place in a particular house or
area that place is simply lit up. It is one o'clock in the
morning; late summer. A PROSTITUTE stands outside her
street door and SOLLY enters. As she sings he sizes her up
from afar.

PROSTITUTE [sings] : Yours for a short time, how about it
　　　　　　　　　　honey?
　　　　　　　　　　I'll give you five minutes, if you've
　　　　　　　　　　got the money.
　　　　　　　　　　You can have me once or have me
　　　　　　　　　　all night.
　　　　　　　　　　I'm very versatile if the price is
　　　　　　　　　　right.
　　　　　　　　　　I can be naughty if you pay me cash,
　　　　　　　　　　Now don't be so bashful, come and
　　　　　　　　　　have a bash.
　　　　　　　　　　If you want what I've got you can
　　　　　　　　　　have it honey
　　　　　　　　　　I'll give you five minutes if you've
　　　　　　　　　　got the money. [She beckons
　SOLLY].

SOLLY: Do you mean me?

PROSTITUTE: Why not? I'm not particular. I'll take
anyone, as long as they're not jockeys or fishmongers.

SOLLY: What's wrong with jockeys? Some of my best
　friends—

PROSTITUTE: Whores are not horses. They tend to dig
their heels in and treat the bed like a winning post.

SOLLY: What's wrong with fishmongers?

PROSTITUTE: They stink, besides—you've got to draw the line somewhere. Come on, don't let's waste time.

SOLLY: Changed my mind, I thought you were fatter.

PROSTITUTE: You don't know what you want—B- off, go on.

SOLLY: But maybe I could stretch a point just this once.

PROSTITUTE: Make up your mind or it'll soon be closing time. Now come on, I want cash on delivery.

SOLLY: How much will you charge me to have a chat?

PROSTITUTE: Cut it out. What do you take me for? None of that kinky stuff for me, at least not unless you make it worth my while.

SOLLY: You mean you charge more for talking? Why?

PROSTITUTE: 'Cos I've heard it all before. How much do you think psychiatrists charge for listening? Five quid for five minutes, that's the fixed rate.

SOLLY: I could become a Catholic and they'd listen for nothing.

PROSTITUTE: Take it or leave it, that's the standard charge.

SOLLY: How much do you charge ordinary rate for the ordinary thing?

PROSTITUTE: Three quid and no beating about the bush.

SOLLY: Three quid? You're a profiteer! It was only thirty bob before I left.

PROSTITUTE: You're living in the past, grand-dad, prices are rising all the time.

SOLLY: Sorry I wasted your time, fact is I've been day-dreaming in the middle of the night. I'm flat broke—stony—skint—haven't even got a bed for the night—take a look at the soles of my shoes.

PROSTITUTE: You're breaking my heart.

SOLLY: I'm hungry too, haven't eaten for days.

PROSTITUTE: Don't come the old acid with me. You might have heard of sentimental tarts with soppy hearts but yours truly is not like that—times are hard, can't even walk the streets these days. The likes of you should be shot, you've got no morals, no principles, that's your trouble.

SOLLY: Well, this is as far as I can go tonight. [*He sits on his case.*]

PROSTITUTE: Your mother should see you now.

SOLLY: My mother! Mum! I can just see her now. I was bad to her but she forgave me—she knew in her heart of hearts that I wanted to help her—she was a famous debutante—Martha Goldberg—I dragged her down and she died in the workhouse—I was just too late—I arrived in my Rolls to take her to the south of England.

PROSTITUTE: Poor boy—[*she shakes herself.*] What! You've got the spiel all right. You never had a mother. Bet you could melt the heart of a judge. Well, I'm off, I hear the Swedish Navy are pulling in tonight. I hope you don't catch cold and die of pneumonia. So long. [*She goes.*]

SOLLY:

[*A* POLICEMAN *enters and watches* SOLLY.] My watch is stopped; wonder if I can pawn it for a few bob? [*He doesn't see the* POLICEMAN.] What can I do about kip tonight? Coo, I could kip right here and now I'm so tired —so here we are back in the old country—It's so old it's got one foot in the grave and the other foot's got ingrowing toenails. [*He takes his shoes off, and his socks, and starts cutting his toenails. The* POLICEMAN *who was just about to pounce, has temporarily held off*.] What am I gonna do for cash? For the old lolly? Must think of something. But there's one thing I'm sure of—I'm not gonna work—never! Never!—never! [*He stands on the case— mocking the Hyde Park orators.*] Comrades, if you want work you can have it, as for me, work's too much like an occupation—I've committed no crimes, work is all right for workers, just the job for the working class, but for Solly Gold? There's only one thing he wants, money! And there's only one way he wants to get it—by doing nothing.

POLICEMAN: What do you think you're doing?

SOLLY [*jumping off case and quickly putting on his shoes*]: Hello, Officer—I remember you from way back. I've just returned from a world trip and do you know the world's nothing to write home about. They wouldn't let me stay in the States so I returned here—to little old England, the greatest little country this side of the Channel.

POLICEMAN: What are you doing?

SOLLY: Isn't it obvious? I'm out here studying the stars—contemplating the infinite.

POLICEMAN: I'll contemplate your what-you-may-call-it if you don't move sharpish. What have you got in that case?

SOLLY: My worldly goods, Officer.

POLICEMAN: You're a saucy bastard, aren't you. Open up.

SOLLY [opens it]: One toothbrush—you know—for cleaning the teeth. [Goes through the motions.] One shoe brush —for brushing the shoes and one clothes brush for— Three brushes and a brain, that's all I've got.

POLICEMAN: Where have you come from?

SOLLY: Started on the boat as a dishwasher. By the time I got to Gib I was head steward, but by the time we got to Tilbury, I'd lost everything in a card game. That's the way it goes—up and down—everything's up and down. Ever been to Australia?

POLICEMAN: No.

SOLLY: Do yourself a favour—never go.

POLICEMAN: You said they threw you out of America. Why?

SOLLY: Because I was a member of the blue and white shirts when I was five.

POLICEMAN: What were the blue and white shirts?

SOLLY: How should I know? But I'm going to get into the States, you see. It's my spiritual home. It's dog eat dog there, that's the way I like it.

POLICEMAN: Ain't you no family?

SOLLY: No—no family—no one. [Sings] My mother got struck by lightning, my father crashed in a plane, my sister drowned in the Serpentine, my brother got shot down in Spain. My cousin died in a madhouse, my aunt from the sting of a bee, my uncle jumped off a skyscraper—Oh what's gonna happen to me.

POLICEMAN: I'm on my rounds now and if you're here when I come back you'll be for it. [POLICEMAN starts to go.] Spiv! Lazy good-for-nothings—

SOLLY: I resemble that remark. He should try living on his wits. Believe me it's a damn sight harder than your union would let you work—and I'm always on duty—twenty-eight hours a day. [*He shouts after the* POLICEMAN, *then picks up case and moves, but after a few feet he notices light in a window of a tailor's shop: he knocks on the door and falls on his face on the doorstep.*] [*groans*] Oh help me—help me— oh God—

[*The* TAILOR'S WIFE *comes to the door, opens it.*]

RITA [*calls*]: Joe! Joe! Come here, someone's in trouble.

JOE: Who isn't? [*He is busy sewing in the interior.*]

RITA: But he's on our doorstep.

JOE: So? We won't charge him any rent.

SOLLY [*desperate*]: Help me—oh lady—I'm in terrible trouble. [*He pulls on her skirt and at the same time tries to look up her legs; she doesn't see this.*]

RITA: We've got enough of our own, son.

SOLLY [*loud*]: I'm so choked—you're a Jewish woman, aren't you? Sholem Alecheim.

RITA: I don't care what your name is—what do you want?

SOLLY: I'm gonna die—I'm spitting blood. Oh God, that it should happen to me. I'm gonna die.

JOE: Tell him please not on our doorstep—bring him in. [*He is helped inside.*]

RITA: Just take it easy, son—try and relax.

JOE: What's he doing out this time of night?

SOLLY: Oh I'm all water, my legs are just like water—I can't go on. Take me too—kill me also. [*He collapses on the floor.* JOE *won't leave the machine so* RITA *pulls him into a chair.*] I'm just like water—water.

JOE: Rita, fetch him some water.

SOLLY: Haven't you got something a bit stronger?

JOE: Rita, bring him some of that Palestinian wine.

SOLLY: I prefer brandy if you've got it.

[RITA *brings him wine.*]

JOE: I'm only a poor tailor.

SOLLY: All right, I'll settle for this, I'm not so particular——Oh no, I don't believe it—Becky—where have you gone?

RITA: He's delirious.

SOLLY: Nice wine—thank God I found you up.

RITA: You'll always find us up—he says he can't afford to sleep.

JOE: All right. [*to* SOLLY] So, what's your story?

SOLLY: I can't talk, not yet. Could I have another glass of wine?

JOE: All right. Now listen, you don't feel so well, have a little rest, put your feet up and in two minutes you'll be as right as rain and be able to leave.

RITA: He drives me mad. Joe, can't you see he looks like death, what's the matter, 'fraid you'll lose a few stitches? Work is all he knows. Never marry a tailor. [*She tells* SOLLY] He borrows a few hours from the next day, then a day from the next week and a few weeks from the next year and then he dies owing all that time. [*She goes to* JOE] What's the matter with him, Joe?

JOE: I don't like the look of him.

RITA: He's a Jewish boy, he can't be bad.

JOE: Yeah? What about Schnorrer Morry?

RITA: Can't you ever get away from that machine?

JOE: You can grumble; did you ever go without?

RITA: Yes, without you, all my life. I'm married to a sewing machine. [*Returns to* SOLLY] You feeling better, son?

SOLLY: Oh, Becky! Becky! What's the matter with you? Why don't you jump—save the children—the children! Becky, my poor wife—all burned. [*Bursts into tears.*]

RITA: It's good to tell someone.

SOLLY: I'm a traveller, I only heard before. I live in Glasgow—and my wife—oh—God rest her soul—died this morning with the children.

RITA: Died? Oh, you poor feller.

JOE [*leaves machine*]: How?

SOLLY: Oh, it was such a big fire, there were twenty engines, masks they had on. They all got burned to death, my Becky, my little Renee, the twins, Michael and Angela they were so beautiful. Becky had long black hair—she was a picture.

RITA: The good die young.

SOLLY: Becky tried to save them—she stood on the parapet

with all the children in her arms—little Renee, she was such a lovely dancer—tap and ballet. What can I do?

RITA: Let me make you something to eat.

SOLLY: No, I couldn't, I'm all choked. All right, if you insist, a chicken sandwich with some mustard pickle or some smoked salmon—nothing much—something light. [RITA *goes off to prepare it.*] I must go to Glasgow— now! I must give them a decent burial.

JOE: Stay here tonight, go tomorrow morning.

SOLLY: I must fly tonight—I'll have to charter a plane.

JOE: Of course, I understand.

SOLLY: I wonder if you could help me? God is good, in times of stress. He sends good friends. Listen—I need a few quid for the plane fare—the banks are closed and I must fly tonight.

JOE: How much?

SOLLY: At least twenty-five—yes, that will cover me. Oh, Becky, Becky, by my mother in the grave I'm sorry—forgive me, I tried to be a good husband.

JOE: I'm afraid I can only afford five.

SOLLY: That's no use, make it twenty then.

JOE: What about ten?

SOLLY: I'll tell you what, I'll settle with fifteen and try and manage with that.

JOE: All right, fifteen it is!

SOLLY: It's a deal.

JOE: Done!

[*They shake hands on it.*]

SOLLY: It's only a loan, mind, I'll send it back tomorrow morning.

JOE: There's no hurry, wait till the afternoon. I'll get it. [SOLLY *lies back, smokes and pours himself another drink.* JOE *meets* RITA *coming in with sandwiches.*] I must be crazy, I'm lending him money.

RITA: It's good to know you've got a heart; he's the first person you've lent money to in the past twenty years.

JOE: Ah well, he's different—you can see it, it's obvious, he's a decent boy in trouble. I'm a good judge of character.

[JOE *goes off and* RITA *brings the sandwiches to* SOLLY.]

SOLLY: You're so kind—how can I repay you? [*Stuffs the sandwich into his mouth.*] You're too good. I bet no one appreciates you.

RITA: You can say that again. My husband takes me for granted.

SOLLY: When you're dead, then he'll appreciate you, just like me and Becky.

RITA: Try and look forward now, we have to get over things, life goes on.

SOLLY: You're very nice, you're an angel. Has anyone ever told you that? You've got a light in your eyes; does he ever say a kind word to you?

RITA: He hasn't got time. He's not a bad boy exactly, just got no time.

SOLLY: I'd have time for someone like you, I would—you're so nice—oh comfort me—my Becky is dead. [*She pats him on the shoulder and puts her arms around him.*] I'm so lonely. [*He pretends to cry and soon he is completely embracing her and touching her hair.*] Oh, you're lovely, so lovely, just like my Becky.

RITA: No—no—I shouldn't—
[*She tries to break away as she realizes he is getting amorous.*]

SOLLY: Don't leave me—I need you—

RITA: Please, you'd better stop.

SOLLY: You're just my size. I'm mad about you.
[*He tries to kiss her but she breaks free and still they speak quietly, urgently.*]

RITA: How could you? With your wife just dead? No-one's ever done that to me.

SOLLY: How should I know what I'm doing—I'm so sad and emotional.

RITA: With your wife just dead how could you do it?

SOLLY: Don't tell your husband, he wouldn't understand. I'll come back some other time—I'm mad for you and so unhappy.

RITA: Men make me sick.

SOLLY: Me too. Forgive me, for poor Becky's sake.

RITA [*wanders off and looks in a mirror*]: How could you do that to me?

[JOE *returns.*]

JOE: Here you are, fifteen quid.

SOLLY: You're a pal, how can I repay you?

JOE: With money.

SOLLY: I'll be on my way now; God bless you all, my Becky will be so pleased, I mean as she looks down on all this. Good-bye! May you live long and die happy—may you live to be a hundred and three.

JOE: Don't do me no favours.

SOLLY: You're one in a million, both of you. I must fly now.

[*He leaves the house and lingers outside, but the light goes off for a moment.*]

JOE: Nice feller, ain't it funny how the good always suffer?

RITA: How could he do it to me? [*She rejoins her husband.*]

JOE: Well darling, I gave him the money.

RITA: Money? You bloody fool! Schlemiel. Why didn't you give me away while you were about it?

JOE: I wish I did.

RITA: Go on, back to your sewing, you silly so and so.

JOE: Why don't you go to bed? I've got a busy night ahead.

RITA: Yes, I'm going to bed and don't wake me up whatever you do—'cos the answer's no. You've had it from now on; you don't know how to treat a lady—you don't appreciate me. It's alright, people still think I'm attractive. I'm not finished yet. Good night.

[*She goes to bed, the tailor continues sewing and the light in the room darkens.* SOLLY *is now seen again, counting the money. The* PROSTITUTE *comes up to him.*]

SOLLY: What happened to the Swedish Navy?

PROSTITUTE: They've got an attack of German measles on board. Bang goes another night's business. I'll have to sleep. My my, you've got a wad there. I'm in the wrong racket.

SOLLY: How much you charge for all night?

PROSTITUTE: Special rates for night work—time and a half.

SOLLY: Do me a favour. I want it cut price. How much?

PROSTITUTE: A tenner.

SOLLY: Come off it, I'm only a poor working man.

PROSTITUTE: Oh alright, nine.

SOLLY: Make it three.

PROSTITUTE: You out of your mind? Don't you know about the cost of living index? Seven pounds ten and that's my final word.

SOLLY: Four pounds ten, on the nose.

PROSTITUTE: You'd auction your own mother—all right, five quid and not a penny less.

SOLLY: Right, it's a deal.

[*They shake on it.*]

PROSTITUTE: Let's go.

SOLLY: You're not as fat as I would like but you can't pick and choose all your life. [*They exit into her door and the stage darkens completely—now there is a passage of time and the stage lightens again and it is dawn—a cock is heard crowing and* SOLLY *comes out of the* PROSTITUTE'S *door, yawns and does some exercises.*] A cock crowing? In Whitechapel? Impossible. [*It crows again. He looks over a fence beside a third house.*] Chickens—that's handy. Come on you pretty little darlings —come and get stuffed. Oh boy, that takes me back . . . chicken soup, stuffed neck, chopped liver, giblet pie. There's one, two, three, five, eight, eleven birds in all, and one lovely rooster—beautiful bird. Looks as if you've had a heavy night like me. Never mind—I'll cut your throat and then you can have a long sleep and then I'll flog you and your girl friends down the lane.

[*He is about to climb over the fence when an* OLD LADY *comes out of the house with some food for the chickens.*]

WOMAN: What do you want?

[*He jumps back quickly but soon relaxes.*]

SOLLY: I want you. I'm the bird inspector.

WOMAN: Bird inspector? What do you want? Where are you from?

SOLLY [*more to himself*]: As a matter of fact I've been inspecting a bird all night. I'm from the Ministry of Agriculture and Poultry; I've been inspecting your birds.

WOMAN: What's wrong with my birds?

SOLLY: What's right with them? They're having a nervous breakdown. This is a serious business.

WOMAN: Please sir, I can't help it; since my husband died I've been struggling to carry on alone.

SOLLY: Your husband dead?

WOMAN: Yes, a month ago, did you know him?

SOLLY: Of course I did, who didn't.

WOMAN: Who didn't know my Hymie? Who didn't know him and love him?

SOLLY: Wonderful Hymie, with the heart of gold. As a matter of fact he owes me some money.

WOMAN: Money? He never owed anyone.

SOLLY: I mean the government. He never paid his last instalment of the Chicken Registration fee—He owed us ten pounds.

WOMAN: Chicken Registration? No, I didn't know—he took care of everything, I'm so lost without him. I'll pay you.

SOLLY: Poor Hymie, the world won't be the same without him.

WOMAN: It's good to talk to you—I haven't spoken to a soul since he died. You make me feel better—I'm glad you liked my husband so much.

SOLLY [*looking over the fence*]: The birds will have to go of course.

WOMAN: Why?

SOLLY: Neurotic birds are a menace to society—they're totally maladjusted and what's more I'll have to kill them here and now, I'm afraid. And that will of course be another six pounds disposal fee—

WOMAN: Take them, kill them. Who can be bothered feeding them anyway? Who eats eggs since Hymie died? Here, six pounds.

D*

SOLLY: I'm letting you off light—because I like you and Hymie was a friend of mine.

WOMAN: Thank you, thank you—I know, you're very kind. Death is an expensive business—all I've done since my husband died is lay out, lay out.

SOLLY: I hope I'm not leaving you too short.

WOMAN: As my husband always said, you can always find money for bread and coffins.

SOLLY [puts away money]: Now please, I will need a sharp razor to cut their throats.

[She goes inside and he jumps over fence and inspects the birds. She returns and hands him a cut-throat razor. He sets to work though we cannot see his hands or the birds but very soon amidst a flurry of sound and feathers, he emerges with a cluster of dead birds.]

SOLLY: We'll send you receipts.

WOMAN: One minute, do you know anyone who could use some clothes? I've got some, my husband's things, they're in marvellous condition. I can't bear to see them anymore.

SOLLY: I might be able to help you out, let's have a look.

WOMAN: Do me a favour, pull out that trunk. [He puts the chickens down and pulls out a large suitcase.] Only the best, as you can see—take it all.

SOLLY: A Rabbi's clothes? [He holds up some jackets and trousers and soon lifts out some rabbi's clothes.]

WOMAN: But you knew my husband was a rabbi, didn't you?

SOLLY: Who didn't know? From Tel Aviv to Tell me the Tale he was famous—the best rabbi in the racket. It's just that I didn't think you'd part with such personal items.

WOMAN: You're right, I wouldn't. Don't touch the Rabbi's clothes and his Bible. Take everything else—I can't bear to see them anymore. I must go now and sweep up. Thank you. [She goes inside.]

SOLLY: These clothes are not worth a light—she must be blind, they're all moth-eaten, but this Rabbi's gear might come in handy—and I hear there are some very hot tales in this black book. Well, Solly boy, you're not doing too bad—last night you had sweet Fanny Adams and this morning you're worth twenty odd nicker, a dozen chickens and this odd clobber. You're in business. [*He kneels down and prays*] Oh, Rabbi Hymie—forgive me but I mean well —I'm a bad boy, but I promise to spread love and happiness everywhere I go—cos money don't bring happiness so I'm gonna take it away from them. [*He puts the clothes and the chickens in his case.*] Watch out, world, I'm coming! Hendon! Golders Green! Hampstead Garden Suburb!— I'm knocking on your door! [*He does a little dance and some mock prayers*] I'm Rabbi Solomon Goldstone, I'm knocking on your door, with a new kind of religion and a brand new kind of law, if you can't get in heaven, he'll fix it in a flash I've got the right connections, if you have got the cash.

[*He exits hurriedly.*]

THE CURTAIN FALLS

The next day. Interior. Living room of the house of MORRY
SWARTZ. *Known as The Castle. First because they've named
it that and secondly because they've tried to furnish it and
make it appear very grand. The furniture is in a mishmash of
styles—good taste and the appalling are side by side. A garish
glassy cocktail bar, for instance, stands next to a great Gothic-
looking bookcase, without books. A suit of armour, and
animals' heads all around. A television screen set in an
antique case. Peach mirrors all around the room. The huge
ugly table is set for a wedding although it appears the
wedding feast has almost been finished. This castle is in
Golders Green. Around the table the people are eating
furiously,* SARAH SWARTZ *is dressed as a bride. She
is attractive in a slightly overblown way. Beside her is the
groom,* ALAN FINK, *a nervous, slight boy, dressed in a
dinner jacket. Next to him his parents sit—*HERBERT FINK,
*in a flashy American get-up, and his intense wife. Next to
them sits* ROMAINE SWARTZ—*a buxom girl in late
twenties—she seems very hungry, as usual. And there is her
brother* MELVIN—*who wears a sports blazer and flannels
—he is always slightly aloof and seems to despise the sur-
rounding people. Next to him* MILLIE SWARTZ, *a rather
attractive woman who tries to look younger than her years,
heavily made-up and wearing a lot of expensive jewellery.*
MORRY SWARTZ *is not at the table but is feeding a bird
in a cage—he too is dressed in a dinner jacket but he has his
slippers on. There are streamers and balloons about. When
the curtain goes up there is a silence for a while as we just see
the spectacle of people stuffing themselves.*

MILLIE: Morry, come back to the table, we're supposed to be celebrating.

[MORRY *takes no notice, but is swaying with a champagne glass in his hand.*]

FINK: Come on, Alan, make a speech.

ALAN: I've already made four.

FINK: Make another one.

[*All except* MELVIN *and* MORRY *bang on the table with their forks.*]

ALL: Speech! Speech!

ALAN [*he pulls* SARAH *to her feet and they cuddle*]: Mum and Dad! My dear Mother- and Father-in-law, Melvin, Romaine, my darling wife—I promise to be a loving husband to bring you breakfast in bed for the first three months, to look after the shop and make lots of money.

[*They all clap.*]

SARAH: I'm so happy, I could cry.

MILLIE: Don't do that, your eyeblack will run.

SARAH: I could eat him, he's so handsome.

MRS FINK: What a handsome couple, don't they look lovely together?

MILLIE: Yes, it's a good arrangement.

FINK: Your turn next, Romaine.

ROMAINE: Don't do me no favours. I don't trust men.

FINK: Alan, you've got a lovely girl there, cherish her. She's a lovely well-made girl and you're a lucky well-off boy. Look, he's blushing, you naughty boy. Bet you can't wait for tonight, eh? It's lovely to see young people coming together. Wish I had my time over again—that's the way I used to like them—well covered.

MRS FINK: Herbert!

MORRY [*sings*]: Here comes the bride, short, fat and wide,
See how she wobbles from side to side,
Here comes the groom, skinny as a broom,
If it wasn't for the bride he would have more room.

[*All laugh nervously.*]

MRS FINK: Aren't we having a lovely time? I love a party.

This is the happiest day of my life, by my life. Don't they look lovely together? I could cry.

MILLIE: Why you?

MRS FINK: I don't know, brides always make me cry.

FINK [*he is very tipsy and holds a drink up*]: Please God by me—I'll sing a song now.

[*The others take it up.*]

ALL: For they are jolly good fellows, for they are jolly good fellows, for they are jolly good felel-ows,

[*At this moment* SOLLY *walks in and holds up a solitary chicken. He is now dressed in the Rabbi's clothes.*]

SOLLY: And so say all of us. [*They are all astonished.*] I rang the bell, but I heard singing so I came in.

MORRY: Please excuse us, we're all upside down.

SOLLY: It's all right, my son, it's good to see people happy. What a lovely house.

FINK: Isn't it marvellous? What do you think of it? Do you know it cost twenty thousand to build.

MRS FINK: It's just like a palace, you could eat off the floor.

MORRY: Excuse us, but we're right in the middle of a wedding.

SOLLY: Carry on, it's so nice to see such a happy family gathering.

FINK: This is a nice stroke of luck, a Rabbi calling on our children's wedding day. Heaven's happy with this match.

MRS FINK: Who wouldn't be? Look at them, they're so lovely.

MILLIE: Well, Rabbi, what can we do for you? How much money do you want?

MELVIN: Mother! You do go on—money, money, that's all you talk about.

SOLLY: Business can wait.

MORRY: Have a drink with us, please.

MRS FINK: Drink the health of our children.

SOLLY: Some of that Three Star brandy please. No soda.

MILLIE: What charity do you represent?

SOLLY [*holds up his glass*]: Lechaim.

MELVIN: Can I go now? I have a game of squash booked.

FINK [*points to couple*]: So have they.

MILLIE: No, you can't go. What's the matter with you? [*She pinches his cheek and he squirms*] He's so highly strung and sensitive. Are you feeling all right darling? Let's feel your forehead. Spit out three times and go and eat some fruit. Well, Rabbi, it's nice to see you in this house.

MRS FINK: Perhaps he'd like to bless the house—believe me, it's worth it.

MILLIE: All right, why not? We've got everything but it can do no harm.

MORRY: We've got nothing, we kid ourselves.

ROMAINE: Oh, Daddy's getting all philosophical again.

MELVIN: Dad's right and we're a load of hypocrites.

FINK: It's a lovely party, isn't it? And soon our dear children will be pushing off on their honeymoon.

MORRY: Thank God.

MILLIE: I agree, it's good at last they'll almost stand on their own feet. After all, you push them out of you—into the world—and then it seems you have to push them right through life. And now at last they're gonna push off. It's not fair—they leave you so suddenly—look at her, she's only a baby.

FINK: Some baby.

[SOLLY *takes another drink, walks around the couple, digs* ALAN *in the ribs and kisses* SARAH.]

SOLLY: Have a nice time, don't be greedy—in life. Love thy neighbour as—[*He starts kissing all the women on the forehead, lingers over* ROMAINE.] Be fruitful and drink lots of malt and may you have peach mirrors in your house and apricots on your table.

MILLIE: They're not moving out yet, we've still got them for a little while—until the architects have finished their house. Then they'll move away; they grow up and leave you.

MORRY: What do you mean? Look. Rabbi, see that building next door? [*Shows* SOLLY *through the window.*] That's how far they're moving.

MILLIE: They've got the best of everything—I've seen to that. It cost a fortune, but who's complaining?

MELVIN: There she goes again. Must you always mention money?

MILLIE: I'd like to see you manage without it.

MORRY: For once I agree with your mother. I wouldn't care if you worked—you're supposed to look after the shop but what do you do all day? You're out playing golf and in the Turkish baths, trying to be like an English gentleman—Ghandi was more of an Englishman. Something for nothing, that's all you want. I had to work for it.

MILLIE: He's not that bad.

MELVIN: He's almost right, but can I help it if I don't belong?

ROMAINE: There he goes again, don't belong. Go out and don't belong—just fifty years or so.

MELVIN: Shut up, you, you silly fat cow.

SOLLY: Children, children, remember the Sabbath day and keep it holy.

SARAH: But this isn't the Sabbath.

SOLLY: I never said it was. You must learn to respect your parents.

MILLIE: That's what I keep on telling him, he's killing me—killing me.

MELVIN: You're a long time dying.

SOLLY: Peace, peace, my children. We must forgive and love each other.

MILLIE: All right, Mel darling, I'll buy you your glider.

ROMAINE: I want a car.

MORRY: Two years ago she bought him a sports car and last year she bought him a yacht, and now, a glider. We've had the ground and the water and now we'll have the air. What happens when we run out of elements? I suppose next year it'll be a spaceship. All right, let's change the subject. Rabbi, it's a great honour to have you here; tell us the purpose for your visit to our humble—big house.

SOLLY: I'm Rabbi Solly Gold, at your service. I bring the word of God, I spread love and happiness. I'm on my usual pilgrimage, through Golders Green and I pass this way but once—for today of all days is the day of days.

ALAN: You said it, today's my wedding day.

FINK: And tonight's the night.

SARAH [*pinching* ALAN'S *cheek*]: Isn't he lovely? I could eat him.

SOLLY: Apart from that, it's still a very special day.

MRS FINK: It's a holiday or festival or something, isn't it?

FINK: No, I know them all.

MELVIN: It's the Amateur Gliding championship today.

ROMAINE: It's just another Sunday.

MORRY: And I've got backache as usual and a splitting headache.

MILLIE: And I've got heartache and headache and stomach-ache—

SOLLY: I'm ashamed of you all. All of you. Look at you! Call yourself good Jews? And you didn't even know it was Rabbinical Chicken Sunday? I'm disgusted.

MILLIE: Rabbinical Chicken what?

MORRY: Forgive me, Rabbi, but I don't follow religion— too many hypocrites.

SOLLY: You've all heard of Mother's Day? And Father's Day? And Doomsday? Well then, you surely must know that seven years ago the American Reform Orthodox Proxy Rabbis' Association proclaimed this Chicken Sunday. In the old days it used to be a great Hasidic feast. Surely someone must know the famous song?

[*Sings and dances again.*]

> On the second Sunday of December,
> Don't forget to remember,
> Give, give and give some more,
> To the Rabbi at your door.
> The third Sunday that comes in May,
> That most auspicious Rabbinical Day,
> Give, give and give your all,
> To the Rabbi who comes to call.
> On the Fourth Sunday in July,
> If a Rabbi passes by,
> Give, give! Don't ask why
> It's Rabbinical Chicken Sunday.

FINK: Of course, now I remember. I was only reading about it the other day.

SOLLY: Then, as you know, the idea is for an esteemed Rabbi, like yours truly, to go humbly from door to door, giving a chicken as a symbol of life and collecting a small amount for charity.

FINK: Ah, charity—what a lovely word that is. I'm a Mason, Rabbi, and that's the basis of our creed. Ever thought of going on the square? I'll propose you.

MILLIE [takes out purse]: We always give to charity. That should be my middle name. Romaine, my purse. Millie Charity Swartz. What charity this time?

SOLLY: The Rabbinical Chicken Sunday fund for the Prevention of Cruelty.

MILLIE: Cruelty to who? Chickens?

SOLLY: Cruelty to anyone.

FINK: You're a man after my own heart. Here, let me give you something. [Hands SOLLY a note.] Honestly, I give, give and never think about it. [Turns to the others.] Just gave him a fiver. Why not?

MILLIE: But we don't want a chicken, we've just eaten half a dozen. I'm beginning to look like a chicken.

MRS FINK: I never get tired of chicken.

SARAH: Neither do I—I love them casseroled.

ROMAINE: I prefer them fricassee with breadcrumbs.

MORRY: Take no notice of any of them. Put the bird on the table. Go on, Millie, give the Rabbi some money. As a guy named Bacon once said—

MILLIE: Please don't mention that word, this is a kosher house. What will the Rabbi think? You give him the money, you want the bird.

MORRY: Who should I make it out to? [Takes out cheque book.]

SOLLY: Please, please. I'm surprised with you—you must surely know that truly spiritual organisations don't believe in banks. It's unholy—it's usury, it cuts across the holy act of giving from one to the other.

MORRY: How much?

SOLLY: Shall we say ten pounds?

MILLIE: Expensive chicken!

SOLLY [*taking money from* MORRY]: Fine—wonderful. Now, let's forget all about money and get down to business, the business of blessing. [*To* SARAH *and* ALAN] What kind do you want? The special super de luxe deep significant kind, or the simple blessing of the bedchamber?

SARAH: How much do they cost?

SOLLY: Let me see—[*takes out little book, consults it.*] The significant cabalistic eternal marriage blessing costs enough —mind you, it's worth it—two hundred and fifty pounds.

MORRY: The man who thinks up them charges should be in charge of my business.

SOLLY: It all goes to charity mind you.

FINK: Our children deserve special prayers. After all, God can't be expected to be tuned in everywhere—we must have a strong transmitter. And the money goes to charity after all, don't let's stint ourselves. Mr Swartz, you can afford it—if it was my house I'd give willingly.

SOLLY: Good, I'm glad to take that attitude. According to the law you must pay—

FINK: Me? Oh— How much does the cheaper blessing cost? You know, the bedchamber lark?

SOLLY: Only twenty-five pounds, and it's a pretty good blessing. For as the good book says: When the bedroom is happy every room is happy.

MILLIE: Very true.

FINK: We'll have to have that one then—I haven't got the loose change here and I've left my cheque book at home —I'll owe it to you, don't forget to remind me.

SOLLY [*points to* MORRY]: He'll lend it to you, won't you, Mr Swartz? Of course he will. [MORRY *nods slowly and gives* SOLLY *the money.*] That's twenty-five pounds this gentleman owes you. Now on with the blessing. Oh, what a wonderful couple they are—they take my breath away. All I can say is they deserve each other. How I envy them—wish I could get married.

MORRY: Why can't you? Rabbis can.

SOLLY: I was married once. She was beautiful. Miriam. She died in childbirth.

MILLIE: I'm so sorry.

SOLLY: That's all right—we have to get over these things; besides, now I've taken my vow of chastity . . . Right, now the—let me see—the bedroom all-purpose blessing.

[*He takes up wine and starts to mumble gibberish and sways backward and forward.*]

Mayyoulivelonganddiehappy. PleasegodbyyouyoushouldlivesolongmayyougetwhatIwishyoufrompurimtoshobosnochmachgodunitetheminmorewaysthanonewhatsdonecanneverbeundonemazelmazelmazeltovmazelmazelmazeltov.

[*He now repeats this over and over again and claps his hands until he virtually hypnotises himself and starts dancing suggestively around the couple. He dances faster and faster while all the others watch with amazement. When* SOLLY *stops dancing he shrugs, all the others seem rather stunned and dazed.*]

FINK: Your Hebrew was the funniest I ever heard.

[SOLLY *sits down at the table and eats a chicken leg with great relish.*]

SOLLY: This is a lovely house.

MRS FINK: It's a palace. You could eat off the floor.

FINK: It's a castle. Believe me, a king could live here. And Rabbi, come here, look at these peach mirrors—all embossed—what do you think of them? I tell everyone about them. They cost the earth.

MORRY: I hate them, they're designed to make you look better than you are. Every day I feel lousy but the mirrors make me look in the pink of health.

MELVIN: Mirror mirror on the wall—who is the peachiest of us all?

FINK: Do you know how much this house cost?

SOLLY: You told me. But tell me, Mr Swartz, who are you that you can afford such opulence?

FINK: You mean to say you never heard of him? Didn't you see that full page ad in the *Jewish Chronicle* last week? This is Morry Swartz—the Morry Swartz—The Shoe King. He's rich, he's famous—haven't you heard the jingle on Tele? Swartz's Shoes—Swartz's Shoes are the Shoes for You. Get some, get some, for your wife, and your children too. My son married his daughter. His shoes are the best.

MORRY: Don't you believe it, I never wear them—they cripple me. Don't talk about business, it's a millstone round my neck. Let's change the subject. What synagogue are you from?

SOLLY: Synagogue? Oh no, I'm a peripatetic rabbi—I travel. Of course I have many synagogues under me, for between you and me—I don't want to boast, but I'm a fully fledged Synog. Regalia and all. You should be ashamed of yourselves—don't you know your own religion?

[*They all look ashamed.*]

I have now renounced ceremony, severed myself from paraphernalia and am having a Sabbatical year, for the whole world is a place of worship. Every house is a synagogue.

MR FINK: I think I read about you in the *Daily Express* and the good work you are doing.

SOLLY: Of course you did, though I shun personal publicity. I've just returned from the provinces where I've been making fifty conversions daily.

ROMAINE: But Jews don't go in for conversion.

SOLLY: Don't be ridiculous, I've been converting the Jews back to their own faith.

MORRY: You've got your work cut out.

SOLLY: I'm so ashamed, of all of you, everywhere I go the same story—everyone only interested in money, no thought for the spiritual.

MILLIE: What's the name of your organization?

SOLLY: The Liberal Orthodox Hasidic Reform United Union of Peripatetics.

SARAH: Well, Mummy, it's time we started on our honeymoon.

MILLIE: Oh darling, I'll miss you.

SOLLY: Going somewhere nice? Bournemouth? Cliftonville?

ALAN: No. We're going to the Cumberland Hotel at Marble Arch.

SOLLY: Eh?

SARAH: What's wrong with that? All sorts of interesting

foreigners come and go and it's opposite the park and it's not too far away.

ROMAINE: And the food's smashing.

MILLIE: Five miles away is far enough—she's never been that far from me. Don't forget to phone me tonight, darling. If there's anything you want or want to know, I'm here at the other end of the phone. And remember I'm always here and you've always got a home here.

MORRY: Alan, look after my baby and we'll look after you.

ALAN: Don't worry, Dad, she's in safe hands.

SARAH: You ready, Alan?

ALAN: What do you think?

MELVIN: Thank God for that. Now I can get to that game —I'll drop you off in my car.

SARAH: No thanks, we're taking Daddy's Rolls.

[*There is now a lot of kissing and pinching and crying by the women and back slapping by the men, then all the people talk in a group near the door as* ROMAINE *and* SARAH *exchange a few words.*]

Don't worry, Romaine, it'll soon be your turn.

ROMAINE: Who's worried? Make sure you have their barbecued trout—it's out of this world.

SARAH: I wish it was you who got married today, really I do.

ROMAINE: I've got no time for men. But be careful of their horseradish sauce.

SARAH: I know it's going to be lonely for you without me around but maybe I'll find a nice boy there for you.

ROMAINE: Men are horrible, they only want one thing. Of course, the speciality of the house is smoked salmon rolled up with capers and stuffed into cold Scotch salmon.

SARAH: Oh I do wish you could get married—you've got such lovely eyes.

ROMAINE: I told you I don't trust men. You going to cook for Alan or employ a cook?

SARAH: I want to cook myself—I can make omelettes. Oh look at him, he seems half-starved.

ROMAINE: What he needs is plenty of lockshen soup, gefilte fish, apple strudel, cheesecake.

SARAH: You're so clever, you must teach me.

ROMAINE: And steaks—lots of steaks, for breakfast. It's the latest rage—and salt beef always goes down well.

SARAH: You're so good, so good, you deserve a man.

ROMAINE: Don't do me no favours.

ALAN: Coming, darling?

MELVIN: Well, Sis, Alan, lots of splendid luck and all that sort of rot and play the game and all that kind of thing.

[*He hurries out and he is followed by* SARAH *and* ALAN.]

MILLIE [*shouts after them*]: Wrap up warm—don't forget, phone me.

MRS FINK: Alan! Don't forget your tablets—well, they've gone now. Suppose we'll go also.

MR FINK: Can't we stay a little longer? Play cards or watch Tele or something, after all our families are now united? Come on, Romaine, put some records on, let's be lively.

MILLIE: All right, let's all go to the other room and play Canasta—I feel funny tonight.

MRS FINK: Believe me, Millie, I've also got the shivers— I know how you feel. My baby got married—

[*They all start for the other room but* SOLLY *and* MORRY *don't move.*]

MILLIE: Coming, Morry?

MORRY: No, I don't feel well.

MILLIE [*to the others*]: You all go, I'll be in in a moment.

[*They all go in.* SOLLY *goes to the bar and drinks.*]

MILLIE: You drive me mad you do. If you don't act a bit more sociable I'll brain you.

MORRY: I can't stand them.

MILLIE: You're ruining everything.

MORRY: Everything ruined anyway. I wanted Alan for Romaine, you married off the wrong one.

MILLIE: Well, at least we got one of them off our hands. Alan's a good boy, he's a plodder.

MORRY: Can't stand his father!

MILLIE: Well at least he's not badly off—even if he is stupid.

MORRY: He's nothing, just nothing in trousers.

MILLIE: He's a turf accountant, rolling in it.

MORRY: Turf accountant? In my day they called it bookie. He hasn't got two pennies to rub together. Street corner spiv.

MILLIE: He's got an office with a typewriter and two girls working for him.

MORRY: I bet!

MILLIE: Besides, he must be respectable, he's a Mason.

MORRY: That explains everything.

MILLIE: He's got marvellous connections.

MORRY: I need unconnections. We'll never get poor Romaine married now.

MILLIE: Why not? She's got nice eyes.

MORRY: Let's face it—she's fat, she waddles, and she's no chicken. I told you to tell that marriage broker that I wanted a husband for her and not Sarah. Sarah could always find a husband.

MILLIE: She'd have got swept off her feet for a lowlife who only wanted her for her money.

MORRY: What about Alan? You think he's marrying her for love? Every time he looks at me, cash registers ring in his eyes.

MILLIE: I know, but this is different; we chose him, it's respectable this way. Anyway, who wants Romaine married? She's such a good girl around the house—no romantic nonsense about her.

MORRY: We sold the wrong one—the wrong one.

MILLIE: Do me a favour, go to sleep—you're uncouth. A rich man with nothing. Look at him. At least I know how to treat guests, even if I don't like them.

[*She goes into the other room and we can just see them in there playing cards.* ROMAINE *is dancing rather sadly around the card table.*]

SOLLY [*giving* MORRY *a drink*]: One thing I don't understand, if you're so rich, why so few guests?

MORRY: Who do I need to impress? Anyway, I don't like anyone, not even myself. I'm surrounded by enemies, all after my money.

SOLLY: You're right, and listen, your enemies praise you but your friends tell you the truth, and I'm telling you that there's something missing in your life.

MORRY: I don't trust no one. I love my children but what's the use, they're spoilt and take no notice of me. I love my wife, but we're miles apart—getting further away every minute. I'm finished.

SOLLY: They're sucking the life out of you. Bloodsuckers, that's what they all are.

MORRY: Riches? You can keep them. All my life I slaved. For what?

SOLLY: It's obvious to me you're a highly spiritually developed man. Ah well, it's time to be gone.

MORRY [breaking away from his own thoughts]: No, no, Rabbi! Please don't go! You give me a certain peace, when you sit beside me.

SOLLY: I've work to do, my son.

MORRY: Please spare me a little longer, I want to talk to you. I feel I could pour it all out, you have such a beautiful face. Please, please, just for a few minutes.

SOLLY: Oh well, if you insist, my son. [He helps himself to another drink.] Maybe I can help you, though I do want you to understand that my time is valuable.

MORRY: I'll make it worth your while. It's worth anything to me, just to get it all off my chest.

SOLLY: All right then—just relax. Sit down. [Using the method of a psycho-analyst, he makes MORRY lie flat on a settee.] Tell me everything, confide in me, God is listening to you.

MORRY: I'm afraid of dying. I'm also afraid of living. Everyone fiddles. My accountant is a crook; so is my doctor and my solicitor. I don't trust my wife; she tries to look too beautiful—who for? Me? After all these years? So I hired a private detective to watch her and now I've had to hire another one to watch him.

SOLLY: That's right, tell me everything—unburden yourself,

MORRY: My son is a no-good snob, my wife nags, nags,

grabs, grabs, and now I'm left with Romaine on my hands.
Till the day I die I'll see her fat podgy fingers eating
Turkish delight and marshmallow.

SOLLY: But she's attractive! Lovely! A big girl, full of—

MORRY: Too bad you took that oath of chastity. You would
have made a lovely husband for my Romaine. Too late
now.

SOLLY: So what can I do for you?

MORRY: I'm useless, not going anywhere, not getting anywhere, except under the ground. I'm crippled with pain,
so Rabbi, what can I do?

SOLLY: One minute! It just dawned on me—of course, now
I remember you.

MORRY: Do the synagogue boys know me then?

SOLLY: You started down the lane, didn't you, with a shoe
stall?

MORRY: Yes, I started humble.

SOLLY: And you're still a humble man—God is pleased
with you. Didn't you then start a small shoe shop in the
Mile-end road?

MORRY: That's me.

SOLLY: And then you built up your shoe empire.

MORRY: Do you know, I'm shoemaker by appointment to
the Queen of Tonga.

SOLLY: My mother once brought me to your shop in Mile-
end—you served me yourself, don't you remember?

MORRY: Does a prostitute remember all her customers?

SOLLY: You saw we were poor so you gave me the pair of
shoes, for free. Providence has brought me to you to repay
that debt—that wonderful gesture of a man, with such
humanity—shush—don't talk—I'm trying to get in touch
with the angels now. Marvellous things are going to
happen to you.

MORRY: Rabbi, you're a wonderful man, I envy you. So
you're a poor boy, like myself. Well, you made good, maybe
there's still a chance for me.

SOLLY: I'll see what I can do. I'll put a word in.

MORRY: I know you. I know I do—as if I've known you for
years. What did your father do?

SOLLY: He was a great composer and my mother was a ballerina, she used to dance at the Palladium, didn't you ever hear of Bertha Goldskya?

MORRY: Not offhand.

SOLLY: Now, let's get down to hard facts—how much are you worth?

MORRY: Who knows? Between half a million and a million. It fluctuates. But what's the use? Has any single pound brought me a single ounce of happiness?

SOLLY: You could always give it away.

MORRY: You kidding? You're not married to my wife. Anyway, I don't really want to give it away. I mean I worked so hard for it. That's my dilemma.

[*They have been drinking continuously and both are staggering around.* MORRY *more so than* SOLLY.]

MORRY: When I was a kid I was happy.

SOLLY [*puts his arm around him*]: Tell me about it.

MORRY: Seven of us—happy kids, all sleeping in the same big bed.

[*He takes some cushions and lays them on the floor.* SOLLY *does the same.*]

The bedroom small, can't you see it? My father struggled and my mother worried and we played. I was rich then, caterpillars in boxes and every day was an adventure. Mummeeeeeeee! Throw me down a peneneeeeeeee! And don't you remember the pillow fights and feathers everywhere?

SOLLY: On guard!

[*He hits* MORRY *over the head with a pillow,* MORRY *is sent flying and feathers are flying everywhere.* MORRY *gets up and hits* SOLLY *over the head. Soon they are fighting and laughing with everything they've got.*]

MORRY: Hurray! Hurray! Charge! Confetti—Hiphip—Hip-Hooray—[*He suddenly stops and becomes doubled up with pain.*] There it is—Oooooooohhhhhh—I've overdone it, I'm finished. [*He gradually lies down.*] Ohhhhhhohohoh—I'm dying—I'm done for.

SOLLY: What can I get you?

MORRY: Stay here. Just speak to me, your voice soothes me. Will God forgive me? I'm dying. Will he forgive me, Rabbi?

SOLLY: He hasn't got much choice with me to help you. Don't speak now—you're doing all right.

MORRY: Oh my stomach. Oh my back. Oh my God.

SOLLY: Listen—I want you to stand up.

MORRY: You crazy! If I stand up I'll fall over.

SOLLY: If you stand up you won't fall over. I have spoken.

MORRY: Leave me to die in peace.

SOLLY: Have faith in God! Stand up—He will heal you. Stand up. I promise you—you won't fall over.

MORRY: All right, for His sake I'll chance it—Oooooohoho-hooo. [*He staggers up.*]

SOLLY: There you are—oh ye of little faith.

[*Unintentionally* SOLLY *slaps the old man on the back.*

MORRY *is hurled to the floor again.*]

MORRY: Oh! You've killed me! [*He writhes and moans and turns over and over in great agony.* SOLLY *quickly makes for the door but suddenly* MORRY *stops and stands up*] That's it! The pain's gone? You've done it! I'm cured. You don't understand—I can stand up straight with no pain! It's a miracle! A miracle!

SOLLY: Of course. What did I tell you?

MORRY [*he kisses* SOLLY *resoundingly on the forehead*]: For years I've suffered and now I'm well, thanks to you.

SOLLY: It's the work of God, I'm just His instrument.

MORRY: It's a miracle. And to think I doubted. He sent you to me—I can't believe it—how can I thank you? How can I repay you?

SOLLY: We'll find a way.

MORRY: Stay here with me—stay here for a time—for a few days. Please be my guest.

SOLLY: I told you my time is precious—there are others who need help . . . people starving . . . I'm the best collector this side of the Thames.

MORRY: I'll make it worth your while—I'll give you more

than you'll collect in a month. But you must stay, I need you. You can help me.

SOLLY: All right, if this is the will of God, who am I to argue? I'll stay for a while . . .

MORRY: Oh, we'll have a marvellous time, you and I together! Have a drink, I'm young again. I'm reborn. I can move, I walk, I can dance! It's a miracle. Thank you, thank you. Can you dance—Kazatzka—I haven't done it for years.

[*He dances wildly to the music that comes from the other room.* SOLLY *claps his hands and they make a terrible noise. The family and the* FINKS *come in from the other room—stand around in astonishment as* MORRY *dances into the other room followed by* SOLLY *clapping. The phone rings; everyone rushes for it but* MILLIE *gets there first.*]

MILLIE: Hullo! Oh—it's them! They've just arrived—they're in the room.

MRS FINK: What's it like?

MILLIE: What's the room like? Oh, it's all pink—and silver—overlooking the park . . . they can see the speakers on speakers' corner . . . how thrilling—what's the weather like? Oh yes, of course.

ROMAINE: What's the food like?

MILLIE: Did you hear that? They haven't eaten yet—the waiter's just taken their order.

FINK: Tell them to behave themselves—I mean they can do what they like but tomorrow's another day.

MILLIE: Alan, your father sends his love. Wrap up warm, darling—the nights are drawing in. I'm so happy for you, you naughty girl.

MRS FINK: Tell him to take his pills.

MILLIE: Take your pills, Alan.

[MORRY *comes dancing back into the room,* SOLLY *stops clapping.*]

Bye-bye—Dolly. Ring me later—Soon. Alan, look after her, and if you can't be good be careful . . .

MORRY: Tell them, God is Good. I'm cured at last and Rabbi Solly Gold did it. [*Carries on dancing.*]

MILLIE *hangs up and they all once more turn to* MORRY *who continues his dance with* SOLLY. *They stand staring in amazement as*
THE CURTAIN FALLS

SCENE THREE

The next day. The curtains are drawn and the lights are on. It seems like the middle of the night but in reality it is eleven-thirty a.m. SOLLY *enters in a very flamboyant looking dressing gown, goes to the cocktail cabinet and drinks, goes to the peach mirror and smiles at himself.*

SOLLY: This is the life for me, I was born for luxury.
[*He takes another drink and* ROMAINE *comes on— also in dressing gown. She touches him on the shoulder, he jumps.*]

ROMAINE: Talking to yourself, eh?

SOLLY: I was talking to God.

ROMAINE: Go away, you can't fool me. I'm not like my father.

SOLLY: Can I get you a drink?

ROMAINE: A bunny hug, please.
[*About to hug her.*]

SOLLY: With pleasure.

ROMAINE [*backs away*]: A bunny hug is Advocaat and cherry brandy.

SOLLY: Oh, I'm sorry, I'll get it. You must excuse me but I want to make people happy and I thought that was what you wanted.

ROMAINE: Wait till I tell my father.

SOLLY: Well, if you don't want it, at least you need it— that's obvious.

ROMAINE: Wait till my mother comes down. [*She takes the drink and drinks it.*]

SOLLY: Your father knows what he's doing—he understands the intricacies of religion.

ROMAINE: He understands nothing, he's a fool.

SOLLY: He can't be a fool if he made a fortune.

ROMAINE: Most people who make money are mad—they're all a bit touched.

SOLLY: My Aunt Sophie had a fortune and she was untouched.

ROMAINE: How long are you staying?

SOLLY: How long do you want me? I can help you.

ROMAINE: Don't need help.

SOLLY: We all need help. Come, my daughter, think of me as a friend.

ROMAINE: Not too close.

SOLLY: Confide in me. Tell me everything.

ROMAINE: There's nothing much to tell.

SOLLY: You're very deep, I can see it. I'm trained to search your inner depths. You're a restless spirit. I can see great fires raging in your soul. Oh, thou fairest of women—

ROMAINE: I'm starving.

SOLLY: Thine eyes are as a dove's.

ROMAINE: You been listening to Housewives' Choice?

SOLLY: Thy hair is a flock of goats.

ROMAINE: Cheek! I shampooed it last night.

SOLLY: Thy mouth is comely and thy breasts are like two fawns—

ROMAINE: How dare you! You're a dirty old man.

SOLLY: I'm not, that's in the Bible—here read!

ROMAINE: You're still a dirty old man.

SOLLY: I'm not old.

ROMAINE: Wait till I see my father, he'll throw you out—Man of God!

SOLLY: Wishful thinking, my daughter. I have not behaved improperly. I will admit though to being human. Under this habit is the same old habit—the desire for a beautiful girl like you.

ROMAINE: Wonder what's in the fridge for breakfast? How about some steak?

SOLLY: You know how to please a man. Why is it that you're not appreciated in this house? Why do they always leave you out?

ROMAINE: How do you know?

SOLLY: God knows everything, and I've come to tell you
that you deserve better for you're the most beautiful woman
I've ever seen.

ROMAINE: You trying to get round me?

SOLLY: The angels are doing their nut over you. I'm going
to help you get what's coming to you, get what you deserve.
Your body is a poem conceived by the love of God and my
imagination.

ROMAINE: Come off it, you know I'm fat.

SOLLY: Not fat, well built, a big girl—a real woman, with
everything in its place and plenty of it. A wonderful sight—
paradise, the promise of bliss.

ROMAINE: Of course, I'm reducing. At least I'm trying—
I'm going to cut down on potatoes tomorrow.

SOLLY: Don't! Stay as you are—you're lovely. Beauty is
in the eye of the beholder and behold thou are fantastic—
colossal—a double feature—I'm here to show you how
much you're wanted.

ROMAINE: Some boys whistled me last July.

SOLLY: Oh, if I wasn't a Rabbi—if I hadn't taken my vow!
My wife! God rest her soul, would understand, I'm crazy
about you.

ROMAINE: How would you like your steak?

SOLLY: Overdone—almost burnt to a cinder.

ROMAINE: I like the opposite—very rare—

SOLLY: Go quickly before I forget that I'm a holy man.
    [She smiles and goes into the kitchen.]
    [He rubs his hands and looks at reflection in mirror.]
Careful, Solly my boy. Careful, go slowly or you'll spoil
everything. [He reads the Bible.]

ROMAINE [calls from kitchen]: Come and watch me cook!

SOLLY: You trying to lead me astray? [He now fights with
himself.] Careful, boy—take it easy. Oh, what's worth more
to me? A fortune or a fat girl? Nothing's ever easy, is it?
[He still fights with himself.] No! Moneymoneymoney-
money!

ROMAINE: Come on, come on and watch me. I'm sorry I
was cross with you before. I got you all wrong.

SOLLY: No, I can't come now, I'm reading. [He reads,

E   129

becoming more and more excited.] This is it! Here it is!
I've got it! Solly, you're marvellous! It's a cinch. A cinch,
a winner! It's all here, in black and white—it can't fail.
[*He can hardly contain his pleasure. He drinks to his
reflection in the mirror.* MORRY *walks in briskly.*]

MORRY: Wonderful morning.

SOLLY: How do you feel?

MORRY: On top of the world, thanks to you.

[ROMAINE *comes in.*]

Hello, darling. [*He kisses her.*] How are you? Isn't it a
lovely day?

ROMAINE: You feeling all right?

MORRY: All right? I'm alive at last—free. Make me some
breakfast.

ROMAINE: But you never eat breakfast.

MORRY: This morning I feel hungry. Just something light
there's a good girl.

ROMAINE: Bit of toast?

MORRY: No, some grapefruit juice, some cereal and to
follow, some fried kidneys and eggs.

ROMAINE: Something light? Oh, I see. Daddy, you kill me.

MORRY: Don't be saucy or I'll cut you off.

ROMAINE: Cut you off! Cut you off! That's all he knows,
I feel like a water supply.

MORRY: Come on, there's a good girl—let's not argue any
more. I'll buy you a pound of marzipan whirls.

ROMAINE: With almonds inside? Daddy, I don't know
what's come over you, but it makes a change. [*She goes
into the kitchen.*]

MORRY: I've got a good idea. Let's go to Brighton in my
Rolls, lay on the sand, then maybe we'll go to the Wax
Works. Or, I forgot—no sand at Brighton. How about
coming to the East End and having a salt-beef sandwich?

SOLLY: No. Now listen, do you trust me? Do you—place
—yourself—in my—care?

MORRY: Absolutely! For some reason I trust you with my
life. I dreamed and dreamed last night—wonderful dreams
—you may be a stranger but you're not so strange as my
own family.

SOLLY: Good! Now! Concentrate. I'm going to make a real mensch of you. First I've got a message for you.

MORRY: From the Stock Exchange?

SOLLY: Somewhere more important.

MORRY [*incredulous*]: More important than the Stock Exchange?

SOLLY: I've got a message from God—for you. He spoke to me last night.

MORRY: Go on—you're a liar.

SOLLY: Would God talk to a liar?

MORRY: I'm sorry, I didn't mean it. A message for me?

SOLLY: When I knocked on your door I had a vision. And when I saw your face I saw a purple light, and when you spoke I knew my search was over.

MORRY: Purple light?

SOLLY: How can I tell him, I said to myself—how? How can I prepare this humble man for the news—for his mission. The Almighty said—'Speak, speak!'

MORRY: Don't leave me up in the air—for God's sake, spit it out.

SOLLY: All night I lay awake arguing with the angels telling them that you were not ready. There I was praying and weeping. All the stars in the sky burst into the room, a great halo covered the universe, and a golden rainbow stretched from Golders Green to Stamford Hill. Then, just at dawn, amongst a choir of assembled archangels the Holy One spoke again: 'Behold—I send you Elijah the Prophet—'

[ROMAINE *comes in and* SOLLY *quickly stops gesticulating.*]

ROMAINE: We haven't got any grapefruit juice.

MORRY: Grapefruit juice? What are you talking about? Go away!

ROMAINE: That's more like it. Now you're yourself again. [*She goes off.*]

SOLLY [*continues*]: 'And he shall turn the heart of the fathers to the children. Behold nations shall come to thy light and kings to the brightness of thy rising . . .'

MORRY: Please tell me, what does it all boil down to?

SOLLY: I've come to proclaim you the Messiah Of The World. [*He kneels before him.*]

MORRY: Me? Don't make me la- -ugh.

SOLLY: It's no laughing matter but a time for jubilation. For you and me and the whole world.

[ROMAINE *comes in to lay the table.* SOLLY *quickly gets up until she goes out again.*]

MORRY: Would it be all right if I had a cigarette?

[SOLLY *nods.*]

Like one?

SOLLY: What brand? [*Looks*] All right. [*Takes one and strikes a match*] You'll catch the whole world alight. [*As he talks he forgets the lighted match and burns himself.*] It's hard to believe, I know, but you must believe.

MORRY: But Rabbi, you can't mean it. You're joking.

SOLLY: I never joke. Certainly not on matters like this. [*He keeps his fingers crossed and offers up a silent prayer for himself.*]

MORRY: Me? The Messiah! Me? Little Morry Swartz? Go on, you're having me on. Me? The Messiah? [*He looks at himself in the mirror.*] I've got bloodshot eyes.

SOLLY: You should have seen Moses. Look at me—listen— I've come to help you, Morry. Look—I'm telling the truth, by my life. Tell you what I'll do—want another miracle? All right. Will that please you? Ye of little faith, I'm sur- prised at you—and you all ready to be the Messiah. Didn't I perform a miracle on you last night?

MORRY: Yes, you did—but—

SOLLY: That was the first sign—to make you stand up and believe in me.

MORRY: But why me? Why do they have to pick on me?

SOLLY: Why not you? Morry, listen. Do me a favour. Do yourself a favour. You are not the Messiah yet—Oh no— not by a long chalk. Hahahah. Did you think—no, there's a long way to go and I've come to take you there—to pre- pare you.

MORRY: But I'm a hypocrite.

SOLLY: Who but a good man would admit that?

MORRY: When I pray my words are empty. I can't get through.

SOLLY: I've got a direct line.

MORRY: I have no real love or reverence for anything—

SOLLY: That's because you haven't been alive till now.

MORRY: Would you swear on the Bible? That what you've said is the truth, so help you God?

SOLLY: Of course I would. [*Puts his hand on the Bible while crossing the fingers of the other hand.*] I swear on the Bible that you Morry Swartz are destined to become the Messiah.

MORRY: It must be true—I feel marvellous. Know what I'm going to do?

SOLLY: What? Pray?

MORRY: No, I'm going out in the garden—something I haven't done in years. [*He goes out.*]

SOLLY: Please, God—you there? If you are there, forgive me, feinlights—I'm doing it for your good. You see— all right so I'm a bad boy. To forgive is human—I'll make it up to you . . . I'll make a bit of cash and make myself happy, and if I'm happy—well, we're all sailing—So listen, do me a favour—and if you're not there—and don't exist— what am I talking for anyway?

[ROMAINE *comes in with* MORRY'S *breakfast.*]

ROMAINE: Where is he?

SOLLY: In the garden.

ROMAINE [*shouts from door*]: Dad! Your breakfast is ready! [*She puts it on table then brings* SOLLY'S *breakfast and* SOLLY *starts eating.* MORRY *comes back in.*] This the way you like your kidneys, Dad?

MORRY: You mad? You know I never eat a big breakfast— who feels like eating anyway at a time like this? Now leave us alone, we're having a business discussion.

ROMAINE: Suppose I'll have to eat my steak in the kitchen. Business discussion! First he wants breakfast then he doesn't. Drive you mad, he does. [*She goes back into kitchen.*]

MORRY: How we going to do this, Rabbi? How will we convince others?

SOLLY [*he furiously cuts into his meat*]: You'll convince others by your simplicity, by being humble. No miracles. Oh, ye of little faith, you will say, isn't life a miracle? I'll help you, Morry, don't worry.

MORRY: Who'll help you?

SOLLY: Now get on with your breakfast, you need to build up your energy for the election campaign.

MORRY: Look at me—ha ha—the Messiah! And I'm only a small man.

SOLLY: So was Napoleon.

MORRY: Look what happened to him.

SOLLY: Well, what about my father? Look what happened to him, and he was only a small man.

MORRY: What happened to him?

SOLLY: He was the first man to swim the Atlantic, wasn't he?

MORRY: You said he was a composer.

SOLLY: Can't a crazy composer go swimming?

MORRY: Rabbi, I only hope I prove worthy of my task. This is the happiest day of my life. I want to tell everybody. At last I've got something to live for.

SOLLY: Now listen, be a diplomat—not a word to anyone, not yet. It's too soon—they're not ready yet for the shock. They're not so spiritually advanced. This must stay our secret until God says otherwise—otherwise you'll be a laughing stock. You know how people are.

[ROMAINE *enters.*]

ROMAINE: I've finished my breakfast. The steak was like butter.

SOLLY: Mine was like leather.

[MILLIE *enters in her dressing gown, looking like death.*]

MILLIE: Did the phone ring?

ROMAINE: No!

MILLIE: Why not? What's the time?

ROMAINE: Getting on for twelve.

MILLIE: What? Why didn't someone call me? I feel terrible. Oh, oh, what a night I had—and I've got such a day in front of me.

SOLLY: Maybe I can help you.

MILLIE: No one can help me—you can only help yourself. I didn't sleep a wink.

SOLLY: Is it the international situation that's worrying you, my daughter?

MILLIE: International? What? What are you going on about? And stop calling me your daughter—I'm old enough to be your mother. It's the servant situation that's worrying me. Other people's worries don't keep me awake. I've got enough of my own; my baby got married, my son's driving me to the grave and my husband to the workhouse —and she's [*points at* ROMAINE] driving me to the mad-house.

SOLLY: If you go to all those places at once it should be very interesting.

ROMAINE: Would you like some breakfast, Mummy?

MILLIE: Couldn't touch a thing. I've got the shivers, and I've got daggers in my head, and my heart is pal—

ROMAINE: Made some lovely kidneys for Dad, who doesn't want them now. [*She puts the plate in front of her mother.*]

MILLIE: No, I couldn't. Do me a favour, you know I never eat break . . . [*she sniffs plate and starts eating very ravenously.*] Such a day in front of me—an appointment with the hairdresser at two, the dressmaker at three, and the chiropodist at four and the dentist at four-thirty, and I told Sandra I'd go with her to a tea dance at five, and then this evening to the theatre with Estelle to see that wonderful play about homo-sexual-ality, and on top of all that I've got to find a new maid.

[*The phone rings.* ROMAINE *and* MILLIE *dash for it.* ROMAINE *gets there first.*]

ROMAINE: Sarah! Darling, how are you?

MILLIE: Give me that phone—I'm your mother. [*She snatches it away.*] Hello, Dolly—Sweetheart. How are you darling? Did you sleep well? What? You poor girl, never mind, you'll get used to it. [*She turns to tell the others.*] He likes to sleep with the window open. Had breakfast yet? Was it nice? Bed comfy? How's Alan? Send him my love.

Tell him not to worry and remember this is your honey-moon. What's that?—As quick as you like. Good-bye. [*She puts down the phone.*] They're coming to lunch. She misses us.

MORRY: But she's only just left.

MILLIE: It was last night. She's homesick. Blood is thicker than water.

[MELVIN *comes in dressed in blazer and white trousers.*]

MELVIN: Lovely day. Seen the papers? What's it going to do?

MORRY: We're on the brink of another war.

MELVIN: I didn't mean that. Is it going to rain? What's the forecast? [*Takes a newspaper, reads the back page.*]

MORRY: The back page—that's all he knows—and on the front page the world's doing its nut. Look at him, the English Sportsman, the Cricket fixtures, the rugger scores—

MILLIE: You hungry, darling? Some nice fried fish in the fridge.

MORRY: I know what he needs, and I don't mean lock-shen soup.

MELVIN: Think I'll have a bash on the tennis court this morning, a nice brisk game to start the day. Has Derek phoned?

MORRY: Aren't you going to work?

MELVIN: Aren't you?

MORRY: How dare you talk to me that way—who paid for everything—who poured out his heart?

MILLIE: Melvin's not too strong, don't nag him.

MORRY: Look at him—the Sportsman. Tallyho Moishe.

MILLIE: How dare you chastise my child like that?

MORRY: He's a stuck-up snob, a delinquent with cash, a Teddy boy of the tennis court. Listen, I'm talking to you.

MELVIN: Really, this is all rather beneath me. He does go on. I'm going in the garden, can't stand the atmosphere here. [*He goes.*]

SOLLY: Morry, remember all will change by your attitude by love and understanding—don't excite yourself. Let's go for a nice drive and look at trees.

MORRY: Yes, you're right you're so right. Melvin, forgive me.

MILLIE: Now something is really up. Morry, I'm worried about you.

MORRY: I'm in good hands.

SOLLY: As I told your husband, you must learn to love everyone—or how will you love yourself and if you don't love yourself, who will love you?

MORRY: He's so right. Well, Rabbi, what about our drive?

MILLIE [*fussing with breakfast things*]: Come on, Romaine, don't leave it all to me.

[*She and* ROMAINE *go into the kitchen.*]

SOLLY: Morry, if only you could get rid of your family for a little while. They clutter up the place so—I can't concentrate.

MORRY: Now you know how I've suffered all these years.

SOLLY: Can't you send them on hoiday? I must have peace to work. They inhibit me. I don't mind Melvin around—he's a fool—but the others must go.

MORRY: But how? How? If only I knew a way.

SOLLY: He'll fix it.

MORRY: He's got his work cut out. She'll never leave me, never. Never let me out of her sight.

SOLLY: You leave it to me—I guarantee by tonight we'll have the place to ourselves. Let's go. [*He calls to* MILLIE.] Don't worry, Mrs Swartz, I'm taking care of your husband.

[MORRY *and* SOLLY *leave.* MELVIN *comes back in and then* MILLIE *and* ROMAINE *follow.*]

ROMAINE: He's going mad.

MILLIE: Going? Going? He's gone. Went years ago.

ROMAINE: I don't trust that Rabbi.

MILLIE: Where was I? What was I doing? Must get a maid, number one. Melvin, there's ice cream in the fridge. Have some and be a good boy. I must get dressed.

[*Doorbell rings.*]

Oh, who can that be?

[MELVIN *goes and voices are heard outside.*]

It's them Finks again, they make me sick.

[*The Finks enter.*]

Hello, Sadie, I was just speaking about you.

FINK: Only good, I hope. You didn't mind us dropping in, did you, Millie? After all we're related now.

MELVIN: 'God gives us our relatives. Thank God we can choose our friends.'

FINK: Heard from the children, Millie? [*He sits down, smokes one of* MORRY'S *cigars and takes a lot of drink.*]

MILLIE: They just phoned me.

MRS FINK: How are they?

MILLIE: They sounded so happy.

MRS FINK: I know, they were the same when they phoned me an hour ago.

MILLIE: They're coming to lunch.

MRS FINK: What a coincidence, I'm dying to see them.

FINK: It will be so nice—a happy family gathering! What's nice for lunch? Eh, Romaine?

MRS FINK: Can I help, Millie?

MILLIE: Yes, get a chicken in the pressure cooker as quickly as possible. Now you must excuse me for a few moments— I must get dressed and I've got a thousand and one things to do. [*She goes.*]

FINK: Well, Romaine, it's your turn next. Who's going to be the lucky man—

ROMAINE: I'm not getting married—I like laying in bed in the morning. Anyway, men are all the same—only after one thing . . .

FINK: Good thing, otherwise where would we be? Still, I don't know why you can't get off. Nice, well built girl like you. Wish I had my time again.

MRS FINK: I'm sure she's going to make someone very happy; meanwhile come and help me make lunch.

ROMAINE: Lunch, lunch—We've only just had breakfast! That's all they think about in this house—food, food!

[*She follows* MRS FINK *into kitchen.*]

FINK: You're a sportsman, aren't you, Melvin? Do you ever shoot any nice wild—er, birds, on your travels?

MELVIN: I've bagged some grouse, and a partridge once.

FINK: You're a dark horse, you know what I mean? You're

a sport and I'm a sport—couldn't we go out together and
perhaps you could show me some high life in some low
dives. Ain't that clever?

MELVIN: You're drunk.

FINK: I'm an outdoor type like you, but I love indoor sports.
Anything between eighteen and twenty-five, and female of
course—

MELVIN: Please, Mr Fink, I think I've heard enough.

FINK [*digs him in the ribs*]: I'm only human, out for a bit
of a skylark in the dark—

MELVIN: Have you no morals? What about your wedding
vows? Play the game, for God's sake.

FINK: I was only kidding. My wife's a girl in a million.
What do you take me for? I've got a son as old as you!
Never mind, Melvin—no offence, no harm meant—I won't
hold it against you that you got me all wrong. I have these
jokes. I understand you. Course I study a bit cycle-logy
myself; what you need is a bit of this and that and one
must never forget the other. Would you like to be a Mason?
I'll propose you. Marvellous—the little case and the badge
and the lovely apron—it's a brotherhood . . . a real brotherhood . . .

[*He almost slumps forward as he drinks and drinks.
ALAN and SARAH appear.*]

ALAN: Hello, Dad, been celebrating?

[*FINK jumps up, kisses SARAH and slaps his son on
the back.*]

FINK: Sadie! Sadie! They're here. Hello my boy. Yes!
You've got that grown-up look.

MRS FINK [*rushing in*]: Alan! How are you? Did you
take your pills? Sarah darling, how are you?

SARAH: Ecstatic.

ROMAINE: Enjoying your honeymoon?

SARAH: Smashing! Where's Mum?

ROMAINE: Upstairs. Well, how's married life?

SARAH: Smashing! Where's Dad?

ROMAINE: Out. What's the hotel like?

SARAH: Smashing. Where's Dad gone?

ROMAINE: For a drive. What's the food like?

SARAH: Sma— Not so hot.

ALAN: She's marvellous to me, Mum—she thinks of every-thing. I married an angel.

SARAH: Oh isn't he lovely, I could eat him. [*Pinches his cheek.*]

ROMAINE: Save your appetite, there's chicken for lunch. [MILLIE *enters dressed up with lots of very expensive but garish jewellery.*]

MILLLIE: You're here! And no one told me, darling! You look lovely.

MRS FINK: They make such a lovely couple.

MILLIE: Taking care of her, Alan? Good. Dolly, you look pale.

SARAH: I feel fabulous, Mummy. That hotel is out of this world.

MILLIE: You're thinner.

SARAH: Mummy, I only left yesterday.

MILLIE: I don't care, I've got eyes, haven't I? I'm so happy for you, you bad girl. It's not fair, you're only a baby. Come over here, Dolly, and tell me all about it.

[SARAH *and the other women sit on the settee chatter-ing quietly while* MILLIE *paints her nails.*]

FINK: Melvin, come here, have you got to know my boy yet? I think you've got a lot in common. Have a chat—be friends—it's nice to be happy. [*He drinks some more.*] Oh, this is the life for me . . . I'm so sleepy. [*Dozes off.*]

MELVIN: Do you like sport?

ALAN: Who don't? Like a nice game of football, myself.

MELVIN: Cricket?

ALAN: No, it's a bit slow for me. Now football—

MELVIN: Rugger? No! Ever been yachting? Ski-ing?

ALAN: It's all a bit hard on the old calf muscles, ain't it? I have a flutter on the pools each week.

MELVIN: Well, what do you play?

ALAN: I like a nice game of football, myself.

MELVIN: I loathe soccer; what about swimming?

ALAN: I'm afraid of water.

MELVIN: Do you ride?

ALAN: Sure, but only on buses, hate the underground. I like a nice game of football, myself.

MELVIN: There must be some other sport you like. What about running? Or tennis?

ALAN: I don't mind a game of ping-pong.

MELVIN: Ah! Table tennis, not a bad little game. As a matter of fact, I'm the champion player of Hampstead Garden Suburb. Care for a game?

ALAN: Well, I'm not so hot, you know—

MELVIN: Be a sport, come on—I have a table in the other room. Don't worry, I'll go easy with you.

ALAN: You'll lick me hollow.

MELVIN: It's the spirit that matters—Don't worry, just relax.

[MELVIN *leads* ALAN *into the other room and now we can see them playing in there—*ALAN *wildly rushing to catch the ball with his bat and* MELVIN *being very calm.*]

ROMAINE: The chicken must be ready; come and help me, Sarah.

[*Off they go.*]

MILLIE: I wonder where that man is.

MRS FINK: They're all the same. I'll lay the table.

[*She and* MILLIE *start laying the table.*]

FINK [*in his sleep*]: Come on, boy—come on—Silver Flash —Silver Flash—you're there, you're almost there—come on all my money's on you.

MRS FINK: Wake up Herbert. [*She shakes him.*] Look, he's sweating. Wake up—you're dreaming.

FINK: Where am I? Where? What did you wake me up for? I had a pony on that dog! And he was skating in.

MRS FINK: It was a nightmare. You look worried.

[*In the other room,* MELVIN *is now frantic and rushing around while* ALAN *is calmly lobbing the balls.* ROMAINE *and* SARAH *enter the living room with the chicken and some vegetables, and everyone sits down.* MELVIN *comes in sadly followed by the beaming* ALAN.]

ALAN: I won, what about that, Sarah? I won. Can I join your club, Melvin?

MELVIN: I let you win, to encourage you. Who cares about stupid ping-pong, anyway?

ALAN: I won! I won; since I've been married I feel like a new man. Did you see that, Dad? Did you see me win?

[MELVIN sits down.]

FINK: What? You won? Bravo! I'm proud of you! What did I tell you, Melvin?

[When he sees MELVIN'S attitude he speaks more harshly to ALAN but much softer in tone.]

You bloody fool! Trust you, what did you go and win for? We don't want enemies in this house—now play him again and lose next time.]

[MELVIN gets furious.]

Better luck next time, Melvin.

MELVIN: Shut up! You silly fat slob.

MILLIE: MELVIN!

ALAN: Don't you talk to my father like that.

FINK: Don't defend me, Alan, he was only joking.

ALAN: I'll punch him on his stuck up nose.

MILLIE: Don't you dare talk to my Melvin in that tone.

ALAN: I'll knock his block off.

MELVIN: Worming their way in here, oh go back to Stamford Hill.

MRS FINK: Alan's too good for her, he's a boy in a million.

MILLIE: HIM? TOO GOOD FOR HER? AM I DREAMING?

SARAH: Don't talk about my husband that way.

MILLIE: Stay out of this, Dolly.

ALAN: Don't talk to my wife in that tone.

MILLIE: You've married beneath me.

MELVIN: Sozzled old sex pot. I'll take on both of you.

ALAN: If he doesn't stop sneering, I'll knock him out.

MILLIE: Over my dead body.

ALAN: PIPE DOWN.

SARAH: Don't talk to my mother like that.

[FINK tries to separate the boys and MRS FINK tries to pull him away.]

FINK: We're related now, we're related.

MRS FINK: It's all a mistake.

[*They are all at each other's throats when* MORRY *and* SOLLY *enter. They break, start eating furiously and* SOLLY *whispers to* MORRY.]

SOLLY: Stop! All of you. Stop eating!

[*Some are shocked and some splutter.*]

MILLIE: Oh, my God—what's the matter?

SOLLY: There must be no more flesh eaten in this house.

MORRY: That's right. No more meat.

MELVIN: I absolutely agree with you.

SOLLY: From now on this is a vegetarian house.

[*He says a few words of gibberish, as if praying.*]

FINK: Sounds like a good idea.

MILLIE: Shut up. No more meat?

MELVIN: You gone potty?

SARAH: Mummy, what's the matter with him?

SOLLY: He has decided. No more steak, no more liver, no more fish, and no more chicken.

ROMAINE: I'll die without meat.

SOLLY: The next one to eat flesh will be banished from this house.

[MILLIE *and* ROMAINE *eat.*]

All right, you brought this on yourself.

MILLIE: Isn't it time you were going, Rabbi?

MORRY: Show them a miracle—teach them a big lesson.

SOLLY: No, why should I waste miracles on them? Would they believe it if they saw? Clear them all out of the room —all of them—they offend my eyes.

MILLIE: Right, now I've heard enough. I must ask you to leave. Mr Fink, please help me—Alan, Melvin.

MELVIN: Be a good chap, go quietly.

FINK: Can't we talk this over?

ALAN [*hiding behind* SARAH]: Sarah, whose side am I on?

MILLIE: Call yourself men? Look at you!

MORRY: I'm the boss in this house, and I'm taking over. I'm wearing the trousers from now on and the Rabbi is my guest; if you don't like it you can lump it—and Mr Fink, please don't come so often.

MILLIE: How can you talk to our guests in this way? What's come over you?

MORRY: For once I'm saying the things I believe.

SOLLY: You've all strayed from the path of righteousness, there must be a change before God can enter.

MELVIN: Yes, it is rather stuffy in here. Toodlehoo, have fun. [*He goes.*]

MILLIE: Morry, shall I send for the doctor? Do you want a rest?

MORRY: I've had a rest too long. Carry on, Rabbi—the house is yours.

SOLLY: Let's all be calm, my children, and remember the wise words of the Khama Sutra. Now I want you all to go onto your knees, and think sensuously about life— become ecstatic, at one with the pulsing beat of the throbbing universe. The fast begins tomorrow.

MILLIE: Fast?

ROMAINE: I'll die.

MILLIE: Look, what do you want? Just tell us. For charity? A bit more money? Here you are—just take it and go— [MILLIE *takes money from her purse.*]

SOLLY: You don't understand. I'm staying until the new heaven on earth is proclaimed—but don't worry, we're preparing for it right away—for Morry Swartz is to be the first acolyte.

MILLIE: Morry, listen, this is me—Millie, your wife. This will break our marriage.

MORRY: This will make our marriage.

MILLIE: This man is dangerous.

SOLLY: Of course I am. Because I'm going to wipe out pride, to drive out greed and hate, and place in its place love. And then there'll be a new heaven on earth.

MILLIE: Oh, how much will it cost us? I can't have a Rabbi in the house—what will the neighbours say?

SOLLY: Halleluiah, eventually.

MORRY: Darling, don't upset yourself—don't cry. How lucky we are to have this illustrious saint in our own living room.

MILLIE: If he doesn't leave this house right now, I will.

MORRY: You can't leave me.

MILLIE: That's what you think.

MORRY: But I need you.

MILLIE: It's him or me.

MORRY: He must stay.

MILLIE [*cries*]: I've never been so insulted in my life. Romaine, pack your bags, we'll show him. I'm going as far away as possible.

SARAH: Where to, Mum?

MILLIE: Bournemouth! He'll see, he doesn't think I'll do it! Romaine, I said pack the bags.

MORRY: Good luck to you, my love—you deserve a holiday. We both need a rest from each other.

MILLIE: What? How could you? After all these years? That settles it. Romaine! Will you go and pack those bags? [*She punches her daughter.*] I'm going to teach you a lesson once and for all. [*She is about to stomp out and she pushes* ROMAINE.] Sarah, don't stay in this house, it may be catching. [*She goes out.*]

FINK: You're overwrought, Morry, I understand.

MORRY: Good-bye, Mr Fink.

> [FINK *goes out after* MRS FINK. MORRY *speaks to* SARAH *and* ALAN.]

You going to Bournemouth with your mother?

SARAH: What, and break my honeymoon? Not on your life. We're going back to Marble Arch. Bye-bye, Daddy, I wish you better.

> [*She kisses her father and leaves with* ALAN.]

SOLLY: Now we're in business.

> [FINK *furtively appears as he puts on his coat.*]

FINK: Did I hear someone mention business? Can you cut me in, gentlemen? I've got connections.

SOLLY: We're going to be a very limited company.

FINK: Too bad. I want you to understand, Morry, that I sympathise with you completely. We men should demand equality. I love the way you stood up to her.

SOLLY: Good-bye, you old hypocrite.

FINK: Good-bye, Rabbi, I love your sense of humour—they need putting in their place—they need a firm hand.

MRS FINK [*off*]: Herbert? Where are you?

FINK: Coming, love. [*He hurries off.*]

MORRY: Peace at last; all my life, for fifty years I've had screaming people around me, and you pulled it off.

SOLLY: Oh I can see you now—virgins dancing around you and children, dressed in white, pelting you with rose petals. Shush! Listen!

MORRY: What is it?

SOLLY: A revelation. Shush—go on—I can hear you.

MORRY: Is it the Lord?

SOLLY: Shush! Yes sir, I've got that clear! We will do what you say—by my mother in the grave—yes, sir. I understand—whatever you say. I've got the message and I'll pass it on! [*He turns to* MORRY.] See them go? Radiant angels, look at them, what charm they have, did you ever . . . Oh what do you think of those purple cloaks and those golden clouds like chariots—[*Sings*] Bring me my bow of burning gold . . . Look!—just look at their haloes—Good-bye. [*He waves at space.*]

MORRY: Who are they?

SOLLY: Gabriel, Michael, and Raphael, of course. Didn't you see them?

MORRY: I'm not sure.

SOLLY: What, you didn't even see them?

MORRY: I—think I did.

SOLLY: I should think so too. Did you get the message? Surely you got the message?

MORRY: Almost—but it was a little blurred—please repeat it for me again.

SOLLY: It said that we must search for your throne—

MORRY: Yes, yes, I got that—where?

SOLLY: In the West End—it was plain enough. It once belonged to King Solomon and now it's going to be yours.

MORRY: What have I done to deserve all this? Why should I be chosen? I'm not worthy. How much will it be?

SOLLY: We must pay the earth if necessary. Don't worry, we'll beat them down. For the moment how about you and me going to Morrie Bloom's and having some salt beef?

MORRY: But I thought we are vegetarians?

SOLLY: Don't be silly, that's for them, not for us. We must set the example but that doesn't mean we must follow it.

MORRY: I don't like that. I want to be pure. What's good for my Millie and everyone is good enough for me. Besides, I really feel now for the souls of little animals.

SOLLY: Have it your own way but don't you see, how can we convert people to vegetables unless we go among the meat eaters? And where will we find the meat eaters? Why, Bloom's, of course. And how can we go to Bloom's and not eat salt beef? Do me a favour. Use your head— don't worry—you'll lead the world and I'll lead you.

[*He pushes* MORRY *off.*]

Morry Swartz, the saviour—certainly saved me. Solly boy, you're in for the big time at last. How much shall I take him for—And why not? I like to see a Yiddisher boy getting on. [*He lights a cigar and follows* MORRY *off.*]

THE CURTAIN FALLS

A few days later. The living-room is almost in total darkness. A single shaft of light piercing the gloom reveals MORRY *sitting on a throne. He looks very uncomfortable. Now we see that the room is almost empty. The only furniture is a few chairs, a settee and a small table on which stands a tape recorder. The Messiah is playing. After much fidgeting* MORRY *gets off his throne, goes to the tape recorder and switches it off.*

MORRY: No. I don't feel right—I miss Millie. And let's face it, no Messiah would miss my Millie. Why hasn't she phoned?—No, I'm not cut out for this Messiah caper. And if I'm no Messiah he's certainly no Rabbi. Oy I miss my Millie—Mind you I'm happy. Never been happier. I wish she was here to share my joy. How can I be happy without her?—I must have been mad to believe. But you believe what you want to believe—And I've had fun—But if my Millie doesn't come home today I'll have to go to Bournemouth tomorrow. Meanwhile—charities? Yes! More thrones at this price? I can do without. Pity I'm not the real McCoy, still, Messiahs don't grow on trees.

[MORRY *wanders off.* MELVIN *enters, pulls the curtains open and the daylight streams in. He starts excercising.* SOLLY *enters and sees the throne.*]

SOLLY [*Excitedly*]: Morry! Morry! Your throne has arrived. [*He rushes off in one direction as* MORRY *enters from another. Then* SOLLY *comes on again.*] Have you seen your throne?

MORRY: Certainly. I signed for it.

SOLLY: There! Not bad for a hundred and fifty quid. [*He sits on it and smokes a cigar.* MORRY *sits on the floor.*]

MORRY: Please let me smoke.

SOLLY: Please don't be so childish—you must practice frugality and economy. Self-denial is the way to sainthood.

MORRY [*peers at throne*]: He said it was solid gold—I can't see it.

SOLLY: It's spirit gold. Can't you see the aura? It looks like wood but it has a spiritual inner tube.

MORRY: When is the coronation?

SOLLY: Be patient. Aren't you happy with the day drawing near?

MORRY: I miss Millie.

SOLLY: Look, sit down here and realize your true responsibilities.

MORRY [*sits down*]: I feel better now. It was a miracle the way you came into my life. Any message from your mother, Melvin?

MELVIN: No.

MORRY [*rising*]: I must phone her. I want her to know that I want her to be happy—that I want her to be Queen Millie.

SOLLY: No, sit down. She must come to you, in her own time.

MORRY: It's the first time we've been apart.

SOLLY: Now, listen. For a few days now you've been worried. Well, it just won't do. It's not easy being Messiah. You've just got to grow up and stand on your own feet. You're not allowed to worry, you've got to radiate happiness and calm.

MORRY: Look, have a heart. I'm only just indentured, don't expect me to be a fully fledged graduate. You sure she didn't phone, Melvin?

MELVIN: Dad, leave me alone. I'm practising for the Maccabee games this evening.

SOLLY: I shall walk out on you if you continue like this.

MORRY: Please be patient with me. I'll be all right.

SOLLY: Go into the garden to study cloud formations—add up the large ones, then add up the little ones and take one from the other and take away the first number you thought of.

MORRY: Thank you. There are moments when I lost heart. Thank you for being so firm and nice to me.

[*He goes out counting on his fingers, trying to remember* SOLLY'S *instructions.*]

SOLLY: What are you doing standing like that? You hoping to become the Prime Minister of Israel? Why do you waste all your time with muscle stuff?

MELVIN [*stands upright*]: Look, I don't tell you how to pray. So don't tell me how to play.

SOLLY: At your age you should be having a good time with girls.

MELVIN: Not interested.

SOLLY: All this sport is a cover up for the things you're really longing for.

MELVIN: Nice advice, coming from you.

SOLLY: Sex is nice, it's here to stay. You can't get away from it, it follows you everywhere. Don't swallow it, wallow in it—find yourself a nice girl, not too nice. When I was your age I knew my onions.

MELVIN: You?

SOLLY: Girls were my downfall before I picked myself up. It was the fat girls—oh, fat girls were the ruin of me and the making of me. I still have a soft spot for them.

MELVIN: You surprise me.

SOLLY: Listen, a dog collar doesn't stop a man being a dirty dog. Mind you, I don't mean myself—I'm finished with all that now. Do yourself a favour—sow your wild oats on fertile feminine ground. Throw away your discus, take up the challenge.

MELVIN: But I'm shy—how do I start?

SOLLY: If you see a skirt, follow it. You're a man now—follow your natural instincts. Forget all about games, that sort of game—and play the game of life. A woman is the prey and you are the beast—and do they love it. Follow your natural inclinations—haven't you got any? You must have. Put some brilliantine on your hair, a smile on your face. [*He illustrates all this for* MELVIN.] Then saunter amongst them, looking supercilious, debonair, aggressive, like a lion, like a peacock—

MELVIN: All at the same time?

SOLLY: Like this: Inscrutable—slinky. Pout your nostril all the while and clench your jaw.

[MELVIN *tries it.*]

And you'll be a wow. Go amongst them, boy—there are masses of waiting virgins—go and break their— . . . hearts.

[*He leads* MELVIN *out.*]

Come, I'll help you choose the right suit.

[ROMAINE *and* MILLIE *enter.*]

MILLIE: It must be the wrong house.

ROMAINE: Oh, Mummy—

MILLIE: Oh, Dolly—what can we do? We're ruined! I'll kill him—kill him—Where's everything? [*She weeps.*] I'm finished, finished.

ROMAINE: Mummy, don't cry, pull yourself together—[*she cries*] Ohohohohohohohohoho!

MILLIE: Romaine, I'm ashamed of you, always going to pieces in a crisis. Stop crying and be a big girl. [*She looks round the room.*] Oh my lovely television set—where is it?

[*She cries again and now they lean on each other and both weep.*]

This is the end. I'll pull my hair out, I'll scream—I'll faint, I'll kill myself. Have you got a cigarette?

[ROMAINE *gives her one.*]

Turn your back for five minutes—I'll kill him.

ROMAINE: I told you not to go. I warned you against that Rabbi.

MILLIE: If we didn't go you'd have been head over heels in love with him.

ROMAINE: Me? Bloody cheek.

MILLIE: I saw you falling for that snake in the grass.

ROMAINE: Me? You think I'd throw myself away on that low-life?

MILLIE: That swine.

ROMAINE: A villain!

MILLIE: Crook. Rogue.

ROMAINE: Monster. Maybe it wasn't him.

MILLIE: Who else? Oh, we're ruined. My Sheraton! My cocktail cabinet, my virginals! He's taken everything, and your father's gone off his rocker. That's where you get it from.

ROMAINE: What are we going to do?

MILLIE [*goes to phone*]: The police, that's the only thing. [*Dials.*]

ROMAINE [*stopping her*]: You out of your mind? Find out first who's taken the furniture. Who you going to accuse?

MILLIE: That terrible man! Don't you see, we've got to get him out. He's after our money.

ROMAINE: Who isn't? Listen, if you call the police it will get into the papers and we'll be the laughing stock of the neighbourhood.

MILLIE: Better a laughing stock with money than being respectable and broke. Your father's mad—stone bonks. I must call the police.

ROMAINE: All right, if he's mad they'll take him away, then there'll be a whole legal rigmarole. Meanwhile we'll all be starving.

MILLIE: Sometimes you use that stupid brain of yours. You're right. But I still say you've fallen for him.

ROMAINE: Fallen? May I drop down dead on this spot if I have! [*she sits quickly on the small settee.*]

MILLIE: Darling, don't swear your life away, it's precious to me. Love is blind. You've done nothing else but talk about him since we left. I'm not a fool—you make me so mad. Feeling better, Dolly? My whole family's turning against me.

ROMAINE: Do you honestly think I'd fall for a rat like that?

MILLIE: Yes. Never mind, he's enticed you the way he has Morry. He's hypnotic—you know, like Rasputin.

ROMAINE: I never met him.

MILLIE: What have I done? Am I bad? Haven't I given to charity? Why should it happen to me?

MELVIN [*breezes in*]: Lo, Mum. Lo, Roroe. Back already?

MILLIE [*falls on him*]: Melvin! Darling! What's happening?

MELVIN [*releasing himself*]: You're smothering me.

MILLIE: What's been happening here?

MELVIN: Oh, I don't know. Something or other. Must dash now—I'm late as it is.

ROMAINE: But where's the furniture?

MELVIN: Oh yes, it's gone isn't it? And about time too—it was simply gasters.

MILLIE: Are you feeling all right?

MELVIN: Now, Mummy, please—later. I'll be late for the games.

MILLIE: Where's your father?

MELVIN: Your husband is contemplating. Well, tata for now.

[*She won't let him go yet.*]

MILLIE: And where's that snake of a Rabbi?

MELVIN: He's a very nice chap and I won't hear a word against him. Since he's been here the house has been tolerable.

MILLIE: What's he doing to your father?

MELVIN: I don't know and I don't care. [*He goes.*]

MILLIE: When I see that Morry I'll kill him.

[MORRY *wanders on, looking very happy. He sees* MILLIE *and he kisses her.*]

MORRY: Hello, Millie—how are you darling? Two weeks passed already?

MILLIE [*she stifles her anger*]: I only stayed away two days. Do you think I'd trust you here any longer? Look what's happened already. What have you been doing?

MORRY: Looking at the clouds. I never knew they were so beautiful. Have you ever looked at the clouds, Millie? Shall we both do it together now? And there are birds in London—and trees. I've never seen them before.

MILLIE: He's gone cuckoo. Listen Morry, come to your senses.

MORRY: All my senses are working overtime. I can smell and hear and see and touch.

MILLIE: This Rabbi is a phoney. Did you see his credentials?

MORRY: Do ask I for the credentials of God? He is honest and beautiful. The most trustworthy person I ever met.

MILLIE: How do you know?

153

MORRY: I know because I know.

MILLIE: How do you know you know?

MORRY: Because I'm happy. Really happy.

MILLIE: How do you know you're happy? You're not happy. You only think you are. He's taking you for a ride—I feel it in my water.

MORRY: It's a lovely journey and at the end of it I shall be the Messiah.

ROMAINE: Messiah?

MILLIE: Messiah? Romaine, shut up—don't interfere. Listen Morry—carefully—take it easy. Did you say Messiah?

MORRY: Yes, very soon now I shall be ready, when I reach perfection.

MILLIE: He won't make a Messiah, he'll make a mess of you, you bloody fool. You're sinning—do you know you're sinning?

MORRY: Thought you didn't believe in God. Sinning against who?

MILLIE: Sinning against me—against you—against everything. Listen, Morry, look at me—I'm your wife, your other half. How can you be a Messiah? You're overwrought. I understand. There ain't no such person as God and thank God there isn't, because if he existed you'd really go to hell, and please God, soon you'll realize all this and come to your senses.

MORRY: All I want is for you and everyone to be happy. Don't get angry with me. I'm so happy.

MILLIE: I could ki—

[Turns to ROMAINE as if to show her they must bear with him for the moment.]

It's just that you're getting old, Morry, old and scared.

MORRY: I must go now and see the new moon rise. [He sails off.]

ROMAINE: Poor Daddy. Isn't it funny, he's happy and we're sorry for him. Poor Daddy.

MILLIE: We'll have to humour him. I'll even become vegetarian to please him now. How could he change so quick? He wouldn't trust a fly till that Rabbi came along.

ROMAINE: Everybody believes what he wants to believe, believe me.

MILLIE: Oh shut up you! It's all your fault.

ROMAINE: But I told you I didn't trust him.

MILLIE: Now be quiet will you, and stop bickering. We've got to think of a way to make him see, somehow. But we mustn't let the Rabbi know that we suspect he's a phoney.

[SOLLY *enters and says*:]

SOLLY: Hello, my daughters, how was Bournemouth? Still kosher and Godless?

MILLIE: Hello, Rabbi, glad to see you looking so well, and I'm glad to see you looked after Morry.

SOLLY: Where is he?

ROMAINE: In the garden watching the moon.

SOLLY: Good, I'll find him. Well, welcome home. Are you thoroughly cleansed and vegetarian now?

[ROMAINE *is about to protest when her mother shuts her up.*]

MILLIE: What else? It's wonderful. Nuts and raisins for breakfast, turnips and lettuce for lunch, and carrots for supper.

SOLLY: Good! Good! You've got a glow on your face. [*He goes off.*]

MILLIE: May he rot, may he burn—may he get run over and smashed—may he drown.

ROMAINE: And all at once.

[MR *and* MRS FINK *and* ALAN *and* SARAH *enter.*]

SARAH: Mummy, you're back. [*They kiss.*]

ALAN: What's the matter, where's the furniture?

MILLIE: Sarah darling, we're in terrible trouble.

SARAH: I know. I've been having nightmares.

MILLIE: The Rabbi is a charlatan—what can we do?

ROMAINE: He's fleecing us—taking us for a ride.

FINK: I told you so.

MILLIE: No, you didn't.

FINK: I could have told you so.

MRS FINK: Shut up. It was a palace here, a real palace. Where's the furniture? Where?

FINK: The woodworm ran away with it. [*Nobody laughs.*] Hahahahahaha! I'm only trying to cheer everyone up.

ALAN: What's it all add up to?

MILLIE: My Morry thinks he's the new Messiah, no less. [*She weeps.*]

ROMAINE: And that Solly Gold is getting all our money and Daddy won't hear a word against him.

FINK: I knew it. I can smell a crook a mile off.

MRS FINK: What will the neighbours say? [*She cuddles* ALAN.] Oh, my poor boy.

SARAH: To hell with the neighbours—what about us?

FINK: Open and shut case. Leave it to me, let Fink think— Simple—the police. [*Goes to phone.*]

MILLIE: What? And let my Morry be the laughing stock of all the world?

ROMAINE: They'll take him off in a strait-jacket.

SARAH: And we'll be starving while the lawyers argue.

FINK: Poor Morry—what can we do?

ALAN: We must think of something.

[MORRY *wanders in.*]

MORRY: Hello everyone. Lovely evening. I just saw Sirius and Orion, and heard the music of the spheres. I'm no longer just Morry Swartz of Golders Green—I'm Morris Swartz of the Universe. I'll see you all on the great day. Toodleloo. [*Wanders out again and the women cry and the men shake their heads.*]

SARAH: He overtaxed his brain.

MILLIE: He never had a brain—only an adding machine up there.

ALAN: Hold it—I've got an idea coming up! Shush . . .

SARAH: Isn't he marvellous? I could eat him.

ROMAINE: Not yet, wait till he comes out with it.

ALAN: Got it! [*Claps his hands.*] That Rabbi Whatyoumay-callit, must confess directly to your father, must say he's a complete phoney, now how? How can we get him to confess?

[*They all walk backward and forward thinking.*]

Who would he tell the truth to? Who has he got a weakness for?

[ROMAINE *is somehow now in the centre of a circle of walking people, they all stop together, turn and stare at her.*]

ROMAINE: What's up? What have I done?

SARAH: It's not what you've done, it's what you're going to do.

ALAN: I've seen the way he stares at you. You'll have to do it.

ROMAINE: Do what? I'm getting out of here.

[*She tries to go but* MILLIE *stops her.*]

MILLIE: Dolly do you love me? Do you love your father? Do you love luxury? Well, then, you'll have to help us all.

FINK: Only you could make him confess.

ROMAINE: But I don't trust him.

MRS FINK: This time you don't need to.

SARAH: Lead him on a little, get him hot under the collar—

ALAN: Tell him you're passionately in love with him but unfortunately you couldn't give yourself to a Rabbi—

FINK: Tell him it's against your principles, but you could make love to a layman—

ROMAINE: Are you all mad or something? What do you take me for?

MILLIE: A good girl. And when he confesses that he isn't a Rabbi, lead him on a bit more—tell him you don't like good boys—

ALAN: And when he confesses that he's a crook . . . [*Thinks for the next move.*]

SARAH: You'll switch on Melvin's tape recorder.

MILLIE: And when Daddy hears the tape, we'll be rid of that worm.

ROMAINE: I won't be left alone with him.

MILLIE: You'll be all right, don't worry.

ROMAINE: Do you think I'm gonna sacrifice my purity for rotten money?

FINK: You've got to lose it sooner or later.

MRS FINK: Herbert, shut up. Listen, Romaine, we all have to take chances—

ROMAINE: You're all against me.

ALAN: Whatever happens, we'll sympathize and understand. We're depending on you. I expect you'll pull it off.

ROMAINE [*she almost weeps*]: I'll be expecting all right, with that snake in the grass. Mummy, look at me! I'm your daughter. Your own flesh and blood. Don't leave me alone with that monster.

MILLIE: Listen, your purity, my darling, is worth all the tea in China, all the gold in Hatton Garden. Don't worry, we won't let it go too far. If you scream we'll break the door down—but don't scream unless you can help it, they cost enough. He'll confess. After all aren't you a lovely girl? And why not, why be ashamed of what you've got?

ROMAINE: Oh go on then, go, leave me alone. What do I care? [*She does a great tragedy act and falls on the sofa.*]

MILLIE: Good luck, Dolly—a lot's at stake.

ROMAINE: Telling me!

FINK: We'll wait in there and be as quiet as little mice.

ROMAINE: Don't look through the keyholes—I'll be embarrassed. Promise?

ALL: Promise.

MILLIE: What about the tape machine?

SARAH: It's all ready. At the crucial moment just switch on, like this: [*She demonstrates and then they all troop into the other room and shut the door.*]

ROMAINE [*overplaying*]: What do they care? Do they consider my feelings? I shall run away! [*She overweeps and then stops as she sees herself in the mirror.*] How marvellous. I looked like Anna Magnani just then. [*She smiles and poses in front of the mirror as if to make herself look enticing, then she weeps again.*] Oh, what do they care—leaving me with that shark.

> [*She switches off the main lighting and the indirect lighting now makes the room look seductive. She sprays perfume upon herself and then puts on a soft tango. She settles down and starts to eat Turkish Delight but changes her mind and then, fixing her dress to look more sexy, she dances to the music seductively. Then we see* SOLLY. *He comes on like a furtive fly, in quick, sharp*]

*jerking angular movements, as if drawn by an irresistible
impulse. He is about to go directly to her, but goes to the
adjoining door, where the family are, and locks the door
on this side. When she sees this she starts to get panicky
but carries on—dancing. He pours her a drink and gives
it to her.]*

SOLLY: May I have this dance? [*He pushes her into a
dance.*] Do you come here often? What a smashing bit of
overtime you are. [*He pinches her.*]

ROMAINE: I think you're crude.

SOLLY: Sorry, I get carried away by your beauty—what I
mean is, God worked overtime when he created you.

ROMAINE: Never knew that Rabbis drink, and dance, and
pinch girls.

SOLLY: What else? All work and no play makes Jacob
a very miserable geezer. Haven't you read the Song of
Solomon? But anyway—you are so marvellous I could even
leave my religious world for you. Let's sit down. I want to
give you some spiritual instruction.

ROMAINE: No, no, I'm afraid.

SOLLY: Foolish lady, I'll look after you. Sit down, I'll
make it worth your while.

ROMAINE: I shouldn't really. [*She sits down.*]

SOLLY: Doing what we shouldn't is one way of finding out
the mysteries of creation.

[*She leans down to switch on the machine and as she
does so he kisses her. First she struggles but then she sub-
sides into his arms and does not touch the tape recorder.*]

ROMAINE: Now listen! I'm giving you a chance to get
away.

SOLLY: How beautiful are thy feet in sandals—

ROMAINE: I've got corns.

SOLLY: The joints of thy thighs are like jewels.

ROMAINE: And they're staying in the safe because you're a
thief. But I'm giving you a chance to run. Run, before
you're caught.

SOLLY: What are you talking about? I've got nothing to
be ashamed of.

ROMAINE: I don't know why I'm telling you, but I don't

trust you, so don't try and get round me. You're a bad boy and you know it.

SOLLY: Me? I'm a—angel, a saint. Ask anyone.

ROMAINE: Listen. There's no time to lose.

SOLLY: Enough of this.

ROMAINE: You're no good.

SOLLY: What's good? What's bad? Relative terms, my daughter. Thy navel is like a round goblet.

ROMAINE: Cheek! How dare you, you've never seen me!

SOLLY: Enough of this, let's get down to something serious —let me kiss you, let me love you! Thy belly is like a heap of wheat.

[*He tries furiously to embrace her, but she keeps freeing herself. It's almost a chase.*]

ROMAINE: That's the last straw.

SOLLY: Forgive me, I get carried away. I was only quoting from the Bible.

ROMAINE: Then it should be banned.

SOLLY: Nonsense, it's beautiful—have you ever read it?

ROMAINE: No, but I've seen the film. Please, listen, there's no time to waste.

SOLLY: All right, spit it out, what's it all about?

ROMAINE: Now he hears. Solly, my family are on to your game, they are trying to get me to make you confess. I'm the decoy.

SOLLY: On to my game? Confess? Confess to what?

ROMAINE: You can trust me. I'm on your side. I must be mad, but I am.

SOLLY: Why should I trust you all of a sudden?

ROMAINE: Because here's the tape machine that I was supposed to switch on when you started confessing.

SOLLY [*as she shows him the machine*]: Tape machine? What are you talking about? I'm a servant of the Lord.

ROMAINE: Solly, Solly, oh Solly boy, you can trust me.

SOLLY: Why should I?

ROMAINE: Because I want to see you get away. Because you're romantic. Because I've fallen for you, for a tyke like you. My mum always told me I was no class. I've fallen right down.

SOLLY: Don't believe you.
   [*She kisses him.*]
   Well, maybe I believe you a bit—kiss me again.
   [*She does.*]
   Yeah! Oh, Romaine—I could feel your whole heart pouring into that kiss.
ROMAINE: I want to help you. Can't you see that? Tell me about yourself.
SOLLY: All right, I admit I'm not a Rabbi. I'm a liar, a lobos, a gonif. You know—I take things from people who can afford to do without. But I'm the best con man in the business—
ROMAINE: Maybe, but fancy doing your tricks on my father, he's such a good man.
SOLLY: All right, so now you know. Happy? I'm a lay-about. I'm a thief. That lets me out . . . [*He turns his back and is about to go when he turns back and smiles.*] Run away with me.
ROMAINE: Where?
SOLLY: Anywhere.
ROMAINE: Run away? No, I couldn't.
SOLLY: Why not?
ROMAINE: Why not? Why not? I love my luxury.
SOLLY: Now's your chance to really live.
ROMAINE: I couldn't run fast enough to keep up with you. Besides I'm too selfish—I've got so much to give that I need a lot in return . . .
MILLY [*off*]: You all right, Dolly?
ROMAINE: Fine—fine. Hurry, hurry—Solly, Solly, time is pressing.
SOLLY: Nobody here understands you—how deeply romantic you are. Just like me. Chasing the stars, looking for kicks and only getting kicked in the teeth. Look at you —you're a child of the sun, a victim of circumstance holding on to your chastity—saving it all for a rainy day. But why be a pessimist? No one can love you like me. You're fat and I love you that way. I'll take you to the life of luxury you dream about—a life of romance in the best hotels, as much Turkish Delight as you want, we'll go to Rome,

F   161

Miami, Glasgow. Hiding and flying—romance on the run. Snatched hours of passion in hotel bedrooms; different places, different faces. Romaine your humdrum life is nearly over. Solly Gold is taking over.

[*They kiss.*]

ROMAINE: That settles it. I'll get my things.

SOLLY: Don't bother. I'll buy you everything new on Broadway next week.

ROMAINE: With what? On peanuts and prayers?

SOLLY: With the money I've got from your father already and the money I'm getting from him in a minute or two.

ROMAINE: Oh, Solly, I was forgetting that. It's so dishonest.

SOLLY: Is it dishonest to make him happy for the first time in years? You'll help me.

ROMAINE: I'll never forgive myself.

SOLLY: You don't have to—God will. We'll fill a suitcase full of fivers and be on our merry way.

ROMAINE: It is true, he is much happier.That can't be bad, can it? What about the police?

SOLLY [*he jumps*]: Please. I don't like bad language. That word makes my blood run cold. We'll go to the docks tonight and get a boat. Let's call your father now.

ROMAINE: One minute, I'm not coming with you unless you marry me.

SOLLY: Don't you relish sin? Silly girl—all right! I'll marry you, on the other side.

ROMAINE: On the other side of where?

SOLLY: Tell you when we get there.

ROMAINE: Just one thing more—are you sure you're not married?

SOLLY: Absolutely, definitely not—I cross my heart, that's the truth so help me God. Come on—

ROMAINE: There's just one other thing.

SOLLY: I love the way you're so concise. What is it?

ROMAINE: Where did you get the Rabbi's clothes?

SOLLY: From an old lady in the East End.

ROMAINE: You must take them back, I'm superstitious.

SOLLY: Let me burn them, let me chuck them away.

ROMAINE: No! We'll take them back to her on our way to the docks.

SOLLY: It's too risky.

ROMAINE: If you love me you'll do it—just this once, for me.

SOLLY: I must learn the art of blackmail from you. All right, and now I'll find your father. Wait here for me.

[*He pretends to go but hides and watches* ROMAINE.]

MILLIE [*off*]: You all right, Dolly?

ROMAINE: Sure.

MILLIE [*off*]: How's it going?

ROMAINE: Perfect.

SARAH [*off*]: Got the recording yet?

ROMAINE: Not yet, be patient.

[SOLLY *is obviously satisfied with her, and goes before she sees him. Now she poses herself in front of the mirror.*]

Oh God forgive me, but I must grab the opportunity. Why not? Eh? Oh romance, Romaine—romance at last.

[SOLLY *brings* MORRY *on.*]

SOLLY: Well, Morry, the great day approacheth and verily I say unto you that a purple light surrounds you. Sit on your throne.

MORRY: How we doing, Rabbi? What's the score?

SOLLY: Great news. We're almost there—I saw half a dozen angels at Golders Green station today—they're assembling and now rejoice even more so, for your blessed daughter Romaine has become a disciple. She has repented from her evil ways and stands before us, devoting herself to the cause.

MORRY: About time too.

ROMAINE: Daddy, darling, how you feeling?

MORRY: Never felt better in my life.

ROMAINE: Solly, let's go now.

SOLLY: Yes. Now listen, Morry, Romaine and I are going on a pilgrimage.

MORRY: That's nice.

SOLLY: But you can't come with us.

MORRY: That's sad, it's so lonely becoming the Messiah sometimes.

SOLLY: We must go to sordid places to spread the word, to the docks and get love and give love. You must be unsullied—think only of higher things. And then we're going to Westcliff-on-Sea where we'll distribute charities to the Jewish Society for the Prevention of Cruelty to dead Poets and to the Sisters of Nathaniel Greenbaum. We'll need a little money for this purpose.

MORRY: How much?

SOLLY: Not too much, a few to begin with—about—erm— five thousand?

MORRY: That's a lot of money.

SOLLY: It's to help the needy, the lonely, the sick, the lost, the sad dreamers and happy destitutes.

MORRY: Well that includes practically everyone alive. I'll get it. You going to give all this away tonight? Good. Money must go to those who need it. As for me, what else is it but bits of metal and paper around an idea? Five thousand. Hope I've got that much loose laying around . . . [MORRY goes off.]

ROMAINE: I don't like it. Daddy's out of his mind.

SOLLY: We've burnt our boats now and we're in this to- gether—sink or swim. Don't worry. [He calls out] Morry! There'll be plaques up to you all over London, 'Morry Swartz, the Saviour, saved our hospital'. 'Morry Swartz lived here'—'Morry Swartz ate here'—

[MORRY enters with some packets of money and tosses them to SOLLY.]

MORRY: Don't want no plaques, just a plain bit of marble when I die, saying: 'He tried to do good'. Hope that keeps you busy.

[As SOLLY stuffs it into the suitcase.]

ROMAINE: Daddy, Daddy, are you happy giving this away?

MORRY: The more that goes the happier I am.

ROMAINE: What about your life's work? You worked so hard?

MORRY: My life's work is just beginning. Listen, darling,

in this world you own nothing but your bones and even they let you down in the end. You come in with nothing and go out with nothing—and you're nothing unless you realize this, at least, now and again.

ROMAINE: Come on, Solly, time's getting on.

SOLLY: Contemplate, Morry. Pray for us all, especially me. We'll see you in the morning.

ROMAINE: Forgive me for everything.

MORRY: There's nothing to forgive. Go in peace. The way you both look, so lovely, I could kiss you. As a matter of fact I will. [*He does so.*] I'm so happy because before I only thought I was rich, now I know I am. Good-bye.

ROMAINE: Good-bye, come, Solly.

SOLLY: Good-bye, Morry—you're a lucky man. I'm carrying all your worries from now on.

[*He holds up the case and follows* ROMAINE *off.* MORRY *picks up the Bible that* SOLLY *has left behind, sits down and reads from it.*]

MILLIE [*off*]: Romaine! You ready yet? Romaine? Are you there?

SARAH [*off*]: Romaine? Did you do it? Why doesn't she answer?

[*The door is tried and they furiously push it from the other side.*]

MILLIE [*off*]: Romaine! Stop playing about. It's locked on the other side. Romaine! You all right? Darling where are you?

[MORRY *goes to the door and unlocks it just as* FINK *is about to fling himself against it. They all fall into the room.* MORRY *goes from them and sits on his throne.*]

MILLIE: What are you doing?

MORRY: Sitting down.

SARAH: Where's Romaine?

ALAN: Gone?

MORRY: Gone with the Rabbi.

SARAH: Gone where?

MILLIE: What do you mean? Oh my poor baby.

MORRY: They've gone on a pilgrimage. She's in safe hands. Don't worry.

SARAH: Daddy, don't you realize, he's a crook! A no-good, good-for-nothing. He's not a Rabbi.

FINK: I'm afraid you've been taken for a ride, Morry; it happens to the best of us.

MORRY: Don't worry about me, Fink. Go home and settle your own problems.

MILLIE: Take no notice, Herbert. Morry, you ought to be ashamed of yourself. Oh, my daughter! He's carried her off.

SARAH: That would have been difficult.

MILLIE: What's going to happen to her? I knew it.

MRS FINK: Call the police, Millie, call the police.

MILLIE: What? And have her dragged through the Sunday papers? I'll never live through it. Yes, I'll have to.

MORRY [reads from Bible]: Praise him with the sound of trumpets, with the stringed instruments and the pipe. Praise him upon the loud cymbals—

[MILLIE crashes two metal trays together. Everyone jumps except MORRY. MILLIE also jumps.]

MILLIE: Will you shut up! He reads the Bible. Will that bring your sanity back? Don't you see? He's taken your furniture, your sanity, your money and your daughter. I suppose you won't be happy till he takes me!

MORRY: That's an interesting thought. [Returns to the Bible.]

MILLIE: Phone the newspapers. Call the police. [SARAH goes to the phone.] Oh my money! Oh my poor baby. Oh my money. Listen Morry. Just listen to his confession. [She switches on the tape recorder. The Messiah blares out.]

MORRY: Ah, my music.

THE CURTAIN FALLS

SCENE FIVE

We are back in the East End. It is early morning. The
TAILOR *is seen working away in his house, sewing frantic-*
ally. SOLLY *comes on followed by* ROMAINE *who carries*
lots of cases. She seems all in. SOLLY *is dressed in very*
American-looking clothes and he carries the Rabbi's clothes in
a small bundle. The TAILOR *comes to the window and hides*
as soon as he sees SOLLY *but watches them all the time.*

SOLLY: I could have slept for another six hours.

ROMAINE: So could I, normally, but the boat leaves in an
hour.

SOLLY: I'm starving.

ROMAINE: I'm not, except for your kisses.
  [*They kiss.*]

SOLLY: Here's the house. I'll dump it on the doorstep.

ROMAINE: Oh no you're not. You're giving it to the lady in
person and apologize.

SOLLY: She won't be up this early.

ROMAINE: We'll wake her up.

SOLLY: You're very cruel. Look. The door's open . . .
Obviously she still trusts people . . . let's go inside. [*He
calls*] Yoohoo—yoohoo—
  [*Soon they are inside and we cannot see them.* JOE, *the*
  tailor, jumps up and goes to a door in his house and calls
  his wife.]

JOE: Rita! Rita! Get up—get up quick! Rita, for God's
sake get up—
  [RITA *rushes in in her nightclothes, she is distraught*
  and almost panicking.]

RITA: Joe, what is it? Is it bombs?
  [*She tries to dress herself hurriedly and gets everything*
  in the wrong place.]

JOE: Shush! That swine's come back.

RITA: Thank the Lord. I thought the world had come to an end.

JOE: And guess what?—he's got with him that missing heiress, what's her name—Rona Swarb or something—

RITA: Missing heiress?

JOE: Wake up. The one who's in the papers. The one that reward's for. You phone her mother quickly while I keep them here. The number's in the paper.

RITA: All night he works. All night. I just want to get some sleep. I'm fed up with you and the whole business.

JOE: Do as I say. We'll make a few hundred and I'll take you on a cruise. Quick!

[*She quickly runs for the newspaper and then goes into a back room.* JOE *comes out of his house and creeps towards the next house just as* SOLLY *comes running out with* ROMAINE; *they are chased by the old woman who is throwing things at them.*]

WOMAN: Get out of my house!

SOLLY: I've come to pay you back—to make it worth your while.

WOMAN: What do you take me for? Think you can buy me after what you did?

[*She hits him with a stick and he takes shelter under his coat. He brings out several pound notes and waves them about.*]

SOLLY: Truce! Truce! Is this flag the right colour?

WOMAN: Thief! Liar! Rogue! Crook!—Police . . . [*She suddenly stops and takes the money.*] Get out of my sight. [*She is about to go inside.*]

SOLLY [*to* ROMAINE]: See darling, anything can be bought with money, especially people. When pound notes flash, principles crash.

WOMAN: I can't afford principles. They won't buy my husband's tombstone.

[*She is about to go in and* SOLLY *is about to go off with* ROMAINE *when* JOE *grabs him.*]

SOLLY: Must you be so passionate?

JOE: So, you've returned to the scene of the crime?

SOLLY: Can't we talk this over like English gentlemen?

ROMAINE: Leave my Solly alone or I'll murder you.

[As JOE *gets off him* SOLLY *gets up.*]

SOLLY: I'll explain and settle everything.

JOE: Wish there was a copper about; they're never around when you want one.

SOLLY: I agree with you. And it all comes out of the tax-payer's pocket.

[RITA *comes out.*]

JOE: Well, what have you got to say for yourself?

SOLLY: Help!

JOE: You're a lousy rat.

SOLLY: Let me go and I'll make it worth your while.

JOE: You can't buy me.

SOLLY: I actually came to give you your money back.

RITA: There you are, Joe—I knew he was an honest feller.

SOLLY: Look here's the money. I'll give you twice as much.

JOE: Nothing doing, I won't be bought. I demand justice.

SOLLY: You're living in the wrong world.

[*The* PROSTITUTE *comes from her room.*]

PROSTITUTE: What's all this noise? Can't a nightworker get some decent sleep.

[JOE *is holding* SOLLY *by the arm and* ROMAINE *is trying to pull him in the other direction. The* PROSTITUTE *walks around* SOLLY.]

Haven't we met before?

SOLLY: Perhaps in some previous reincarnation.

PROSTITUTE: I've heard it called some things. Why are you holding him?

JOE: He owes me money.

SOLLY: I've offered to pay him back, twofold.

ROMAINE: It's the truth, honestly it is.

JOE: I don't want to be paid back, I want justice.

WOMAN: He's a thief. He got money out of me, my poor husband's clothes, and chickens.

PROSTITUTE: Come on, Joe, let the poor blighter go, the law will be around if you're not careful.

RITA: Let him go, Joe, we don't want no trouble.

SOLLY: Lady, I admire your common sense. Joe, do what your wife says.

JOE: I'm thinking about this poor girl here. He's a deceiver, leading her up the garden.

SOLLY: It ain't half pretty.

JOE: Don't you see he's no good? [*To* ROMAINE] How can you fall for a type like this?

SOLLY: I'm not a type, I'm a specie.

PROSTITUTE: Go on, let them go. You were young once.

RITA: Never. He never was young.

JOE: Will you shut up?

SOLLY [*as they argue*]: I think you're all marvellous and here's a token of my appreciation.

[*He throws a small packet of pound notes in the air. Eeveryone starts scrambling for them: at this* SOLLY *pulls* ROMAINE *and starts to rush off. The attache case, however, comes undone and pound notes are flying everywhere.* SOLLY *rushes about like a madman and* ROMAINE *sits down and cries. Everyone else desperately fights each other for the money.*]

JOE: He's robbed the Bank of England.

SOLLY: Have you no respect for private property?

PROSTITUTE: Someone's been working overtime.

RITA: Joe, Joe, come inside. [*As she pulls* JOE *she is stuffing pound notes into her dressing gown.*]

WOMAN: Now my husband can have a marvellous memorial.

POLICEMAN [*enters*]: Hello, hello, what's all the fuss? [*They all try to shield* SOLLY *but* POLICEMAN *walks into the centre and sees him.* SOLLY *is sitting on the pound notes now like a chicken sits on an egg.*]

SOLLY: We're discussing the political situation.

POLICEMAN: Looks like a mothers' meeting—what's it all in aid of? Eh? I remember you. Didn't I run you in? Wasn't your mug in the *Police Gazette*?

SOLLY: The only *Gazette* I was in was the *London Gazette* when I was mentioned in despatches, and the *Hackney Gazette* when I was born.

POLICEMAN: I remember you now. You're the loud-mouth spiv I spoke to last week. What are you sitting on?

SOLLY: Lettuce leaves.

[POLICEMAN *tries to drag him up.*]

POLICEMAN: Stand up.

SOLLY: Oh, all right. Bloody law has to interfere.

POLICEMAN: Where did you half-inch these from? Whew! Quite a fortune—talk yourself out of this.

SOLLY: I talked myself into this. This is my personal fortune. I can explain it. I won it.

POLICEMAN: What? On tiddlewinks? All right, come along with me. We'll sort it out down at the station.

SOLLY: Come on, Romaine. Whither I goest thou must go.

ROMAINE: I've never been in a police station before.

SOLLY: Better get used to it.

JOE: One minute, Officer, may I have a word with you?

ROMAINE: Solly, tell him the truth. The fact is we're running away, we're madly in love.

POLICEMAN: Just you two wait there and don't move. [*To* JOE]: Now what is it?

JOE: Don't you recognize her? She's the missing heiress, Don't you read your *Express*?

POLICEMAN: What do you mean—heiress?

JOE: Listen, just keep them here for a while. Her old man's on his way to claim his daughter and to pay me the reward.

POLICEMAN [*loudly to all*]: I've got my duty to perform. There's some dirty business going on with all this money. I'm taking them into custody.

PROSTITUTE: What's the matter with you this morning, George? Why are you so narked? Didn't you get your dropsy from the girls last night?

POLICEMAN: Now you shut up—or I'll run you in also.

SOLLY: Please, Constable—a word in your ear. [*He leads* POLICEMAN *to one side.*] This is not a bribe, it's just a present or a loan. Just turn the other way, will you? I've got a boat to catch. [SOLLY *offers him a wad.*]

POLICEMAN: Right! Bribery and corruption as well. You're for it, my lad.

[*The* POLICEMAN *takes the money, puts it in his pocket and takes* SOLLY *by the scruff of his neck.*]

SOLLY: In that case give me my money back.

POLICEMAN: What money?

[MORRY, MILLIE, SARAH, ALAN, MR *and* MRS FINK *and* MELVIN *enter hurriedly.*]

MILLIE: Oh darling! [*She rushes to* ROMAINE] How are you? Where have you been, you bad girl? I could murder you. You all right, darling?

ROMAINE: I'm so pleased to see you, Mummy.

MORRY: Hello, Solly. How's tricks?

SOLLY: Complicated.

MILLIE: Fancy running away like that, where have you been?

ROMAINE: Lying low.

MILLIE: Naughty girl.

SOLLY: You said it.

ROMAINE [*sings*]: 'Ah, sweet mystery of life, at last I found you.' [*She kisses all the family on the cheek.*]

MILLIE: You'll have to marry him now. You're ruined otherwise. [*To* SOLLY]: You'll have to marry her.

[SOLLY *kisses* MILLIE, *who smiles.*]

SOLLY: Who's disagreeing? Mother.

MORRY: Congratulations.

[*General back slapping.*]

ALAN: Wish you joy.

FINK: Please God, by you.

MRS FINK: May we only meet on holidays.

SARAH: I'm so happy for both of you.

MILLIE: Isn't it wonderful?

PROSTITUTE: Here comes the bride . . .

WOMAN: I love a wedding!

[*Everyone is joyful except the* POLICEMAN.]

SOLLY: You're wasting your time Constable. Back to your beat now, my good man.

POLICEMAN: All right, but I'm keeping my eye on you.

[*He goes off and everyone cheers.*]

ROMAINE: Sarah did you see my picture in the papers?

SARAH: Oh yes it makes your eyes look so alluring.

SOLLY [*To* MORRY]: How can you forgive me?

MORRY: You showed me the way.

SOLLY: But I must confess to you now, I'm not a Rabbi.

MORRY: That I've known for a long time.

SOLLY: You know?

MORRY: Suddenly I came to me senses but in such a way that I see more clearly now than ever before.

SOLLY: But you did believe that I was a Rabbi, admit it. I'm a bloody marvellous actor.

MORRY: Yes, I believed for a time. You see, I'm a simple man and you swore on the Bible. Besides I was bored with life until you came.

SOLLY: Aren't you disappointed that you're not the Messiah?

MORRY: In a way.

SOLLY: And what about my money? This money?

MORRY: It's yours. Call it my dowry for Romaine. Besides, you've earned it. You cured my backache. Hundreds of doctors treated me for years and fleeced me blind and still I suffered. You worked a miracle.

SOLLY: It was an accident.

MORRY: Call it what you like. The point is the pain is gone.

SOLLY: But I must admit, Morry—I've been a bad boy. Can you forgive me for my past?

MORRY: Easily. What about my financial advisers? My solicitor and accountant? And my branch managers? They've been diddling me for years. You're an amateur compared to them.

SOLLY: I'm not an amateur—I won't have you say that.

MILLIE: Relax, Solly, let's all be friends. You're one of the family now. [*She kisses him.*]

SOLLY: I'm so glad you like me now. You had me worried at first.

MILLIE: I feel so much better since you came into our lives. I've become a vegetarian now—on your advice, and it's working wonders. I've lost three ounces in three days— I look so young, don't I? Besides, you've got such a big dowry from Morry, we must keep it in the family—so welcome.

SOLLY: Mother! At last I've got a Mum of my own. My Mum took one look at me and ran away.

MILLIE: No more lies now. We want you to look after the business.

SOLLY: What?

MORRY: It's true. If you can't lick them, make them join you. With you in the business nothing can stop us.

SOLLY: You said it. You're very smart. I'll make it the greatest shoe concern in the universe! I can sell anything, even your shoes. 'Swartzes Everlasting Immortal Soles.' I can sell binoculars to a blind man, roller skates to a cripple. Romaine, Romaine, I'm the happiest guy in the world.

[*He cuddles her but she doesn't react.*]

SARAH: Solly, you're as good as gold.

[*Everyone slaps him on the back.*]

MELVIN: I would like to thank you, Solly, for helping me so much.

SOLLY: You as well? I'm so glad I helped. But tell me how?

MELVIN: I took your advice. The other evening at the Maccabee games I took the plunge and spoke to a girl, and now we're mad about each other. We're going to Israel next week—going to get married. And then we're going to start a new Kibbutz—devoted entirely to the propagation of sports and English sportsmanship. You know, cricket, polo and badminton. She's lovely. What a figure, and can she throw the discus!

MORRY: Come on then, let's all go home and prepare for more weddings.

SOLLY: I feel like dancing.

[*He dances with* MILLIE *and soon everyone but* ROMAINE *is dancing round and round as* JOE *plays the mouth organ.*]

Come on Romaine, back to Golders Green, back to a life of luxury and love.

ROMAINE: I'm not going back.

[SOLLY *leaves* MILLIE. *He wonders if he heard right. Meanwhile the rest of the cast dances around—in and out of the houses—where they drink and eat.*]

SOLLY: What do you mean, not going back?

ROMAINE: I love you, Solly. I want to go forward with you.

SOLLY: But everything's arranged, everything's marvellous. Your family approve of me.

ROMAINE: Well, I don't approve of them. I want us to start afresh—without their lousy money. For you and I to go off into the world with nothing except our love.

SOLLY: Oh God, you've been reading *True Romances*.

ROMAINE: Darling, I want us to start from scratch.

SOLLY: I've been scratching all my life. Sweetheart, I want us to have a little money to start with.

ROMAINE: I want you to work for me—to prove you love me.

SOLLY: I'm going to work. I'm taking over your father's business.

ROMAINE: It's the money or me.

SOLLY: Why do you see everything in black or white?

ROMAINE: What do you want—the money or me?

SOLLY: I want both. Don't you see I was born for luxury?

ROMAINE: Well I've had enough of it.

SOLLY: Come on, darling, I love you, you know I do.

ROMAINE: It's good-bye then.

SOLLY: Romaine, this is no time for a parting scene. What about last night and the night before? What about the things you whispered in the Three Nuns Hotel?

ROMAINE: No! No! No! I don't trust you—I never should. I should have listened to my Mum.

SOLLY: All right, darling, come with me, now. Without the money.

ROMAINE: No, it's too late. You're hoping to get that money later on. I don't want you any more.

[*The family have now stopped dancing.*]

ROMAINE: I'm not going with him.

SOLLY: She's mad.

ROMAINE: He doesn't love me for myself.

MILLIE: Oh darling, you sure?

ROMAINE: Oh Mummy, I don't want a life of poverty, I want to come home with you—[*she weeps.*] He just wanted my money and my body. He didn't really love me.

MILLIE: I don't want my Dolly unhappy, and on such a happy day.

175

SOLLY: But it's all crazy. I do want her! Morry, please try and persuade her—

MORRY: Do you want him, Romaine? Make up your mind.

ROMAINE: No! I never want to see him again, I don't want him or any man—you can't trust them.

SOLLY: Morry, as her father it's your duty to make her see sense. You know I'm right for her.

MORRY: Sorry, my boy. She must make her own decisions. I'm not going to interfere. I learned from you how to be tolerant. Thanks.

SOLLY: All right then, I'll go. [*He reaches for suitcase.*]

MILLIE: Oh no you don't! That's my money—Romaine's money, for her dowry, and as she's not getting married, I'll keep it for her.

ROMAINE: I don't want it.

SOLLY: Well I do. I earned it, you said so.

MILLIE: Well, it's mine now.

SOLLY: But I made you all so happy—you said so.

MORRY: I know, but women! What can you do with them? Good-bye, my boy—thanks for everything. If you're ever passing, drop in for a chat.

SOLLY: A chat! A chat! I say, can you lend me a fiver?

MORRY: Certainly. [*He gives it to him.*]

SOLLY: Can you spare a little more?

MORRY: Sorry. I don't carry much around with me. Come on everyone. Come on Fink.

[*They start to move off.*]

FINK: I told you, Morry, never to trust that man.

MRS FINK: Herbert, shut up.

MILLIE: Feeling better, darling?

ROMAINE: What's for lunch?

SARAH: Chicken, casseroled, and Neapolitan ice cream to follow.

MELVIN: Good-bye, Solly. If you ever want to play hockey in the Holy Land, look me up.

MORRY: Come on, everyone—liven up. Good-bye, Solly— all the best . . . Look after yourself.

[*They are gone, and now the other people go in.*]

SOLLY: [*Forlorn. Looks around, picks up a cigar butt.*] I

made them all happy and I didn't earn a bean and I let a
fortune and a fat girl slip through my fingers at the same
time. One thing I'm sure of, I'm not going to work. No,
work's too much like an occupation—work's all right for the
working class, but for me—it's got to be something better. I
must think of something—something really spectacular this
time . . . I've got it! No, no—[*he walks around the stage.*]
One minute—No. I'm bloody fed up. You can't con an
honest coin these days . . .

*He sits down, picks up some fag ends, rolls a cigarette
and becomes deep in thought as*

THE CURTAIN FALLS

Home Sweet Honeycomb

CHARACTERS IN THE PLAY

THREE MALE SCENE SHIFTERS
THREE FEMALE SCENE SHIFTERS
HEADMAN
HEADWOMAN
MRS TODD
ROBERT TODD
DAPHNE TODD
DANNY TODD
HELEN
REVEREND JAMES

EMPTY STAGE: *At the back there is a blow-up of an assembly of empty silent faces. They stare straight out at the audience. People from the building enter. Four men and four women. These are the* SCENE SHIFTERS. *They are dressed in normal working clothes but as they erect a scene they change into the clothes appropriate to that scene. It is these* SCENE SHIFTERS *who become the firing squad; the people in the madhouse; the police; the warders; the people on holiday, etc. While some of these* SCENE SHIFTERS *may be involved in an actual scene, some others will be anticipating the next and preparing it. Often, during the main action they sit on the side, play cards, smoke and knit. There is a quiet and frightening air of inevitability about them. Sometimes they can erect and stack a scene just one step ahead of the main actors but it is always done with an inevitable planned casualness. Out of these four men and four women, a man and woman give the orders. These are known as* HEADMAN *and* HEADWOMEN. *The other actors often adopt more than one role in the play; even though the role may change (and even the accent) the personality remains the same.*

The scenery is minimal and skeletal.
The SCENE SHIFTERS *set the scene of a block of Council Flats: A Cold, Modern, Claustrophobic structure. Then they bring in a Firing Wall, pitted with bullet holes. Now the men change into firing squad uniforms and the women lead in* MRS TODD *and her son* ROBERT. MRS TODD *is trying to sing a quiet tune in her son's ear; the young man is trying to push her away. He is dressed in black but he has a crimson heart painted over the spot where his heart is. He is put against the wall and the women change into their firing squad uniforms.*

183

The firing squad smoke and chat. There is the noise of people congregating.

MRS TODD *stands centre stage and looks at the audience with arms outstretched:*

MRS TODD: What a lovely big crowd! What a lovely send off for my boy.

[*Now we hear bugles slightly off key; sounding like the Boys Brigade. At once all goes silent except for the ominous, relentless sound of a solitary drumbeat; this gets louder and louder until it is joined by many more drums: the sound dominates everything. Then they stop suddenly. A terrific sense of relief.*]

HEADMAN [*he is chummy and cockney*] [*through his loud hailer*]: Zero! Zero! Testing! One! Two! Three! Testing! Testing! Mary had a little—Ladies and gentlemen, please be patient—everyone will be able to see. Excuse me! [*He consults with* HEADWOMAN. *She puts on gramophone record. A smaltzy tenor sings ' Mamma, this is just to tell you that I'll always love you '.*]

HEADMAN: Hello! Will Firing Sqaud please report to the execution wall.

[*The* SCENE SHIFTERS *reluctantly tear themselves away from a card game.*]

Will the Building Militia report to the Execution Master.

[*They move now to the wall and have a word with* REVEREND JAMES *who instructs them.*]

[*A patriotic song is played. i.e. ' I vow to thee my country ' and the* SCENE SHIFTERS *take up their rifles.*]

HEADWOMAN [*she is respectable, sour and sexless*]: Here is a special announcement. Lemonade is being sold on the stand outside A Block. There will be a Whist Drive, to-morrow at eight-thirty and a parents' meeting on Thursday afternoon.

HEADMAN: Thank you! And now the Reverend James wants to say a few words to you. [*All clap.*]

REV JAMES: Unaccustomed as I am to public speaking, I won't take too much of your time. I know you haven't come here to hear me speak. Hahaha! [*He clears his throat.*]It's a lovely day and we are here enjoying ourselves. And it is Mayday. The people's day. And God's day—for are we not built, er—created—in his—er—image. The Church and the State—recognize—no—nay, rejoice in the growing awareness of civic duty and pride—and so—the foundations are magnified and thus everlastingly—the civic and cultural—duty and responsibility of the church and—er—the church—[*He is lost for just a moment.*] The poor victim—there—Robert Rodd! Robert—Todd! We can pray for him! I repeat, we can pray for him. Do not let any one of us imagine that we cannot pray for him.

MALE S.S.: Put a sock in it. Blimey O'Riley!

REV JAMES: In three minutes he will meet his Maker.

FEMALE S.S.: Three hours if he goes on this way.

REV JAMES: We, servants of—God? Can understand—remember this collar, this habit just covers the same disgusting human flesh. For He alone is the final referee. He is the only chap who understands. No one is beyond mercy. No one is beyond our prayers for mercy, not even a bloke like Robert Todd. Let us pray.

[*They all put their heads down to pray but just for a fraction of a second.*]

HEADMAN: Thank you Reverend James.

[*The mood becomes lighter. Popular dance music is played.* REV JAMES *has a smoke and a lark with the* S.S. GIRLS. *The men smoke and play cards.* ROBERT TODD *just stares ahead looking vacantly at everything.* MRS TODD *looking at her son, goes close and shakes her head. She is joined by the* HEADWOMAN. MRS TODD *is knitting. They converse casually either side of the condemned man.*]

HEADWOMAN [*staring into Robert's eyes*]: Blue, aren't they?

MRS TODD: Yers, all my boys were blue.

HEADWOMAN: Cold for this time of the year, ain't it?

MRS TODD: Yers, it's fresh, it cuts right through you.

HEADWOMAN: Yes, it does cut right through you. Are you sad to be losing your boy?

MRS TODD: No, can't say I'm sad. Yes, he is my son but I'm not sad. I'm glad we decided to put him under.

HEADWOMAN: Well, he may have been no good, but he's certainly taking it well.

MRS TODD: All my boys took it very well. Yes, all my boys took it well. They all ended up this way, you know. Except Danny of course.

HEADWOMAN: Don't blame yourself, Mrs Todd.

MRS TODD: No, I can't blame myself.

HEADWOMAN: You brought them up well, didn't you? You've got nothing to blame yourself for. As I always say, it's better for them to be put under if they're going bad. Good-looking lad.

MRS TODD: All my boys had lovely faces, long curling eye-lashes, beautiful strong little limbs.

HEADWOMAN: He's your fourth, isn't he? Robert?

MRS TODD: No, Jack was my fourth, he's my fifth and Danny is my sixth and last. Danny is the baby of the family!

HEADWOMAN: Will you be putting Danny under? Will he end up like the rest?

MRS TODD: Well, we all end up dead, don't we?

HEADWOMAN: Will Danny go rotten like the rest of your boys?

MRS TODD: It's too early to say, but we live in hopes. We'll know more about Danny by supper time. I'm not like some, I'm not going to blame it all onto my husband. I'm not going to blame it all on him though where they get their black streak from I don't know. Certainly not from my side. Oh Bobby, my little Bobby. My Robert, so headstrong. You can't tell them nothing.

HEADWOMAN: What was the final charge against him?

MRS TODD: Don't you know?

HEADWOMAN: Been too busy to read the report. This is my ninth this week.

MRS TODD: Wouldn't work. Thank God for the Borough Council.

HEADWOMAN: Yes, you can always trust the local council in these execution matters.

MRS TODD: I warned him. I told him. It's not that I didn't tell him. And have I got a weekend ahead of me. All that washing and cooking and the tube of my telly gone. And on top of all that I've got to get Robert a lovely funeral. I've got a lovely bird for roasting.

HEADWOMAN: Ssh. This is it.

[*People cheer.*]

MRS TODD: Ooh, I love this part.

HEADMAN: Now ladies and gentlemen the thing you've all been waiting for. Building militia, are you ready?

[*The* FIRING SQUAD *poise themselves.*]

Mrs Todd, step forward please. Militia men, on her final count of three, when she drops her handkerchief, you will fire.

[*Drums roll and then stop.*]

MRS TODD: Bye bye, Bobby boy.

ROBERT: Goodbye you old cow.

REV JAMES: Have you one final word?

ROBERT: Yes, it's a pleasure to leave this lousy world.

REV JAMES: Squad, take aim, ready.

MRS TODD: One! Two! Fire!

[*As she drops her handkerchief, they fire their rifles.* ROBERT *falls.*]

ALL [*together with massed bands*]: Abide with me, fast falls the eventide. The darkness deepens, Lord with me abide.

REV JAMES: And now let's all have a happy sing-song. I'm sure you all know this old favourite. [*He sings*] 'Dear old pals, jolly old pals'.

[*They all join in and the voices fade. The stage darkens, the* SCENE SHIFTERS *dismantle the building while others erect the Todd House and build Danny's room.*]

MRS TODD [*walking towards her house*]: Coming home for a cuppa, Mrs Butler?

HEADWOMAN: No thanks, Mrs Todd. We're having a bit of a telly party tonight.

[*The wind begins to howl and behind, a picture of television aerials is projected.*]

It cuts right through you, the wind. The nights are drawing in. Toodleloo.

[*The house is now built, a soulless house in bad taste.* DANNY *is in his room lying on the floor.* MRS TODD *is about to enter the house when two of the* SCENE SHIFTERS *stop her. They are carrying the body of* ROBERT.]

1ST S.S.: Mrs Todd, Mrs Todd, this is your house, ain't it? Where do you want him?

MRS TODD: Oh I'm so gormless, I am dim. Robert must be very heavy.

2ND S.S.: Yes, bodies are heavier than people.

[MRS TODD *opens the door. They nearly trip over as they carry* ROBERT *into the house.*]

1ST S.S.: Ooops! Excuse us. Where shall we dump him?

MRS TODD: Oh, just shove it down on the floor.

[*They do.*]

We must order a nice box for Bobby. I always like to give them a nice box. Cup of tea, boys?

2ND S.S.: No thanks Mrs Todd. Wallop and tea don't agree.

[*During this* DAPHNE *enters. She sees her dead brother, holds her little mirror to his mouth and is pleased to see that he is dead.*]

MRS TODD: Well, here's a few bob for your trouble. Have a drink on me.

1ST S.S.: Goodnight and ta very much.

[*They exit and join the others who by now are doing a spot of sentry duty at the back of the stage.*]

MRS TODD: Hello dear, you're home early?

DAPHNE: Boss got fresh again so I walked out. Ain't it dark early?

MRS TODD: It don't improve. Weather gets worse every year.

DAPHNE [*standing over* ROBERT'S *body*]: Look at it! Lazy good-for-nothing. He was always a layabout and he's still a layabout. [*She laughs and prods her brother and then preens herself before an invisible mirror.*]

MRS TODD [*laying up for dinner*]: Don't talk unkindly of the dead, even if he was your brother. Besides, you never know when it's your turn.

DAPHNE: I'm starved. Famished. What's for supper? Where's Danny?

DANNY [*he plays jazz and speaks out to the beat*]: Rise up and get down. [*He follows his own instructions.*] Get down to that sex urge. Put down your banners, pull off your trousers, rip off your tight skirts. Get down and be done.

MRS TODD: I thought it was a passing phase, tried not to face it. He's sinking fast, into himself. We'll probably have to put him under.

DAPHNE: What are we waiting for?

MRS TODD [*bashing at his door*]: Shut up in there! If you don't shut up you've had it.

DAPHNE: Why waste time. [*She looks out of the window. THE SQUAD approach, ready to pounce.*]

MRS TODD [*waves them away. They retreat, reluctantly.*]: Oh, Daphne, let's give him another chance. Let's see if he improves in the next fifteen minutes.

[DANNY *enters the living-room.*]

MRS TODD: Oh, here he comes, Lord Dunkabunk!

DANNY: Hello my dearest Mum, Angel of Mercy, Queen of Light. Hello sis, you old slag. You need a good—blowing up. [*He pinches her cheek.*]

DAPHNE: He's bonkers. Stark stone bonkers!

DANNY: If you're sane thank God I'm mad. Let me squeeze a smile on your tight little face.

DAPHNE: Mum! Keep him away from me.

DANNY: Get stuffed—with sawdust, at least that would be an improvement.

MRS TODD: Danny darling, why ain't you like everyone else?

DANNY: I hate everyone else. I wish everyone was dead except me. That would bring peace to the world.

MRS TODD: For the last time—are you going back to work?

DANNY: No. I've lost the appetite for slavery.

DAPHNE: It will be mercy killing when they put you against the wall.

MRS TODD: Then you'll have no more problems, son, when you're like that lump of dead flesh. Helen's your only hope.

DANNY: I've finished with her.

[MRS TODD *goes to the phone.*]

She twitches when I touch her.

MRS TODD [*dials*]: Helen? Oh Helen dear, would you please be a poppet and pop round . . .

DANNY: How do I know if she's any good in bed if she won't give me a sample. [*He calls down the phone his mother is holding.*] If she won't give me a sample. She twitches when I touch her. Twitches when I touch her!

MRS TODD [*into phone*]: Nothing dear. He sends his love. Toodleloo, see you soon. [*She puts down the phone.*] After all I sacrificed for him. Warn the Militia, Daphne, to stand by for another Todd.

[DAPHNE *rushes out, tells the* SCENE SHIFTERS *and they immediately surround the house.*]

[DAPHNE *returns.*]

MRS TODD: Look at your rotting rotten brother and learn a lesson. Go back to work before it's too late.

DANNY [*stands on the corpse*]: This doesn't scare me. We had nothing in common. I'm Danny Todd, I'm someone! I don't die so easily. They'll never get me.

MRS TODD: That's what all my boys said.

[MR TODD *walks through the militia, has a quiet little joke and enters the house.*]

MR TODD: Evening all! Oh, I see Robert went out all right.

MRS TODD: He died lovely. One little curse, bang, a few bullets and he burst.

MR TODD: Lo Dan! How's my favourite son?

DANNY: You mean your only son.

MR TODD: You always were my only son. You old joker. How's work? Plenty of overtime?

DANNY: I wouldn't know, I've chucked it.

MR TODD: What? Has the rot set in with you? You of all people?

MRS TODD: Calm down, Dad, after all, if he's serious, it's his funeral. Let's change the subject.

MR TODD: It spreads. Spreads. Once it enters the house it's like the plague. Oh, Danny, please tell me you're joking.

MRS TODD: Don't worry, Dad, he'll come to his senses. We'll get another couple of years out of him yet.

MR TODD: I hope so. He certainly seemed good for another three months at least. After all, Danny, you've aways been the apple of my eye.

DANNY: The crab apple with maggots in the middle. How's trade?

MR TODD: People are smoking! Yes, they're smoking. They may not smile no more or buy anything else but they're certainly smoking. Thank God they're going up in smoke.

DANNY: Perforated lungs will be marvellous for yodelling when the world catches alight.

MR TODD: You old joker, you holy terror. Nearly giving me heart failure pretending you left your job.

DAPHNE [to MRS TODD]: He has. Tell him he has. Tell him now. Let me tell him.

MRS TODD: No, don't tell him or he'll blow. Let him enjoy his supper first.

MR TODD [he starts washing]: Yes! Yes! They're smoking. People are smoking. Where's the towel. [He is given it and he becomes submerged in it.]

DAPHNE [to DANNY]: Brave boy! With big ideas. You're afraid to die! Can't even stand up to your own father. Coward.

DANNY: I admit it. I'm scared. So what? If only I could get away from this shower before the storm.

MRS TODD: Lay the table, Daphne dear.
    [DAPHNE does.]

DANNY: If only I knew what to do. There's no one to tell me. No one.

MR TODD [at the television]: What's wrong with the telly?

MRS TODD: Give it a kick.
    [He does. Several.]

MR TODD: I don't like it, don't like it at all.

DAPHNE: It gives me the shivers, the dark screen.

MRS TODD: Father, what are we going to do?
    [There is a real feeling a dread amongst them.]

MR TODD [kicking again]: Don't like it. It's no good.

DAPHNE: I'm so scared.

DANNY: I'm so pleased.

MRS TODD [*cuddling her daughter*]: Don't worry dear, everything turns out all right in the end. God is good.

MR TODD: After all—[*kick.*] It's—not the end [*kick*] of the world—[*kick again*]. Is it? [*He kicks it again and this time it works.*] There you are, leave it to me. Flickering beautifully.

[*Gay music is heard.*]

What's the latest news?

ANNOUNCER [*calm voice*]: Premier says war is inevitable. Thirty or sixty million will be annihilated in the first three minutes.

MR TODD: Really. What's the cricket score?

ANNOUNCER: England all out for fifty-six, India—

MR TODD [*passionately*]: Damn those blacks! Fellow at work said—he took in a Negro, out of the goodness of his heart— The black came off on the sheets. [*He picks his nose.*] Dirty beggars.

[*More telly music is heard.*]

MRS TODD: Supper all.

[*She starts serving as* DAPHNE *reads her weekly woman's mag.*]

DAPHNE: Ooooooh! Read this. Heiress Sally elopes with bald-headed heir.

MRS TODD: All the word loves lovers. They say he loves his mother.

DANNY: Not in the same bed I hope.

DAPHNE: Red Head Weekly will follow the fabulous honeymoon. Have you ordered your copy?

MRS TODD: Father? What do you think of the fresh frozen, ready to heat and eat, succulent fish fingers in golden breadcrumbs and with real lemon?

MR TODD: Delicious! No time? Don't fluster. Feel hungry? Don't worry! Try Fletchers Fish Fingers if you're in a hurry.

MRS TODD: He knows the slogan, he knows it all right.

DANNY: They stink.

MR TODD: Mother, they were beautiful.

DANNY: We've forgotten the taste of things. Smell this.

[*His father does and gobbles it up.*]

MR TODD: What I like about my wife is— She knows how to feed a man after a hard day's work.

MRS TODD: A mother knows what's good for her healthy, growing, hungry family. But I'm worried about my boy.

DANNY: I'm going mad. No I'm not, I'm going sane.

[*On the background is seen a fiery red sky.*]

DANNY: Got a terrible headache. [*He wanders away from the table.*]

MR TODD: Headache? Solved, with Soluble Aspex.

DANNY: Where did the day go? Look at that crazy sunset. I'd better lay off the benz but I must take something if I can't take the day. [*He takes drugs.*]

MRS TODD [*whispers*]: I'm giving you one last chance. Otherwise I'm on that blower.

DAPHNE: Let me! Let me!

DANNY: I've reached the end of my tether. What's a tether?

DAPHNE: The three and sixpenny family size is wonderful value.

DANNY: What a lonely night. Empty streets. No one goes out any more. Dig that moon digging us. One dead world contemplating another.

MRS TODD: And now—a surprise. No more washing up. Eat up your plate Dad because it's your afters. Yes! Munch a mouthful!

MR TODD: Would you believe it.

MRS TODD: The tastiest vanilla and strawberry munch, eat after breakfast, dinner or lunch.

[*They all start eating their plates, except* DANNY. *They laugh hysterically as they do so.*]

MR TODD: Well Mother, isn't it high time we were burying Robert?

DANNY: High time is right. How can I get away from this dump? I'm trapped.

MRS TODD: How can we get through to you?

DANNY: All I ever wanted was love.

MRS TODD: I never thought I'd live to hear you say that.

[*She weeps but* MR TODD *comforts her.*]

DANNY: If only the world would get blown to smithereens,

would get smashed in the next ten minutes. I had such faith in the government, I thought at least they'd bring us destruction. [*He re-enters his room, locks the door: he stands against a wall of stars and seems surrounded by the universe. First he starts howling like a wolf.*] Missile! Missile! Burning light! Across the endless Polar night! I love you war! Man's gift to man! Polaris, Thor and Minuteman! I love you war! I love you war! [*He calls out of the window.*] Death to the human race! Death to the inhuman race!

[*The soldiers of the building squad stand motionless, watching him.* DAPHNE *looks through his keyhole and* DANNY *stands on his head.*]

MRS TODD: Dad, I've been trying to keep it from you. To keep you away from the horrible truth. Danny's gone bad.

DAPHNE [*rushing to the door*]: I'll tell them we're ready then.

MR TODD [*pulling her back*]: Hold your black horses. Danny? Bad? Not really. Why—he's the— That telly again! [*He kicks it.*] Danny is the apple. Where am I? I mean where was I? It is out of the question to contemplate it.

DAPHNE [*pulls her father to* DANNY'S *door*]: Look! Come here! [*She pushes her father down on his knees and makes him peek through* DANNY'S *keyhole.*]

DAPHNE: Look at him smiling. Disgusting monster. Won't even press his trousers.

[*Now she sits on her father's back, as if riding him and at the same time she manicures her nails.*]

MR TODD: It's a disgrace.

DAPHNE: If he doesn't go against the wall and get it over with, well, I don't know who I am.

MR TODD: Who are you? —to tell me these terrible things. To show me this dirty disgusting sight. When your dreams burst it's worse than your worst nightmare.

MRS TODD: Walter! Let's get on the blower. He'll have to go. It's contagion—outright contagion.

MR TODD: Mother, I have given the matter some thought, and I've come to the irrevocable conclusion that I couldn't

possibly help not agreeing with you, so I'm not. Least
not straightaways. The Thames was high today, spilling
over at the top it was, all red and blotchy.

We could bury them together, couldn't we?

MRS TODD: Walter, that's a lovely idea.

DAPHNE: Side by side. I can just see them.

MRS TODD: They'd like that. They were always such pals
together, remember how they used to punch each other and
smash each other's faces in. Smashing kids. Best boys on
the earth and tomorrow lying side by side, best boys in the
earth, in a coffin built for two. Daphne, run to Puke the
florist and order two wreaths of red roses intertwined with
arum lilies. These extra expenses don't half tax the house-
keeping but then—a funeral is a funeral.

DAPHNE: Don't worry Mum, the flowers are on me.
[*She goes off.*]

MR TODD: I'd like a few last words with him. [*He knocks
on the door.*] Can I come in, son?

MRS TODD [*as she starts ironing*]: I tried, didn't I? No
one can say that I didn't try to break his spirit.

MR TODD: Yes Mother, it can definitely be ascertained you
have done your best under difficult circumstances. Open up
Danny! Open this door.

DANNY: Go away you silly sod.

MR TODD: I want us to make our peace with each other.
[DANNY *gets up and unlocks the door and then lays
down on the floor.* MR TODD *enters the room.* DANNY
reads a book.]

MR TODD: Books! That's been your downfall. What came
over you? How did you get lost in books? I gave you a good
education, didn't I? How could you do this to me? When
people hear you read books they'll say I deprived you.
Doesn't the name Todd mean anything to you? Stop
smiling. Have you got no respect for your own death? Stop
smiling! All your blood will be trickling out of you in ten
minutes. Only I can save you.

DANNY [*he gets on all fours and starts rubbing against his
father's legs who tries to avoid him*]: Sorry you old swine,
your world disgusts me. [*He makes cat noises and howls. He

licks his father's ankles.] I lick the unclean and like it.

MR TODD [*jumping on bed*]: Stop it or I'll swipe you.

DANNY: Come on Dad, down on all fours! When everyone else is radio ash we'll take over the remains of the world. Oh, what's the use. We're all yes men. Yes Men! Yes! Yes! Yes! Men in No-mans land. I sing of peace, of men squatting on all fours, chewing grass. Call your squad.

MR TODD: Care for a filter tip? Maybe we can get you commuted instead of executed or committed. [*He smokes.*] I have connections with the Unions.

DANNY: You? A tobacconist? Everyone is a tobacconist, selling each other empty packets of smoke and puffs of hot air. Empty packets of nothing. Sleepwalkers in a chain-smoking semi-surburban slide into oblivion. I'm afraid there may not be chaos. Just endless creeping Croydon.

MR TODD: Furthermore I have ascertained that you will fully appreciate that we have looked into the matter—

[*DANNY is reading. MR TODD looks over his shoulder and for a while enjoys with delight the things he sees. He contorts his head in several upside-down angles*]

What's this? What? —the Bible? That's the end. You're a goner. Erotic literature irrevocably carries the death penalty.

DANNY: Everything carries the death penalty.

MR TODD: Say your prayers, Danny.

DANNY [*kneels beside his bed*]: I exist. Everything exists! Everything in this world, imaginable, unimaginable will soon exist no more. Everything existed and was so beautiful and could have been. [*Now he prays properly, like a child, hands together.*] Dear Bomb! Listen to my last confession. I want you to get into bed with me. How lonely you are, bomb. You need us, you need to pulverize us. Pulverize me. Let me get inside you, you are the fearful dream, that's why I love you, bomb, no one above you bomb! You are the forbidden beautiful desire of us all, the holy father of all of us.

MR TODD: The squad will squash your problems.

DANNY: I'm lonely for the dead. I miss the endless dead, I'm homesick for the universe.

[*He reads and smokes.*]

196

MR TODD [*like a pompous announcer*]: All vestiges of hope have finally faded and now the world hangs—what am I on about? There's absolutely no hope for the bastard.

[*In the living-room* MRS TODD, *still ironing, is chatting to* HELEN.]

MRS TODD: Dad, Helen's here. It's our last chance.

HELEN: Hello Pop—is there any change?

[*He embraces her more than somewhat.*]

MR TODD: I'm afraid we have to face it girl, he won't last the night out.

HELEN [*knocks on the door*]: Danny, let me in. [*He opens the door and she enters.*] Hello Daniel. Stop picking your nose.

DANNY: We all pick our nose, I suppose. We are the bogey men.

[DAPHNE *returns with two wreaths.* MRS TODD *holds her ear against the wall, listening to* DANNY *and* HELEN. MR TODD *looks through the keyhole.*]

HELEN: A fridge with a feedback. No liberties Danny, stop it, naughty hands. Be patient, darling, we've waited so long, why spoil it now? The bridesmaids had their fittings today and I saw decorators. One wall will be all contemporary black.

DANNY: Let me crack you.

HELEN: And the Z plan furniture, on easy easy terms. Fits so snug. And there's the most wonderful rubbish disposal unit and the lavatory works like a dream and we need the deposit for flush fitting carpets.

DANNY: Come on, now!

HELEN: What about the hire purchase?

DANNY: I'm broke. I've given up work for always.

HELEN: I don't want to be a widow before our first baby is born. Would you make our children orphans? Stop mauling me. All this necking and mucking about—stop. It's not safe. Dirty beast.

DANNY: You're stiff like a poker. Stop twitching and I'll make you beautiful.

[*He bites her hand.*]

HELEN: Stop biting me.

DANNY: Let me lift you up. [*He does.*]

HELEN: Put me down! Put me down!

[*He moves towards the bed.*]

No, not on the bed.

DANNY: Let me take a lump out of you. I want to eat you. [*He bites her ankles while the Todds watch and listen solemnly.*]

HELEN: He's gone mad. Help, Mrs Todd—I'm bleeding. Danny, that's the last straw.

DANNY: Let's take all your clothes off.

[MRS TODD *indicates to* MR TODD *that it's time to break in but* MR TODD *prefers to wait.*]

HELEN: Mr Todd! Save me! Save me!

[MRS TODD *gets more frantic but cannot move* MR TODD *who is far more moved at the possibilities in the bedroom.* DAPHNE *indifferently pares her nails.*]

DANNY: I want to see the whole of you, naked at once.

HELEN: Oh save me.

DANNY: I will. [*He bites her toes.*]

HELEN: Oh, he's biting my toes off.

MRS TODD [*to* MR TODD]: If you don't bash the door down I'll bash you down.

MR TODD [*pulling himself together*]: If you don't open up Danny—I'll—I'll—

DANNY: I want to open her up.

[*Drums are heard. The Firing Squad start building the execution wall again. Again the blow up of assembled faces.*]

DANNY [*opens the door*]: Out you go Helen. I saw something in you once, but I never saw it again. You're shell to the core, uncrackable. Goodbye.

HELEN: Good riddance to bad rubbish. [*She leaves and is more than comforted by* MR TODD.] He tried to rape me.

MR TODD: How? How could he? I'll take care of you, little Helen. Come over here. [*He sits down with her on his lap.*] There, there. He bit your little fingers did he now. [*He kisses her fingers.*] Let me kiss them better.

[HELEN *likes this.*]

He bit your ankles and your toes, did he? Dirty pig. Let

me rub it better. You see, I am endeavouring to stimulate the skin, thus, in this circular movement, thereby bringing— Don't cry pretty little Helen, they'll take care of him.

HELEN: Oh Dad, you're so lovely to me. It's just that I wanted so much to be related to you. I wanted you to be my father-in-law. And everything was arranged. But he's no good to man nor beast, let alone me.

MR TODD: If only I was younger.

[*The drums get louder. The sounds of Billy Cotton's band playing 'Wakey! Wakey!' And signature tune playing over loud speaker. The faces on the background get lighter. The* REV JAMES *comes out and benignly smiles and talks to the* SCENE SHIFTERS.]

MR TODD: Come outside Helen and make sure we get a good place. I love outdoor games don't you? Almost as much as indoor ones.

[*He cuddles her and gives her a tickle. She giggles as he leads her out.*]

HELEN: Oh Mr Todd, whatever do you mean?

[*Now the* SCENE SHIFTERS *start dismantling the Todd house around* MRS TODD *and* DAPHNE. *They remove* ROBERT *and now* MRS TODD *stands in an empty space, with* DAPHNE *at her make-up still.*]

MRS TODD: Danny? Can you hear me? They'll be coming any moment for you. Get ready dear. Dress up smart. Give our loving regards to our eternally beloved Robert when you get to the other side. Come on Daphne, bring the wreaths.

[*They go to where the two others wait.*]

MR TODD [*calls out*]: Come on Danny, my old joker. We're all waiting. And I'm proud of you and I'll be watching, not without, I might say, a certain modicum of pride.

HEADWOMAN: This is your fifth son, isn't it, Mrs Todd?

MRS TODD: No, my sixth, my baby.

HEADMAN [*to* MR TODD]: I bet you'll be relieved to be putting him under, eh Mr Todd?

MR TODD: You bet. I hope you don't think it's anything more than mere coincidence. I've always been respectable, paid my debts and travelled on the Central Line. I hope he don't give you any trouble.

[*They all stand waiting and the whole house is gone except the framework of* DANNY'S *bedroom, where* DANNY *stands. The* FIRING SQUAD *take up their positions.*]

HEADMAN: Daniel Todd! Open up! In the name of the Borough Council, the Ministry of Labour and God.

DANNY: They'll never get me. Nor will she. Somehow, when your time is up you want to live. Council flat! One cough and the walls will fall down; like these walls here—they seem very thin—they give to the touch. They call this security and it's just stuck together. Hey, why haven't I noticed this before? You can see the moon through the wallpaper—straight-up. That broke my dream, all night I dreamed I lay awake. And I put my hands to the wallpaper, like this, and that was all that separated the house from the universe.

[*It is very dark outside, just the vague outline of the people waiting and the stars.*]

DANNY: Strange doors start in the corner of my room. Doors I have never noticed before. Cut out of the fading, dying wallpaper flowers. And I pressed my hands onto the petals—like this—and look, there's the street, I'm through.

[*He tears the wallpaper and walks through it.*]

DANNY: I'm through! I'm free! [*He rushes off.*] I'm saved! I'm free!

[*The* FIRING SQUAD *now march to his room and open it.*]

3RD S.S.: The bird has flown.

[*The Family rush up.*]

MR TODD: I knew he'd disgrace us.

DAPHNE: Coward! Fancy words! Crying out for death until it came.

HEADMAN: Ladies and gentlemen, there will be a slight delay. Daniel Todd has scarpered.

HEADWOMAN: I can't say it was entirely unexpected.

MRS TODD: I said so all along. I'll never be able to hold up my head again.

HELEN: No good to man nor beast, let alone me.

REV JAMES: Come along, good people, let's all go back to bed.

[THE TODDS *leave unhappily with* HELEN. *Darkness and solitary drum while* SCENE SHIFTERS *finish dismantling the whole scene. Now the hiss of endless trains on the Underground and when the light comes up huge pictures on backwall suggests tube tunnels and Underground intersections, looking rather womb-like and frightening. The* SCENE SHIFTERS *build a tube station—Oxford Circus. Thousands of faces again, faces of pale-faced people on the back wall.* DANNY *enters, he seems lost.*]

DANNY: Where am I?

HEADMAN: The Central Line.

DANNY: All my life I've tried to avoid the Central Line.

[*The* SCENE SHIFTERS *now hold sections of scenery so that they themselves become a tube train. Then in dead unison keep on going off and coming on again. Included in this section are all the others who are not queuing.*]

HEADMAN: Oxford Circus! Mind the doors.

DANNY: That face seems familiar. And that one and that one. But I thought they were dead. Joe! Susan!

[*The train goes off again.*]

[DANNY *now notices the queue.*]

Hey Robert! You're not dead? Robert, I'm your brother. What are you doing here?

ROBERT: I'm queuing.

DANNY: But you're dead!

ROBERT: Yes, I said I was queuing.

DANNY: But you're dead. I said you're dead.

ROBERT: Yes! Yes! I said I was queuing.

DANNY: What are you queuing for?

ROBERT: How dare you ask such disgusting questions? Once and for all, stop accosting me.

DANNY: Robert! Let me stay with you. I'm your brother. We belong to the same revolution.

ROBERT: If you read the bye-laws you'll see that obscene remarks are not permitted on the Central Line.

DANNY: But I'm your brother.

ROBERT: Inverted inuendos are bad enough but incestuous suggestions are unmentionable.

DANNY: But I saw you die.

ROBERT: Yes, I'm queuing, now get away from me.

HEADMAN: Move along please. Pass along the platform, watch the gap. Mind the doors.

[ROBERT *and the rest of the queue join the train and stand there, strap hanging without expression.*]

DANNY: Bob! Don't leave me. Hey, he's my brother. Leave me alone. He's my brother.

HEADMAN: Pass along please. Watch the gap, mind the doors.

[*The train moves around and* DANNY *moves round with it. The queue of people are now plainly seen as his* MOTHER, FATHER, HELEN, DAPHNE, REV JAMES, *etc, and* ROBERT.]

DANNY: Robert. [ROBERT *turns away and he pulls* MR TODD.] He's my—bro—Dad! [*They all seem dead and take no notice: he now registers all of them.*] Mum! Helen! and you darling—little Daphne. You're dead are you? You're a zombie, well marvellous, I've always wanted to do this. [*He pulls some of her hair off.*] And you Helen, the waxworks haven't changed you one bit. One little bit. Hello Mum. [*He sings and nods.*] When your hair has turned to silver I will loathe you just the same. Hello Dad, drop dead. [*He picks his father's pockets.*]

S.S. FEMALE [*speaking to another*]: So I said to him, I said, if you say that to me, I said. Do you know what I mean I said, do you know what I mean I said, I said, so he said to me, he said—

DANNY: Excuse me, Miss, are you living or dead? You've got a lovely scent on. Excuse me but I just touched you, I just pinched you on the bottom.

S.S. FEMALE: Are you talking to me?

[*She then turns and carries on chatting.*]

[*The train goes round and stops.*]

HEADMAN: Marble Arch, mind the doors. Mind the doors! Shepherds Bush train! Mind the doors.

[DANNY *follows his relatives off and they immediately start queuing. The skeletal train moves off again.*]

DANNY: Excuse me, I'm looking for my brother.

REV JAMES: Who isn't?

[*All the people now queue up behind* DANNY *and* REV JAMES *stands at the top of the queue as if dispensing something.*]

DANNY: What's this queue for?

REV JAMES: This is the queue to queue for the queue, for going upstairs, or downstairs or anywhere. Hurry along please. I've given you a little wayside thought for today.

DANNY: But I'm looking for my brother.

REV JAMES: This is not information. Psalm 109 verse one! [*He starts intoning and all the others become a congregation.*] Hold not thy peace—O God of my praise—for the mouth of the wicked and the mouth of deceit. You still here—what do you want?

DANNY: Are you selling anything?

REV JAMES: What do you want? Cigarettes? How can we be expected to live in the service of God without sidelines. Cigarettes?

DANNY: Yes, I'm dying for some.

[*As the rest become a queue again behind* DANNY.]

REV JAMES: This is the cigarette queue.

DANNY: I can certainly use some.

REV JAMES [*almost intoning*]: You're a half price man. Yes, we sell cigarettes to you at half price.

DANNY: At last, good news. Twenty please.

REV JAMES: Sorry, this is a full price day. You're a half price man.

DANNY: All right then, I'll pay the full price. I don't want to be a half price man. I'll pay the full price.

REV JAMES: Sorry, you're a half price man. We're only selling them at full price. Move along please, you're holding up the queue.

[*As he moves away the others buy their cigarettes and become a train again and move off and come on again and*

*on and on. The people strap-hang and change and queue
and strap-hang.*]

HEADMAN: Marble Arch! Marble Arch! Mind the doors!
Mind the doors!

DANNY [*goes up behind him*]: How can I get out? I must
get out. I must protest.

HEADMAN: Shepherds Bush train! Mind the doors.

DANNY: I want to protest.

HEADMAN: Protest upstairs. Marble Arch.

DANNY: Isn't that funny, sir, everything we see and touch
comes out of the earth. Everything. And goes back into
it. Please I must protest.

[*The stage now is in darkness and the tube people have
gone.*]

Why didn't they recognize me? I must protest.

HEADMAN: Protest upstairs. Marble Arch.

DANNY: I'm so pleased I've stopped loving the human
race. What a relief. I'm trying to get away from my family
and I seem to have managed that at last. I must get away,
I hate this bloody world. I must protest. They didn't even
know me. Good. I could kill them all in cold blood, cut
their throats. Wonder why they didn't recognize me?

HEADMAN: Protest upstairs to your heart's content. Haven't
you heard of freedom of speech? You can stand on a soapbox and yap your mouth off. You have all the time in the
world or four minutes, whichever is the longest.

[*Crowd start congregating.* DANNY *walks towards a
soapbox.*]

DANNY: They didn't recognize me because I've changed. I've
grown up at last. I hate this world. What a relief. Down
with everyone. Hurrah, at last I'm finding my voice. [*He
gets onto the soapbox.*] Comrades— [*He opens his arms
and yells. They all cheer.*]

ALL: BAN THE BOMB! Ban the bomb. Speech, speech.

DANNY: Comrades. We didn't colonize the universe because
of the—

[*The* REV JAMES *is timing him with a stop-watch.*]

—bomb. Hey this is wonderful, I'm finding my voice. No,
we didn't colonize the universe because of the bomb, but

rather, we invented the bomb to give ourselves the incentive and the necessity to colonize the universe. Long live death. Long live the bomb.

s.s.: Ban the bomb!

DANNY: Ban the bomb be damned, drop the bomb.

s.s.: You for the bomb?

DANNY: The thought of the bomb dropping soon, gives me the strength to carry on.

[*The procession of people march off.*]

THEY SING: Men and women stand together, Do not heed the sound of war, Make your mind up now or never, Ban the bomb forevermore.

[*They are all off except* REV JAMES.]

[DANNY *rushes off after them, there is a scuffle and he is flung back onto the stage, bruised and hurt.*]

DANNY: Don't leave me alone, you were cheering me before. I was only looking for my dead brother. Ban the bomb, drop the bomb, what's the odds. What's the use, one single priest listening to me now, and we all know what he's after. I love the bomb, I want to lick its beautiful black body—

[REV JAMES *starts to go.*]

Hey, please don't leave me. An audience of one is better than a spit in the eye.

REV JAMES [*consulting his stop watch*]: Time is up! Sorry Angel, I must fly [*He goes.*]

[*A great explosion is seen on the screen behind the stage. A great mushroom cloud rises, the empty stage now with* DANNY *lying crouched on the floor.*]

DANNY: At last I'm alone. Life is over, thank God.

[*But the stage lights come up and he staggers to his feet. Birds are heard singing. The* FIRING SQUAD *play cards at the back of the stage.*]

DANNY: You can't rely on anything. It makes you sick.

[*A park is projected onto the screen.*]

Hyde Park! Large as life and I thought all London was destroyed. What a night! What a nightmare! I never knew London had an underground city, populated by the queuing and the dead. Mind the doors! Mind the doors! Mind the doors! he said. If every door in this city could only speak they would all be carried away, jibbering. I seem to remember grass. Or was grass a dream? Didn't I once hear about—trees?

[*The* SCENE SHIFTERS *enter in bandsmen uniform and erect a bandstand and then take their places and tune up.*]

DANNY: I love a band. It gives you a sense of security. But fancy playing to no one.

[*Suddenly* MR TODD *enters with a baton in his hand and dressed as a Bandmaster, he takes his place before the* SCENE SHIFTERS.]

DANNY: No, it can't be. It can't be! Dad, hey Dad! What are you doing here?

[*The band starts playing off key but* DANNY *runs up and stops* MR TODD *conducting.*]

DANNY: But he's a tobacconist! You're a tobacconist! What are you doing?

[*The band stop playing and try to attack* DANNY *with their instruments.*]

MR TODD: Alright boys! Take five.

[*They go to the back of the stage where they continue playing cards.*]

Now what's all this? Spoiling everyone else's enjoyment. Eh? Well, there were other people here.

DANNY: That uniform doesn't half suit you Dad.

MR TODD: Dad? What are you on about?

DANNY: You know very well that I'm your son.

MR TODD: You? With your flies undone and egg stuck to your two days growth. No, my boy, I'm a bachelor. Yes, after ascertaining all the law reports about vice in the suburbs and milkmen who seduce the wives of bank clerks, I have ultimately decided that the best possible remedy is to remain a bachelor. I'm celibating. No, it's just a case of misplaced identity. People often remind me of people. [*He starts to move.*]

DANNY: Where are you off to?

MR TODD: The Serpentine, to feed the ducks. You've put me off work for the rest of the day.

DANNY: Can I come with you? I'm lonely.

MR TODD: Of course, my boy. I'm a musician, so I'm not a happy man. No, I'm far from happy I have recently reached the undeniable conclusion that I am far from happy.

[*The* SCENE SHIFTERS *remove the bandstand. The stage goes dark and* DANNY *and* MR TODD *walk without moving.*]

MR TODD: Why am I telling you, a stranger, more than I've told anyone? Sit down here.

[*They sit.*]

I have sexual problems. I think about sex all the time.

DANNY: That sounds quite normal to me.

MR TODD: It's all to do with repression and suppression.

DANNY: That's what Freud said.

MR TODD: Oh, did he also say it?

DANNY: I like you. No, you couldn't be my Dad. You've got kind eyes. I wish you were my father.

MR TODD: That's the nicest thing no one's ever said to me. I'll let you into my secret, I'm not really a band leader. Listen.

[*He plays cool jazz on a trumpet.*]

DANNY: You're wasting your time.

MR TODD: I play in dark places at night. But I keep up a front of respectability. A uniform keeps you safe. I need money for the birds. For the painted queer birds. I need the birds to deprave me. Depravity for inspiration—inspiration for dreams, dreams for jazz and jazz to keep me going, to earn money for the birds. I have come to the ultimate weapon in my armoury—a uniform is as safe as houses. Safer these days. I play in dark places at night.

DANNY: Stop crying, please.

MR TODD: Please put your arm around me.

DANNY: No, I—I couldn't. But listen, you're the first real man I've met. Let's talk—let's be friends.

MR TODD: My condolences my son. There's only one thing I want from you. And I don't know if you know what I mean. And I don't mean what I think you might think I mean.

[*He puts arm round* DANNY. DANNY *removes it.*]

DANNY: Um—Well—I really must go now.

MR TODD: No, no, not yet. It's so romantic here, son. Sit down beside me. Be nice to me. Don't hit me, will you, don't hit me hard on the back with a thin cane will you?

DANNY: Must go. No—I won't—you play marvellous. See you.

MR TODD [*pulls him back*]: Don't hit me. Not with a cane eighteen inches long and an eighth of an inch in diameter?

DANNY: You're very kind, thank you.

[*He takes his hand to shake it.* TODD *immediately pounces on him and gets him into a policeman's grip.*]

MR TODD: Holding my hand, eh? Daniel Todd, I am a plain clothes officer attached to C Division of the Metropolitan Police Force of Greater London, and I am arresting you for indecent behaviour.

[DANNY *hits him.*]

And assaulting a police officer—help—in the pursuance of his—help!

[DANNY *knocks him over and kicks him very hard while* MR TODD *blows a police whistle.*]

[*The* SCENE SHIFTERS *come and erect a door and a little room.* DANNY *doesn't see them but sees the door,* HELEN *stands in the doorway.*]

HELEN: If you're running away from the law, come inside. It won't cost you much.

DANNY: Helen! You on my side now?

HELEN: Quickly, inside.

[*We hear police whistles and* DANNY *follows her inside. It becomes light in the room and dark on the stage.*]

DANNY: It's funny, the things you run away from you seem to rush right into. Helen, please explain.

HELEN: If you've got cash you can call me anything. Come on, quickly, on the bed. [*She starts to strip.*] Don't stand there gaping. Haven't you seen a naked girl before? Give me the three nicker and get on with it.

DANNY: Helen! Helen! I've only got a quid, won't you give me a sample? I'll give you an I.O.U. for the rest.

HELEN: Hurry up. O.K. I haven't got all day.
[*She is lying down on the bed.*]

DANNY: Oh your beautiful body. This is the greatest gift you can give me. Helen, you're free at last.

HELEN: You talk too much. Get on the job.

DANNY: Helen, you represent freedom. The ideal woman of the future. [*He gets on the bed and tries to kiss her.*]

HELEN: Stop it! Stop trying to kiss me, you filthy beast. What do you take me for? Just take what you're paying for. This is a transaction, not a love affair.

DANNY [*he wanders to the door. She is getting fed up*]: We come from a hole in a hospital bed and we can't wait to get back there.

HELEN: Take off your trousers. I haven't got all day. Times are bad.

DANNY: Let me relish this. I'll make it worth your while. This is the first privacy I've had. The world seems to rush through every room. There's nowhere to hide any more, but here at least there's a lovely feeling of the end of the world, a blissful feeling of the end, of the final crack. What a beautiful acid green sky. I'm coming, Helen, with my I.O.U. in my hand, coming to crack you at last.

HELEN: That's what you think.
[*He is about to surmount her when she rushes to the door and throws it open and blows a police whistle.*]

HELEN: Here he is! Seize him.
[*The* SCENE SHIFTERS *rush on on all fours, like dogs and they rush to the door and bark like dogs.*]

DANNY: You lousy cow, give me back my I.O.U. [*He pulls* HELEN *inside and slams the door.*] Oh Christ. A black mass. I've had it.

MR TODD [*rushes on*]: Daniel Todd, prepare to meet thy God, but put your trousers on first or what will the neighbours say.

MRS TODD [*walks on*]: Come on Danny, you can't get away, don't be a silly boy. Mummy loves you.
[DANNY *has been inspecting the wallpaper, and then, as the dogs snap and bark, he triumphantly tears the wallpaper and prepares for flight.*]

HELEN: But I've only just had it repapered.

DANNY: Get the crack covered.

[*The dogs bark but gradually fade. He dashes through the wallpaper, but stays on stage and crouches down and then all activity seems to fade.* THE TODDS *and* HELEN *are gone and the* SCENE SHIFTERS *dismantle* HELEN'S *place.*]

[*Now they reconstruct the firing wall and* MR TODD'S *tobacco shop. Then they all fall down and sleep. A solitary drum beat and then silence.*]

DANNY: The squad are sleeping. That's good. Dad's shop, my luck's in, I'll pinch a bit of dough, make a clean break. They don't know who they're dealing with.

[*He approaches the door of the shop.*]

It wouldn't be the first time I've stolen. What about that time I pinched a toffee apple. There was a worm inside. I took a bite and swallowed the worm. Nothing seemed to go right after that. Do they die inside you or do they grow? Slip the celluloid into the lock and this—should—do—the —trick. [*He opens the door and is pleased with his achievement. On the counter is a till, he quickly takes money out of it.*]

DANNY: Fifteen quid? Poor day. Oh, someone walked over my grave. Something's shadowing me. Why did I think of the worm, just now? Oh Hell—hello—who's there?

[*He backs away and a figure moves towards him.*]

DANNY: Who?

MRS TODD: Hello.

DANNY: Mother! Oh, I know, you don't know me.

MRS TODD: Of course I do, Danny. Am I pleased to see you.

DANNY: Yes, to report me, I suppose. To turn me over.

MRS TODD: How could you say such a thing? That hurts me. That cuts deep, especially coming from my best boy, my favourite, my baby.

[*She tries to cuddle him.*]

DANNY: Well, I always liked you in a way.

MRS TODD: Pinching money from your dad, eh? You know how hard he works for it. Here, give some to me, we won't say a word. [*She snatches most and shoves it down her breast.*] Come over here and sit down. What a lovely head of hair you have, you had. [*She is now caressing and stroking him as he sits on her lap.*] You're thinning. Look at your skinny neck. You've got circles under your eyes and blood streaks in the centre. Your mind's on naughty things, that's why. Naughty little thoughts you lovely little boy.

DANNY: Oh mother. I'm scared. Scared of going home and not going home. Scared of standing up and not standing up. I'm scared of being out and I'm scared of being in.

[*She starts making a cup of tea.*]

MRS TODD: Let's just sit here and have a nice cup of tea, and a sing-song, just the two of us.

DANNY: I'm scared of a tea-cup. It smells of execution.

[*Behind, clouds quickly tear across the sky. Thunder is heard and now all the sky goes ominously dark and then pouring rain.*]

MRS TODD: Pity it's pelting. We're burying poor Bob to-morrow. Oh Danny, there's a wonderful new gadget—it's like a tape-recorder, playing everlasting music inside the coffin. I know you can't hear when you're dead but it's so nice to know that Brahmns Lullaby or Vera Lynn will be singing to your remains. They say it works for ever—and it's quite cheap. We've instructed the undertaker to install one in Robert's box. The song's going to be, I think— [*She sings.*] We'll Meet Again—or maybe, I Ain't Got No Bodee. [*She dances hand on hip and laughs grotesquely.*] There, there, lean against me. [*He does.*] Only your mother loves you. You'll never find anyone else. [*She starts making up.*] I got whistled on the way here, so I must still be quite attractive. Fancy anyone fancying me! Mind you I've lost weight shocking, recently. They like that, mind you some like plump girls.

DANNY: I love the smell of your hair.

MRS TODD: Bought some lovely herrings for supper. Souse them I think. Have funny dreams sometimes, not nice. Do you like my perm? Do you like me all blue? It's coming down cats and dogs and you look starved.

DANNY: Running away is so exhausting. Why does one have to run away? Why can't one walk away from home?

MRS TODD: Lean against me, come on. Cuddle in, all safe, the way you used to. Mummy loves you. [*She sings.*] Go to sleep my baby, Close your pretty eyes. Angels are above you, peeping down upon you from the skies. Great big moon is shining, stars begin to peep, Now it's time for little Danny to go to sleep.

DANNY: Oh Mother, you can hide from the past and hide from the world—but you can't hide from the universe.

[*He is dreaming. The lights change and he walks away from his mother, stands against the backwall where there is a feeling of endless cosmos. Every so often explosions and mushroom plumes arise.*]

DANNY: Danny, you've had it. No I haven't. You can't hide from the hearse. Walk down the street like everyone else. No! walk up the universe. Danny you have had it. No I haven't. Yes you have. Yes, I have. No you haven't. So where am I? People walk on this earth—on this thin pie crust. How fragile civilization is. Forget it you silly sod. Shit on the universe.

[*Drums are heard.*]

Earth waits under the living room, sand waits in the glass. I'm a good looking boy, I could earn a bomb. I ought to settle down, ought to give myself up. You out of your mind? Yes! Yes! Yes! Dust! Dust! Brick Brick House House Street Street Town Town! Woom! Dust Dust. Shut up, dreamer, come down to earth. The Lord is my shepherd and it serves him right. The moon is dying of cancer. See its jaundiced face. It won't last the night out. And the stars, dressed in black will attend her funeral. Never mind moon, we will soon keep you company in the graveyard of space. You with your cancer spores—everyone you shine on will die. It's catching. It's a race —of obstacles. If you're not destroyed on the way, you fall at the winning post. Shut up, this is only a dream and your mother is with you. Mum, you look so lovely against the moon.

[*He has returned to her by now and at this moment his father and the* F I R I N G S Q U A D *seize him.*]

MRS TODD: Alright Walter, take him away.

DANNY: I can't say it was totally unexpected.

[*Now immediate activity as in the first scene. Firing wall built, daylight, faces on wall, dance music playing, cocks crowing, sound of drums and boys brigades.*]

SCENE SHIFTER [*through a microphone, like a radio commentator*]: Well here we are on a truly magificent, beautiful morning. The azure sky is decked in her most delightful translucent gown and the ceremony promises to be absolutely splendid and magnificent. And now the victim is led out.

[*Everyone cheers, including all the family.*]

DANNY: No prayers please. I beg you, no prayers. All I wanted was to find my own way in life, to think for myself, to follow my own star and keep away from the Central Line.

DAPHNE: Put him out of his misery.

HEADWOMAN: This is your sixth boy, isn't it, Mrs. Todd?

MRS TODD: Let me see. Yes, my sixth and last, my baby.

[*An Italian tenor sings 'Mama' on a record.*]

MRS TODD: All I ever wanted was security for them.

MR TODD: Well Mother, they've certainly all got that now. Goodbye son.

MRS TODD: Teta Danny. I'll contact you through the Spiritualist Church.

DANNY: Don't tell me you're crying.

MRS TODD: I'm crying for joy, darling.

HEADMAN: Militia! Take aim! Daniel Todd, please be co-operative and stand right against the wall.

DANNY: I'm not going through with this. This wall looks just as insecure as all the others.

HEADMAN: Take aim, ready—

DANNY: Goodbye!

[*He steps back and kicks through the wall and vanishes.*]

MRS TODD: I don't know what I'm going to do with that boy.

HELEN: And to think I fell for him.

MR TODD: Yes, I have ascertained without a question of the possibility of doubt that he has gone and walked through the wall.

MRS TODD: I'll never be able to hold my head up again. [*The* SCENE SHIFTERS *remove the wall as they are all inspecting it. The lights change.* MRS TODD, *head high, walks off with the others. The* SCENE SHIFTERS *bring on another building but we don't quite see the point of it yet. The play cards are back.* REV JAMES *is left on, but he slips off his dog-collar, as* DANNY *enters.*]

REV JAMES: You seem lost. Can I help you my son?

DANNY: Aren't you the priest who officiates at my funerals? Stay away from me.

REV JAMES: Priest? Now there's a racket, now there's a lousy, rotten, bloody, stinking swindle. Wish I was in it. No, I'm only a poor tramp, down on his luck. For the price of a cup of tea I'll give you a kind word.

DANNY [*gives him a coin*]: Can you help me? I want to escape. Is there a way out?

REV JAMES: No. Once I tramped the country. Now I sleep in the gutters. Accept the inevitable. Let them delouse you every month or so.

DANNY: But they want to kill me. Where can I hide?

REV JAMES: There's nowhere to hide. Give yourself up.

DANNY: But the local council have issued a destruction order for me.

REV JAMES: Take my advice then. Go to the police and demand to be executed by the State. Stand up for your rights.

DANNY: But I want to run away to the countryside, to the green fields.

REV JAMES: Countryside? Don't you know it's all concreted over. And a good job too. I never could abide by nature and all that stuff. Didn't you know that?

DANNY: No—I—I never got away from the city. But I did see a tree once. Honest I did.

REV JAMES [*points to building*]: Go in there and demand your rights. You paid your stamps, didn't you? Demand a State execution.

[*He goes.*]

DANNY: I've had it. Yes, he's right. If I'm going to die it must be the State and not the Borough Council. At least they owe me that.

[*The* SCENE SHIFTERS *turn the building round. It is a section of cells and* ROBERT *sitting at a desk.*]

DANNY: My name is Danny Todd and I'm on the run from the Borough firing squad. [*He sees* ROBERT.] I give up, everyone looks like someone. Someone you want to know, someone you know or don't want to know.

ROBERT: Yes! Yes! Sign here please, no don't worry about the date, just sign.

DANNY: I demand my rights.

[*Already the* SCENE SHIFTERS *are at him, shaving him and washing him and changing his clothes.*]

Section C.5. of the Westminster Bye-laws on Education and Execution stipulate . . .

ROBERT: Another of those clever bastards who know their rights.

DANNY: Therefore, I demand, I absolutely demand a state execution.

HEADMAN [*leads him to a cell, he is not locked in, it is like an ant cell or bee section, other sections also contain prisoners.*]: All right. Don't get excited. Here's your condemned cell. Go put your feet up. How about a nice cuppa? No? I know I'll get you something really nice to eat. Yes, that's the advantage of getting hanged, at least you get a real bloody, juicy steak. I've often been tempted myself. Toodleloo. Make yourself at home, you've got fifteen minutes or so.

[*As he goes* MR TODD *enters.*]

MR TODD: Hello son, I've been waiting for you. [*He keeps on walking round him, feeling and assessing him.*] I'm going to do it.

DANNY: You called me son. At least you admit you're my dad. It's so good to see you, Dad.

MR TODD: They all call me Dad. But that's understandable

under the circumstances. You just carry on calling me Dad, if it makes you feel better. A little loving kindness never goes amiss. Hold still, I'm measuring you—for your nice purple shroud, for the drop and the black box. Are they treating you nice?

DANNY: Smashing. They're treating me smashing.

HEADMAN: Here's your lovely under-done steak.

[DANNY *starts eating ravenously.*]

MR TODD: It's a bit cold out today. So I think we'll do it in here. Don't want to get you all wet. Nasty to go off all dripping wet. I'll give you a little free advice son. Say a little prayer—like— [*He sings.*] All things bright and beautiful—all creatures great and small. All things wise and wonderful, the Lord God made them all. Hmmmmm. [*He clears his throat.*] Let yourself go all limp and you'll hang better. I'll go and get the ligature, see you in a tick.

DANNY [*still tucking into his steak*]: What a nice man. Yes, he's definitely too nice to be my dad.

[*All the people in the other cells watch him. Two* SCENE SHIFTERS *enter his cell.*]

1ST S.S.: Hello Danny, I'm your guard. Please call me Wilf and his name is Mabel.

2ND S.S.: Howdo.

1ST S.S.: Care to play Take Over Bid to while away the time?

DANNY: Rather, this place is like a morgue.

[*They all laugh heartily.*]

2ND S.S.: Smoke? Chocky? Here, have a look at this picture of my wife and kids?

1ST S.S.: Nark it Mabel. Come on Danny, throw the dice. [DANNY *does.*] Well, your luck is in. You're first away. [*They play furiously.*]

2ND S.S.: Take my advice. Buy property as quick as possible.

DANNY: This is a smashing vicious game. I'll buy the Admiralty—No 10 Downing Street, Shepherd Market, The Houses of Parliament and good old Buckingham Palace.

2ND S.S.: May God bless her and all who sail in her.

1ST S.S.: Look at him, luck of the devil.

DANNY: And I'll take the Defence Ministry and the Ministry of Fisheries and Germ Warfare.

1ST S.S.: You can't take it with you Danny boy.

DANNY: And the Commissioners of Inland fallout and Poultry prices.

2ND S.S.: We're bankrupt. We've had it. You've cleaned us out.

DANNY: Tell you what I'll do, because I'm passing on to some real estate. [*He points to the earth.*] I'll bequeath all my earthly property to you.

1ST S.S.: Lovely St Paul's Cathedral. [*He hugs the little effigies towards him and kisses them.*] Beautiful Festival Hall.

2ND S.S.: Sorry chum they're mine. [*He snatches them.*] Take your hands off my Monument.

DANNY: Listen boys, it's only a game. [*He tries to separate them.*]

2ND S.S.: If you don't put down Harwell I'll smash your skull in.

1ST S.S.: You and who else? Give me back my War Office. Take your hands off my Monument.

DANNY: Can't you have some respect for the dead? Well, the nearly dead.

[*He cannot stop them and they start hitting each other mercilessly over the head with iron bars. They both kill each other. DANNY is sickened by the sight.*]

DANNY: I feel sick now. If they think I'm going to go through with it now they've got another think coming. [*He inspects the walls as he talks.*] I wanted my neck pulled with serenity, not with a splitting headache. [*He looks at the people staring at him.*] Besides, I can't stand them staring at me. What's the good of a state execution if it can't be a little more private. I suppose I'm just not the dying sort. Hmmm, as I thought, these walls just seem the same as all the others.

MR TODD [*returning with his ligature*]: Hey, son, where are you going?

DANNY: To have another bash.

MR TODD: But I'm all ready for you. Don't let me down.

DANNY: I've changed my mind. I'm not going to die.

MR TODD: But I must hang you.

DANNY: Hang some more wallpaper.

[*He walks through the walls and the scene fades. All the* SCENE SHIFTERS *come on and start constructing a long wall and gate. Just as* DANNY *comes to it, the lights go on, it is almost a lyrical scene with the sound of birds singing.*]

[*All the people take off their uniforms and lay around on the floor or quietly and happily make love. They all look much happier than they ever did.*]

DANNY: That tramp was a liar. He said all the countryside was concreted over.

HEADMAN: It is, except for madhouses.

DANNY: If this is the loony bin, please let me in. I'm insane. I hate people. I'm a fool, I'm a coward. I'm cynical and bitter.

HEADMAN: You sound ripe enough.

[*He opens the gate and* DANNY *enters. The gate is taken off and the wall also.*]

DANNY: Who are these people? The happiest I've ever seen. They're actually smiling. Hello everyone.

[*They all wave and smile.*]

ALL: Hello Danny.

DANNY: Mum. Look that's my mother.

[MRS TODD *waves.*]

So radiant. Helen! There's Helen, let me go to her.

HEADMAN: Sorry, Dr Lotus first.

[*A small office has been constructed just for this small meeting and is taken off as soon as it is no longer needed.*]

MR TODD: Hello Danny.

DANNY: Doctor, I know this sounds ridiculous, but you've got the same face—as my—

MR TODD: Father? What are you suffering from?

DANNY: From life.

MR TODD: Terrible disease. We'll soon cure you.

DANNY: I don't want to be cured. I want to stay here.

MR TODD [*he takes him out*]: Come and meet the others.

218

ROBERT: Do you play chess?

HEADWOMAN: Do you sing? Do you start the day with music?

DAPHNE: Perhaps you're interested in Drama?

HEADMAN: Do you believe in poetry?

REV JAMES: Do people stare at you in the dark? Do you get up to lovely naughty little escapades?

MRS TODD [*as if reciting, sending it up rather*]: You've got a very knowing face. We believe in peace. And in the world. We want to die of old age in our beds. After a full and fruitful life. We want our children to be happy. Naturally these subversive ideas cut us off from society. But where there's life there's hope—so they say. Let's all have some tea on the lawn.

[MRS TODD *pulls at him but the pull of* HELEN *is stronger. Most of the people go. Flutes are heard.* MR TODD *spies on* DANNY *and* HELEN *as they lay and make love. He has a telescope and he looks through both ends, alternately.*]

DANNY: You're the new Helen, the real Helen. Can I have you now?

HELEN: Of course. Why ask? Whenever and how often you want to.

DANNY: We're free for the first time and it's so easy.

HELEN: We can get married if you want to.

DANNY [*a bit put off*]: When?

HELEN: After tea.

DANNY: I'd rather not.

HELEN: That's all right. Just make love to me then.

DANNY: It's getting dark. Do you know we never see the stars in the city.

HELEN: Don't talk. Just love me. Make me feel something. Make me feel nothing.

[*The stage darkens where they are. The* SCENE SHIFTERS *construct a games room, or a single table for ping-pong. One man stands with a bell, he rings it regularly and ominously while two others play watched by static people.*]

DANNY: Let's go back now.

HELEN: All right, we have our lives before us.

[*They rejoin the others at the table.*]

DANNY: Hello Mother. I've adopted you, you know.

MRS TODD: Don't they look beautiful, Dr Lotus? We're all just like one happy family. They go together beautifully.

MR TODD [*agrees*]: I've watched them. Isn't the world, world, world, lovely.

DANNY: Give us this day. I've forgotten the rest but give us something quickly. Horror.

MR TODD: Let's all play ping-pong. Come away from the wall.

[*The wall is quietly being rebuilt.*]

MRS TODD: Danny and Helen, you and me, love all.

[*They play.*]

DANNY: I want to stay here till I die. I want to stay forever.

MR TODD: Just play the game and serve. Make the most of the fading light.

[*The lights fade and the* SCENE SHIFTERS *bring the gate.*]

MR TODD: It's time you were going, Danny.

DANNY: Going? Who's going? I'm staying.

MR TODD: You were only visiting.

DANNY: Is it just a few minutes I'm allowed. One pinch of paradise. I'm as mad as you are.

MR TODD: I have definitely not established that you cannot be allowed not to stay.

DANNY: Please don't turn me out. Put in a good word for me.

MR TODD: Who with? I'm the boss. Who could I impress? Who could I turn to?

DANNY [*turning to* HELEN]: Helen, this is the one place I've been happy.

HELEN: Sorry. You wouldn't marry me.

DANNY: But you said you didn't want to.

[ROBERT *and* REV JAMES *start playing ping-pong.*]

HELEN: That's true but that's not the point.

DANNY: Mother, please! You're close to the doctor.

MRS TODD: You play ping-pong rather badly. Sorry.

DANNY: I make one last plea. I appeal to you.

MR TODD: What did you do to warrant your commitment to an asylum?

DANNY: I didn't conform. I ran away.

DAPHNE [*sticking out her tongue*]: You looked over the wall.

MRS TODD [*hitting her*]: Shut up.

DANNY: I ran away. I wouldn't work.

HELEN [*as if reciting and in fact all the questions and statements from them, until his ejection is in the nature of recitative send-up*]: Once aware you have a larger responsibility.

DANNY: They tried to dehumanize me.

MRS TODD: Did you denounce them? Publicly?

DANNY: How could I fight all of them? No, I know that's not the point. [*The others stand around him and laugh, except his close relations.*]

DANNY: I stand here with nothing but my madness.

MRS TODD: Did you love your mother?

DANNY: Of course I loved you. But can you imagine a world where a mother would denounce her own son?

MR TODD: Would you denounce your own mother?

DANNY: Yes, but that's natural. No! No! I wouldn't. What we have done to the world is a crime against humanity.

ROBERT: It's no good arguing or struggling, come to the gate.

MR TODD: So come to the gate quietly.

[*The* SCENE SHIFTERS *stand behind him.*]

MRS TODD: Yes, come to the gate, because though we must chuck you out we still feel for you. Come with us.

HELEN: Put your arm round me and her. [*She points at* DAPHNE.] Come along. [*He recoils.*] Around my waist then. Why are you crying?

DANNY: Because the world is going down the drain.

HELEN: By the sound of it you should welcome the end.

DANNY: I do. But I loved life.

MR TODD: Your answers prove that you are absolutely sane.

DANNY: What do I have to do to prove to you that I'm mad?

MRS TODD [*as* DANNY *slowly goes towards her with hands outstretched*]: He's got a nice face—reminds me of—
[DANNY *has grabbed her round the throat. It is all so quiet as he squeezes and everyone watches as she slowly goes down. It is like a ritualistic game.*]

HELEN: I never like to see this. Stop him.

MR TODD: You stop him.

HELEN: No, please, after you.

MR TODD: Ladies first.

HELEN: Age before beauty.

DANNY: There, does that satisfy you?

MR TODD [*casually inspects the corpse*]: She is stone dead.

DANNY [*proud*]: There. Now I've proved that I'm mad. Look at my sacrifice. Killing the thing I loved the most.

MR TODD: That proves you're perfectly ready for the world. Throw him out.
[DANNY *is ejected by the* SCENE SHIFTERS *and the gate is slammed.*]

DANNY: Goodbye Helen. Don't just stand there and wave and cry. Oh sod you all. [*He wanders off.*]
[MRS TODD *is carried off and the scene is dismantled. The* SCENE SHIFTERS *now construct a very modern looking ship and then they return to the back of the stage and play cards.* DANNY *enters and studies the ship.*]

DANNY: A ship? Well, that's a stroke of luck. The river's a good way out of the city. *SS Britannia?* [*He reads the name.*] A good sturdy ship. I'll hide somewhere in her belly.
[*Almost reluctantly the* SCENE SHIFTERS *move from their game and swivel the ship around as* DANNY *searches. He finds a hiding place. No sooner is he hidden when* ROBERT *enters dressed as a sailor and finds* DANNY'S *hiding place.*]

ROBERT: And what have we got here?

DANNY [*almost chirpily*]: Lo Bob! I'm a stowaway and demand a State execution.

ROBERT: Not on your life. You can help me out, I'll take it easy for a change.

DANNY: Suits me as long as I get away. Where's the boat going?

ROBERT: To the last resort.

DANNY: I could do with a holiday.

ROBERT: Who couldn't? Muggins here can't get frozen. Yours truly is not good enough.

DANNY: Frozen?

ROBERT: I'm only good enough to take the privileged classes backward and forward. Fully automated, just two people working this ship. Think they appreciate it? Not on your life. Yours truly can't get a prepacked holiday. Anyway, you can help me out. That's the defrosting room in there—when—

DANNY: Defrosting room?

ROBERT: It's the only way to travel, ain't it? You don't have to hang it out, it's all speeded up. Lucky swines they are, I mean, this way they're sure, what with the artificial weather. Well I suppose it will be my turn one day.

DANNY: Well, who do get the holidays?

ROBERT: All the shopkeepers and foremen and the other middle class scum. Tobacconists and policemen, midwives, you know the sort of people.

DANNY: Well, tell me what happens?

ROBERT: You'll see. You're an ignorant little swine, aren't you?

   [*Noise of happy people.*]

Look! Look! There they come in their charabancs.

   [*Noise of cheering people and rattles.*]

In a few moments solid blocks of frozen people will be coming through that batch. You'll help me or maybe not— You'll be better in the defrosting room. Yes, I've got great influence in the defrosting room. But first they've got to get frosted. Want to look? Over there in that shed.

   [*On one side of the stage all the people in the play are congregated.*]

DANNY: No, I want to be sick.

ROBERT: Well, it's better than being crucified at stations with luggage and kids. No more sea-sickness. A two-week holiday compressed into a few minutes. Lucky so and so's, not having time to think for themselves. The great artificial lamps strung over the last resort is much more beneficial than the sun—and more reliable. And beautiful plastic flowers and plants that never die. Glorious. And purified sterilized water from the proper sea on the artificial beach with lovely hand-made waves. No fear of drowning. Ingenuity. Everything prepacked and prepared. An instant holiday. Holiday of a lifetime.

[HEADWOMAN *and* HEADMAN *are dressed in bright red blazers. All the people saunter on with funny hats on.*]

HEADWOMAN: Centre block Portland Estate! Walk to entrance marked A.

[HEADMAN *holds up a card marked A and they follow him. He draws a zigzag on the floor and then holds up another card marked B.*]

HEADWOMAN: Follow the zigzag to spot marked B and stand on the frosting floor.

[*They lose all sense of identity.*]

Come on, happy holiday makers. Close together now. Hurry up there! Look alive! You're only dead forever. Come on. Now this is quite a pleasant sensation, folks, breathe deeply.

[*They do as they are told and they seem to merge together. A hissing of machinery is heard and the people now resemble a thick mass, a sort of box. When* DANNY *or* ROBERT *pushes them they seem to be solid and move as if one box is moving on ball-bearings.*]

ROBERT: This is the first mass. Gently does it, boy, careful of this little lot.

DANNY: They look like frozen cod with watery eyes. If this is Portland Estate my Mum and Dad are somewhere in the middle of this lot.

[*He pinches one lifeless female in the bottom.*]

[*Behind we see the sea and it appears that the boat is moving at speed.*]

ROBERT: Well we're away and almost there already. Isn't science wonderful? I like your face and I think I could help you in the defrosting room. Yes, I've got influence. Here we are. Great influence in the defrosting room. Great influence in the defrosting room.

[*The sea behind stops and the ship opens out. The people are standing in a mass, against complicated machinery, and canned music.* REV JAMES *is there. He takes off his black clothes and puts on his white clothes and speaks with a very queer lisp.*]

REV JAMES: Oh yes, it's lovely to have you work here.

DANNY: What do I have to do? These machines are fantastic. Do they ever go wrong?

REV JAMES: Oh no. Some of my best friends are machines.

[*He helps* DANNY *push the pile of people over and gets needlessly close to* DANNY.]

REV JAMES: Looks frightfully complicated but it's terribly simple. But pretend that it's difficult, if you know what I mean. Take your time— [*He pushes* DANNY'S *hand on to various knobs.*] That's right! That's right, love. Press down, press down. Sideways green, orange on three blooper pink.

[*The machine pings and whistles.*]

And believe it or not, here we are. People. Already for the artificial shore.

[*The people shake, defrost and the* SCENE SHIFTERS *lose no time in constructing* THE LAST RESORT. *The lights change to a terrifying glare. Piped speeded up fairground organ music races everything to a frenzy and the* SCENE SHIFTERS *work to that frenzy. Everything is made of plastic flowers, plants, etc. And all the people hurriedly change into party dresses, throw streamers and blow blowers.*]

DANNY [*goes to* HELEN]: Helen.

HELEN [*looking through him*]: Which way to the tunnel of love?

DANNY: Dad!

MR TODD: Where do we get our sunburn?

DAPHNE: Clockwork lobsters. I want clockwork lobsters.

[*They all seem not to know him but laugh heartily and smuttily.*]

DANNY: Mother!

MRS TODD: I want some rock. [*Hoots of laughter.*] Virgin on the rocks.

HEADMAN: Hurry up quick, quick quick slow, quick quick slow. [*They all start waltzing.*]
Are you all together Portland Estate?
[*They stop dancing and stand in a circle with* HEADMAN *and* HEADWOMAN *in the middle.*]

ALL: Yes!

HEADMAN: Well, here we go.

ALL: Hooray. You put your right foot in and your right foot out, your right foot in and your right foot out, your right foot in and your right foot out—

HEADWOMAN: Are we downhearted?

ALL: Noooooooo.

HEADMAN: Now all the men will dress like women and the women will dress like men.
[*They start stripping each other and changing into each other's clothes to much shrill laughter.* DANNY *walks around them. He is amazed.*]

HEADMAN: Look lively holiday makers. Keep in step and follow the white line.
[*He draws a white line, a zigzagging haphazard affair and they blindly follow where it goes.*]

HEADWOMAN: Keep together. Quickly, quickly.

MRS TODD: Isn't this lovely?

HELEN: It's lovely.

MR TODD: It's lovely.

DANNY: Listen Helen. [*He pulls her to him.*]
[*The others carry on marching round and round but* HELEN *stares at* DANNY.]

DANNY: I must save you. You're too good for them. Let me get you out of here.

HEADMAN: Stop! [*All the people stop.*] No time to lose. For a jet break-neck whizz bang whiz around the island.

HEADWOMAN [*she hands out items as she speaks*]: Don't forget your balloons and masks and your lucky bags.

HEADMAN: Hurry! Hurry! Wakey, wakey. No time to lose. No time to lose. Are we downhearted?

ALL [*as if their words have been speeded up*]: No! No! No!
HEADWOMAN: Enjoying yourselves?
ALL: Yes! Yes! Yes! [*Still the shrill piped music.*]
HEADMAN: There's genuine sand here, folks. Sit down!
Stand up. We've got a busy programme for tonight is
crazy night. Put your lipstick on, gentlemen!
[*They do.*]
Take out your cigars, ladies.
[*They do and light them.*]
No time to lose. No time to lose. For booze, whiz bang
whizzes but first of all the sunburn. We have thirty-five
seconds so take your time. Hurry, hurry, hurry. Are we
downhearted?
ALL: No!
[*They all follow the* HEADWOMAN *off, laughing and
giggling as they go into the sunburn machine, which
rests at the side of the stage.*]
DANNY: Helen, I want to save you.
HELEN: Which way to the tunnel of love?
[*One* SCENE SHIFTER *brings on a sign, which points
the direction of the tunnel of love. Another* SCENE
SHIFTER *brings on a rowing boat.*]
DANNY: This way my love, this way my darling.
[*He pulls her into the boat and starts rowing.*]
HEADMAN [*offstage*]: Keep together, please. No whispering.
You're enjoying yourselves, not conspiring. Follow the white
line for shrimp teas and striptease. Next stop the Ballroom
for spot cash prizes.
[DANNY *in the boat rows away like mad, is unaware
that he is not getting anywhere.*]
For the sooner we get in the sooner we get out. [*He comes
on and sees the boat.*] Hey, no stragglers! No straying.
Come back here.
[*All the people come on and shout and gesticulate at
the boat. They try to run after it and go through all
the motions of running but don't move an inch. Soon it
gets dark and the boat enters the tunnel of love. There are
now no people on the stage, except* DANNY *and*
HELEN.]

HELEN: Where are we?

DANNY: The tunnel of love.

HELEN: They're coming after us.

DANNY [*still rowing, but everything is quiet now*]: They'll never catch us. All the world loves lovers. Can I put my arm round you?

HELEN [*leaning out of the boat, she cranes her neck and he cranes his to see up her clothes*]: Boats are pulling out after us.

DANNY: You're safe with me. Helen!

[*They kiss.*]

You know who I am, don't you?

HELEN: I feel I've known you all my life.

[*They kiss again.*]

DANNY: Who? Who am I?

HELEN: Danny! Of course I've missed you so, you silly boy. I'll do whatever you say.

DANNY: In this direction. [*He rows again.*]

HELEN: You lead me Danny, I'll show you the way. No, you blithering idiot, not in that direction. [*She pulls the tiller round.*]

DANNY: It's nice and dark. Darling angel, you can trust me.

HELEN: Yes, but not too far. Hands! [*She smacks him.*] You wouldn't respect me if I let you.

DANNY: It's worth waiting for. We must always run away from the others. I don't mind waiting for you, as long as we can be alone.

HELEN: I've saved up something special for you, Danny.

DANNY: They don't realize we're in love. They can't catch us. Let's walk along the shore.

[*Moonlight. The boat is stopped. The sea is heard, waves behind.*]

HELEN: The beach is deserted. How dreamy.

DANNY: Let's dance naked in the moonlight.

HELEN: And die of cold? No. Let's discuss practical things. Like marriage and our council flat.

DANNY: Council flat? Council what?

HELEN: How delightfully the moon dances on the water.

You can touch me down to the waist. Hold me, sweetheart. Kiss me. All right, you can go a teeny weeny bit further.

[*They cuddle but he extricates himself.*]

DANNY: What did you mean—Council flat?

HELEN: You make me so happy Danny. Ooh, I love that. It sends shivers. You're so brave and strong.

DANNY: Look, there's a boat.

[*Just as the* SCENE SHIFTERS *construct the boat again.*]

In the harbour. How sweet, all them fairy lights. Council flat?

HELEN: Ooooh, a boat. Oh Danny, soon as the priest brings us together, I'll give you, you know what.

DANNY: Just let's go away somewhere. Just somewhere.

HELEN: How romantic you are, how handsome.

DANNY [*trying to force her down*]: I want you now. Now. I want you now. On the beach, like in films.

HELEN: Darling, don't you think I don't? The sooner we're joined the better. I can hardly contain myself. [*She forces him off.*] Do you know I don't know what I see in you. When I first saw you, you disgusted me. It made me feel sick to see you with your staring red-rimmed eyes and your ears all sticking out. But I got used to it. I don't notice how ugly you are any more. Isn't love grand?

DANNY: Helen, you say such lovely things. I've never been so happy in my life. Wonder where this boat's going? Let's just sail away.

HELEN: Where honey?

DANNY: Anywhere—so long as we're together. Wonder where this boat's going?

[*A* SCENE SHIFTER *answers him just as he leaves the stage.*]

S.S.: Nowhere in particular.

[*They are all alone again.*]

HELEN: That sounds the place for us.

DANNY [*calling off after the* SCENE SHIFTER]: I say, when does it leave?

VOICE: Right away.

[*The* VOICE *now answers from somewhere inside the ship.*]

DANNY: Mind if we sail in her?

VOICE: Climb aboard. All the world loves lovers.

[*We hear the ship's hooters and funnels and it appears to move as* DANNY *and* HELEN *get aboard.*]

HELEN: We're slipping away. How romantic the sea looks.

DANNY: Yes, it's—blue.

HELEN: And sort of ripples of green.

DANNY: With lights dotted on the surface. It's very big, isn't it?

HELEN: Yes, it's—large.

DANNY: And very deep. It makes me feel religious. I remember my eight commandments.

HELEN: Oh sweetheart, darling, honey lamb.

DANNY: The sea makes me feel sexy.

HELEN: Why?

DANNY: Everything makes me feel sexy.

HELEN: Kiss me like they do on telly. Lean me against the rails and give me a proper film star kiss. Good job I shampooed my hair. Hey— [*She breaks as he kisses her.*] No foreign kisses.

DANNY: Hold on. I've been on this before. Yes I have. [*He opens a hatch and there are all the people frozen together again.*] Well strike a light. There's Mum and Dad, and the rest of them. S'pose the holiday's over.

HELEN: I'm so pleased.

DANNY: Don't they look lovely and happy. And all frozen so nicely. Good old Dad, he's proper tipsy with a bottle of instant whisky in his hand.

HELEN: Yooo-hooo! We're engaged.

DANNY: Don't Mum look lovely. Best mother in all the world. Do you know all this burial and cremating business is all wrong. We should all be frozen when we die, and we could be kept in special fridges in the kitchen, for all our relatives to look at, at family gatherings.

HELEN: Yoo-hoo! We're getting married. I've broken him at last. Oh Danny, you've got me where I want you at last.

DANNY: We're going to have a lovely life. In a lovely

council flat. One wall all contemporary black, and smashing floral wallpaper on the other walls. You know darling, I'm ambitious.

HELEN: Goody, goody.

DANNY: I'm going to be a tobacconist, like Dad.

HELEN: Your words bring joy to my heart.

DANNY: The things you run away from you seem to rush right into. Eh? What was that I said? Sometimes I don't half say some funny things. Remind me never to talk soppy again. Let me squeeze you darling. I love you forever and ever and ever.

HELEN: I love you for ever and ever and ever.

DANNY: And we'll have three frozen succulent kids and live happy ever after. We'll break their spirits when they're really young and make them really happy. Oh, Helen.

HELEN: Oh Danny.

DANNY: Oh Helen.

HELEN: Oh Danny. The things you do to me.

DANNY: The things I do to you. We're the happiest, luckiest couple in all the world.

HELEN: The luckiest happiest couple in all the world.

DANNY: The luckiest happiest couple in all the world. Look, we're almost there. The dear old white cliffs of Dover. But I thought this boat was going nowhere in particular? Still, nowhere—England, what's in a name. How lovely to be home. [*The hiss of machinery as the boat stops. The people start defrosting and start queuing up.*]

HELEN: They're defrosting. Now we can tell them. Yoo-hoo. Dad! He's going to be a tobacconist like you. Yoo-hoo.

MRS TODD: Yoo-hoo. Look, Danny's here, Dad.

DANNY: Lo Mum, hello Dad. Dad, you'd better teach me all the retail and wholesale prices. I can't wait to get started.

HEADMAN: Portland Estate, Centre Block, stand on the right of the white line. Hurry up, stay together. Your train is waiting alongside. Come along.

[*The family are all delighted but they soon settle down.*]

HEADWOMAN: Come along.

MRS TODD [*as the others queue to march off stage*]: Come on kids, squeeze in with us.

DANNY: You got a newspaper, Dad? What's the latest?

MR TODD: Premier says War inevitable. A hundred million must die in the first two minutes. But we mustn't give up hope.

DANNY: What about the big football match?

MR TODD: Black news I'm afraid. Moscow beat Arsenal —five nil.

DANNY [*passionately*]: Damn them! Those red bastards.

HEADWOMAN: Portland Estate! That's right! Off we go, left right! Left right! Queue for the queue, queue for the queue, this is the way to Portland Estate, queue for the queue, queue for the queue.

> [*She leads most of them off marching.* DANNY *energetically joins in with the others. Train noises. The few* SCENE SHIFTERS *left on change the scene to the way it was in the beginning. Faces on the background. The execution wall and now all the people come marching on.*]

HEADWOMAN: Queue for the queue, queue for the queue, here we are back to Portland Estate.

> [*They all cheer.* REV JAMES *comes forward, piously. A young man is led out and put against the execution wall. It is one of the boys who has been a scene shifter.*]

DANNY: Who's he?

MRS TODD: Oh, it's tragic. Harry's boy.

DANNY: Course. I've got a head like a sieve. What's the charge?

MRS TODD: Travelled on the tube without paying his fare. Have to be put under of course. You'll be on the building militia, now, Danny, if you want to be.

DANNY: Love to. I seem to have had a nightmare. To have been away a long time.

MRS TODD: Never mind, son, it happens to the best of us. But you're home now. Oh Danny, I was so worried about you.

> [*She gives him a uniform and* MR TODD *gives him a rifle.*]

DANNY: Oh Mummy, at last I seem to have come to my senses.

[*He quickly changes into his uniform and takes up his rifle.*]

HEADMAN: Daniel Todd, welcome home.

[*Everyone cheers and patriotic songs play. They get down to the enjoyable process of the execution.*]

[*The* REV JAMES *comes forward and* DANNY *with almost greater enthusiasm than the others, diligently lifts his rifle.*]

HEADMAN: Squad! Take aim! Ready! Fire!

[*The rifles shoot and the figure falls as ' Rule Britannia ' plays and the curtain falls.*]

The Lemmings

CHARACTERS IN THE PLAY

Mrs Lemming
Mr Lemming
Norman Lemming
Mrs Jones
Mr Jones
Iris Jones

A Seashore

Before the Lemming family enters no one is seen and there is only sound.

The sea. The waves booming gently. Then seagulls and the sound of children playing and young people laughing. A group of people sing a rather run down version of 'I do like to be beside the seaside'. A gathering of people somewhere offstage and a Salvation Army band starts to play.

SINGING: THERE IS A HAPPY LAND FAR FAR AWAY—WHERE THE SAINTS IN GLORY STAND, BRIGHT, BRIGHT AS DAY—

SALVATION ARMY GIRL [*weedy, anaemic voice, speaks jerkily*]: Good evening ladies and gentlemen. It's lovely to see such a lot of lovely people on such a lovely evening. All over the world at this moment, all over the world, here and now, at the present time, millions are entering the water. There is no escape— The Kingdom of God draweth water. We must all walk into the waves. Are you prepared to drown this morning? For you are going to.

  ['*Rock of Ages*' is sung.]

ANOTHER VOICE: Brother Charlie will now say a few words.

BROTHER CHARLIE: Yes! Y—es! You have heard no doubt the news! Yes! Now! Which means at this very moment every living soul must walk into the sea. Man must be cleansed! Is it the sea's fault? Is it God's fault?

VOICES: Yes!

BROTHER C: You can scoff. You'll be scoffing salt water in a few minutes. You! Unbelievers! Believers! Sinners! Trade unionists! You can get right with God. You can enter the sea with the blessing of the State— You can enter the sea with the blessing of the United Nations—but unless you enter the sea with the blessing of God, your little trip is fruitless. So come on! Be jolly! With Jesus in our hearts and the Salvation Army in our legs let's march and sing! Put a sock in it folks! A jolly rousing chorus as we go!

VOICES: ARE YOU WASHED IN THE BLOOD! IN THE SELF CLEANSING BLOOD OF THE LAMB—ARE YOUR GARMENTS SPOTLESS—ARE THEY WHITE AS—

[*They sing as they walk into the waves and then other groups of people are heard singing.*]

VOICES: SONS OF THE SEA, ALL BRITISH BOYS—SAILING ON THE OCEAN—

VOICES: RULE BRITANNIA—BRITANNIA RULES THE WAVES—

VOICES: OH I DO LIKE TO BE BESIDE THE SEASIDE.

[*The choruses merge amidst splashing of water and the boom of the waves. Seagulls. Marching people, laughing people, Salvation Army band gurgling. Children laughing.*]

OFFICIAL: Women and children first! Women and children first! Don't rush, there's room enough for all of you.

VOICE: So-long Dad!

VOICE: Goodbye Joan!

VOICE: GOODBYE JOAN! IT WAS A WONDERFUL LIFE.

VOICE: GOODBYE HARRY! It was a lousy life.

VOICE: So I said to him, the fact is can we survive long enough to kill ourselves decently—

OFFICIAL: Pregnant mothers and little toddlers will now march into the sea.

VOICE SINGING [*listen with Mother*]: OH THE NOBLE DUKE OF YORK, HE HAD TEN THOUSAND MEN, HE MARCHED THEM INTO THE LOVELY SEA, AND THAT WAS THE END OF THEM.

OFFICIAL: Don't rush! Families stay together!

VOICE: Keep close Ariadne or I'll brain you.

CHILD: Where's my stick of rock?

OFFICIAL: And now the able bodied men and women! I say there! No snogging! Consorting is not allowed. Let's be more dignified than Pompei. Quickly, but take your time!

There's plenty of room inside! Get a copy of the bye laws as you enter.

VOICE: BYE! BYE! Oooooer—ain't it wet.

[*The sound of gusts of laughter then waves and the laughter is drowned.*]

VOICE: And now the old aged pensioners will march into the sea. [*'Boys of the Old Brigade' is played.*]

VOICE: The Trades Union Congress will march into the sea. [*The watery sounds of the 'Red Flag' being played but it is quickly submerged by the lapping of water.*]

VOICE: And now, the Conservative Party will march into the sea.

VOICES: ETERNAL FATHER STRONG TO SAVE, WHOSE ARM DOTH BIND THE RESTLESS WAVE, AGAINST THE MIGHTY OCEAN DEEP—

[*By now the hymn is drowned in water and there is just silence. Then the wail of seagulls. It sounds like a cry for help. There is much fog about. A voice calls. At first it sounds like a seagull but soon it is obviously human. Three people enter.* MR *and* MRS LEMMING *and their son,* NORMAN. NORMAN *is pushing a huge old-fashioned pram. It is crammed with clothes and piled high with little bits of furniture. A chair, a collapsible table. Candlesticks are poised on the top. The candles are alight.* MRS LEMMING *helps* NORMAN *push the pram.* MR LEMMING *saunters behind them. He is very well dressed, as if he were going to a party. He stops and puts a foot on a rock and cleans his shoes with great ceremony, then he tries to see his reflection in the shoe. He repeats the process with the other shoe.*]

MRS LEMMING [*searching around, calling nervously*]: Yooo—hoooo— Yoooo—hoooooo.

MR LEMMING: What you yoo-hooing about? There's no one here.

MRS LEMMING: Sure this is the place?

NORMAN: Sure.

MRS LEMMING [*relieved*]: At last. We lost our way. You and your short cuts, Norman. All the others have gone in already. I'm scared, Harry.

MR LEMMING: We'll have to go in alone. Better late than never.

NORMAN: Well they haven't been gone in long. Their hats are still bobbing on the surface. I'm starving.

MRS LEMMING: Push the pram over here Norman. [*He does.*] I want to cut some bread. We lost our way. The fog frightens me. We lost the others. We shouldn't have lost the others. Now don't wander off. Eat your bread and say a prayer. [*She cuts the bread.*]

NORMAN: I don't want to. [MR LEMMING *starts praying.*]

MR LEMMING: Pray! Pray! Quickly pray.

NORMAN: I don't believe in prayer.

MR LEMMING: That's not the point. Pray!

NORMAN: I don't know any prayers. What shall I pray?

MRS LEMMING: What was that one again? The Lord is my—

NORMAN: Yeah, I remember—what is he?

MRS LEMMING: Never mind. Some more bread, Norman? Eat. Eat it all. [*She forces the bread on* NORMAN. *He reluctantly eats.*] I love to see him eating. That's the most important thing. Believe me, you'll never find another woman like me.

NORMAN: You can say that again.

MRS LEMMING: You know why Adam went so wrong in his life? He never had a mother to lead him, to show him the way.

NORMAN: You can say that again.

MR LEMMING: All right! You all ready now? Norman, you push the pram in the sea, you're younger than me.

NORMAN: But why the pram? I've asked you a thousand times.

MR LEMMING: Ask her? I had a perfectly good taxi to bring us here. She has to come like a refugee. So! Your mother knows best.

NORMAN: It was bloody heavy, pushing it all that way.

MRS LEMMING: It looked nice. Youngsters! That's all they do. Ask questions. So here's the sea at last.

NORMAN: It doesn't impress me. And why do we have to walk into it?

MRS LEMMING: Keep together now! One little family altogether. You and your short cuts. I told you we'd lose our way.

MR LEMMING: I'd like one last smoke before we finalize the ceremony.

MRS LEMMING: You smoke too much. Oh all right! But let's get into the water quickly and get it over with.

NORMAN: Why can't we wait till the morning? I don't want to die just yet.

MR LEMMING: You follow in my footsteps and like it.

MRS LEMMING: Anyway, you're not going in just yet. You've got three minutes left.

MR LEMMING: Yes, the length of this fag. Anyway, who said anything about dying. We're not going to die. We're only going to drown.

MRS LEMMING: I'm worried about you, Norman. You used to be such a good boy.

[*The candles in the candlestick have now gone out.*]

NORMAN: I'm sorry Mother. You know best. Crazy ideas come into my head sometimes. I want to follow you. I know you know best but I just wanted to do it in the morning.

MR LEMMING: Now don't make me angry Norman. If I say walk into the sea you'll walk into the sea.

NORMAN: Yes Dad. Whatever you say.

MRS LEMMING: Ah, he's a lovely boy. Comb your hair! He always was a good boy. I love him! Anyway, who's holding things up? Hurry up, Harry, with that cigarette. [*Suddenly she becomes nervous.*] The candlesticks! Where are the candlesticks! Oh, thank God! Light them Norman and I'll try to remember a prayer. And I'll tell you what we do. Forget about the pram. Dad will stand on my shoulder. No, I'll stand on his and you'll stand on my shoulder Norman and we'll go in like that. And you'll hold up the candlestick, Norman. That way it won't go out until the last moment. [*She demonstrates how to hold the candlestick.*]

MR LEMMING: Almost ready. Few last puffs. Nature's so lovely. That's the advantage being a cab driver; you notice nature—especially on the back seat.

NORMAN: I'm ready.

MR LEMMING: The sea is pious. Positively pious! Believe me. Didn't I always say that all men were equal.

MRS LEMMING: We lost our way. You and your short cuts. I feel lonely—I love a crowd of people. I feel so cold.

NORMAN: I feel so happy, now.

MR LEMMING: Shut up, you're depressing me. You going to miss life, Sarah?

MRS LEMMING: Yes and no. You?

MR LEMMING: No, I can't honestly say I'm going to miss life. Anyway, the cab game was going down the drain. Well, that's me ready.

MRS LEMMING: Light the candles and sing a song. Norman. And stay together. Bend down Harry so I can climb on your back.

> [HARRY *bends down and* MRS LEMMING *tries to stand on his shoulder*—NORMAN *tries to get on her shoulder*—*it becomes impossible*—*they compromise.* MR LEMMING *gives his wife a piggy back.* NORMAN *follows holding high the candlestick.*]

NORMAN [*sings*]: The bear went over the mountain,
> The bear went over the mountain,
> The bear went over the mountain,
> To see what he could see.
> And all that he could see,
> And all that he could see,
> Was the other side of the mountain,
> The other side of the mountain,
> The other side of the mountain,
> Was all that he could see.

> [*The waves boom. Then suddenly a dog is heard barking.* MR LEMMING *drops his wife.*]

MRS LEMMING: A dog? That's all I'm short of.

> [*A dog rushes on. It is very friendly.*]

MR LEMMING: Come here boy.

MRS LEMMING: I don't want a dog going in with us. Can't stand them. People who love pets hate children. Carry on walking Harry. Ignore him.

MR LEMMING: What a lovely little feller.

NORMAN: Hate them. Go on, get away. Dad, lend us your penknife.

MR LEMMING: Sure! Well cared for, ain't he?

[*The dog plays and barks.* NORMAN *grabs it and takes it to the edge of the sea. It yelps.* NORMAN *disposes of the carcase.*]

MRS LEMMING: Well, there was no need to cut its head off Norman. That's going a bit too far.

NORMAN: Didn't like its face. Fancy giving in to people.

MRS LEMMING: Now it's stained the sea all red. Come on then.

[*A motor is heard and a hooter. A caravan-trailer is backed onto the stage.*]

MRS LEMMING: What now? Oh this is too bad.

NORMAN: Well, well. That's a posh-looking job.

MR LEMMING: Another family. That's marvellous. We can all go into the sea together.

[*The men go to inspect it.*]

MRS LEMMING: NORMAN! HARRY! Come back here. We're going into the sea this instant. We must keep ourselves to ourselves. I like company, yes; but they look way above our station.

NORMAN: Oh, what's the hurry Mother? We're going to do it. Don't worry. I wouldn't miss the sea for the world, if you say so.

MRS LEMMING: HARRY! TURN ROUND! We're not wasting another moment. If the sea's good enough for everyone else, it's good enough for the Jews.

[*They all resume their previous suicidal positions.*]

WOMAN'S VOICE: PRINCE! PRINCE! I say, over there!

MRS LEMMING: KEEP WALKING! NO TALKING!

VOICE: I say there! Have you seen a dog?

MRS LEMMING: No, we ain't seen a dog.

[*A clap of thunder is heard.* MR LEMMING *drops his wife again.*]

MRS LEMMING: That's all I'm short of. Thunder.

[*Pouring rain; heavy thunder and lightning.* MRS LEMMING *takes it very badly.*]

NORMAN: Don't upset yourself, Mother. Don't cry.

MRS LEMMING: I made us all look nice. I made us all look lovely and look at us now. How can we go in like this?

MR LEMMING: All right. So we'll wait till the rain stops. [*The trailer opens out, a beautiful tent extension.*]

MRS LEMMING: Hate lightning.

NORMAN: Let's ask her if we can shelter in their trailer. We can dry out.

[HARRY *knocks on the trailer.*]

MRS LEMMING: Harry—come back here . . . [*More thunder.*] Lets stick to our own kind. [*Thunder.*]

NORMAN: Come on Mother.

MRS LEMMING: Oh all right. Harry! Wait for us.

[*A woman emerges from the trailer. She is smartly dressed and sexy looking. But she is trying to look younger than her age. She smokes from a long holder and settles herself in a deck chair.* HARRY *looks at her with delight and waves to his family, indicating them to keep away, at the moment.*]

MR LEMMING [*putting on a posh accent*]: Oh, I say, do excuse me. May I— May we shelter under your er—your awning—for a—

MRS JONES: Oh certainly, of course you can.

[*She hardly notices him, continues reading her magazine. Meanwhile* NORMAN *and* MRS LEMMING *are huddled and shivering together.* MR LEMMING *suddenly remembers them and waves them on.* MRS LEMMING *approaches gingerly: now we can see more of the trailer. Inside we can see a man asleep. A girl comes out with a deck chair. She doesn't look up at all.*]

MRS LEMMING: What a beautiful home! Mind if I take my things off and wring them out?

MRS JONES: Not all of them, I hope.

MRS LEMMING: What a beautiful home! What do you think of this Harry?

MRS JONES: Yes, it is a beautiful house on wheels. Costs six thousand. This is my daughter. Iris. She reads a lot. Iris, say hello.

IRIS: Hello!

NORMAN: Hello!

MRS JONES: And that's my husband! Sleeping. These men. I had to drive us down here. Charles! Charles! Wake up. We're here and we have company! [*She goes into the trailer.*]

MR LEMMING: Isn't it a smashing job, eh Norman.

MRS JONES: CHARLES! [*She shakes him.*]

MR JONES: What? What? Oh why did you have to wake me? [*She comes out again.*] Just when I was having such a wonderful dream. [*He comes out.*] Oh, hello! How do you do?

[IRIS *stops reading and looks at herself in a mirror.*]

MRS LEMMING: How should I know?

MRS JONES: Prince has run away again. Iris come away from that mirror.

IRIS: I feel beautiful today. Do you like my hair up? Shall I grow it long? I feel like doing something.

MRS JONES: She's a silly little bitch, take no notice.

MRS LEMMING: The children of today.

IRIS: I feel like dancing. Why have we come to the sea?

MR JONES: When I was sixteen I didn't ask questions.

IRIS: That's obvious. Why were we drawn to this place?

MRS JONES: Shut up, or I'll slap you round the face. I've been having this all day.

MRS LEMMING: My boy? I can't complain. He does what he's told. Don't you Norman?

NORMAN: Yes.

MRS JONES: Shall we all have a cup of tea? We can't do a thing until this wretched storm is over.

MRS LEMMING: Never say no. We like tea with lemon.

[NORMAN *fascinated by* IRIS *follows her away from the others.*]

IRIS: How old are you?

NORMAN: Seventeen and ten months.

IRIS: What do you do?

NORMAN: Nothing [*He kicks stones—she sits and stares at the sea.*]

MR JONES: Oh, it was a lovely dream!

MR LEMMING: I bet it was eh? Eh? [*Lots of laughter.*]

MR JONES: No, not that sort. [*Throughout him telling the dream, gulls screech.*] It was a wonderful dream. The sirens were sounding and everybody was rushing, rushing to get out of the city. We were all trapped—

MRS JONES: So, what's so wonderful about that? Oh, I hate that sound—what is it?

MRS LEMMING: Seagulls!

MRS JONES: Seagulls? Disgusting.

MR LEMMING: Don't worry yourself. They're only pigeons in disguise.

[NORMAN *wanders back.*]

MRS JONES: So what's so wonderful about this dream of yours?

MR JONES: Can't you wait! You've got to see the whole thing in context—so there I am running, in cotton wool, trying to scream with no sound coming out of my throat. I'm alone. Must get to the outskirts, must get out of the city, before I'm trapped like an ant in a jam jar full of flames. Suddenly I see two pals; there they are smiling, cuddling each other around a lamp-post. They seem glad to see me but their faces are all black. They don't speak so I give them a playful shove and they crumble to nothing. They're just ash blown away by the wind. I run and I get to the edge of the city. Middlesex I think it was. I'm through I think! I'm free—but then I see soldiers across the road guarding the way out with machine guns. 'WE'RE ALL GOING TO DIE' I scream. They just stand there with black faces, stopping everyone. Suddenly the children cry and everyone starts fighting and people do such things to each other that I never could believe that people could do such things. But they did, but nobody dare try to get through— Now I'm coming to the nice part. Everybody is tearing and killing everyone to bits and the sirens scream but then a thousand helicopters rise from the fields and hover above our heads. And inside them I clearly saw the military heads and the Government and an Archbishop. A Lord and trade union leaders, and even a few film stars and then the Royal family. And then I heard someone shout

'They're escaping to carry on the good work in our dominions beyond the seas.' And guess what? They started waving at us! Everyone stopped fighting and we all sang the National Anthem with tears in our eyes, and even though we are all turning to ash, we slap each other on the back. And though we died, it didn't matter any more. Then I woke up.

MRS LEMMING: What a beautiful dream. [IRIS *rejoins them.*]

NORMAN: You remember the last crisis. I was looking out of the window, thinking—at last, no more school, when suddenly my pal shouted out 'they've let us down again Norman. The heads of Government have agreed to meet to sort out their differences'. So it was bloody school again.

IRIS: Aren't you ambitious? Didn't you ever have a dream?

NORMAN: Sure. I wanted to go into the advertising, at first. But going into the sea is far better. I couldn't make up my mind.

IRIS: I'm going for a walk.

MRS JONES: You're not. We're all going in, in a minute, when the rain stops.

IRIS: It's not raining too hard; just for a few minutes. [*She wanders away again.*]

MRS JONES: PRINCE! PRINCE! Well I'd better make that cuppa while there's still time.

MRS LEMMING: Can I help you?

MRS JONES: No, you just rest your feet. I'll manage. [*She goes into the trailer.*]

MR JONES: What are you in? What do you do? I mean, what's your business?

MR LEMMING: Taxi cab. Made a living. Not wonderful but couldn't complain. I paid for everything out of that cab. Lovely house, fitted carpets, central heating, twenty-one inch screen, two indoor lavatories, holiday in Bournemouth, son's education, the lot. See, isn't he a clever boy? Still the cab game was going down the drain, so to tell you the truth I'm delighted to be here.

NORMAN: I feel like going for a walk.

MRS LEMMING: No! There's still lightning.

NORMAN: Mother, please, just for a few moments.

MR LEMMING: Oh let him. We were young once, remember? The younger generation need a bit more freedom.

MRS LEMMING: What for?

NORMAN: Please, I won't go far. It's stopped raining.

MRS LEMMING: All right. For two minutes, while we drink our tea, but stay around the caravan, don't wander.

NORMAN: As if I would. Oh thanks!

MRS LEMMING: AND NORMAN! WAIT! [*She whispers.*] Don't you go near that girl and if she comes up to you ignore her, don't speak to her— [*He is gone.*] And what's your profession—Mr—Er???

MR JONES: Jones is the name and here is my card. I'm in Insurance— Maybe I could interest you in a policy?

MR LEMMING: What for, I don't own a Government.

MR JONES: I was only joking. I'm higher up of course than that—Land of Hope Assurance—400,000,000 assets. Biggest and widest known. Mighty and free that's our motto. Worked my way up you know from almost the bottom. They said 'Jones, you're cut out for better things, you're class—you have a future—this company needs men of your astonishing qualities'. Yes, those were his actual words—

MRS JONES: Charles, a moment—I need you.

MR JONES: With pleasure, sweet one.

MRS LEMMING: It's so lovely to see people who love each other.

[*She is looking at* HARRY *closely, brushing his clothes, now she looks at his hair, then she starts looking into it. When* MR JONES *is taken back by this she pulls* HARRY *towards the other side of the stage.*]

MR JONES: Excuse me, just a moment.

MRS LEMMING: Yes, excuse us too, I've got a few last things to tidy up.

[MR JONES *goes to his caravan while* MRS LEMMING *makes* MR LEMMING *sit down, then she puts a towel around him and starts cutting his hair.* MR *and* MRS JONES *start making tea.*]

MRS JONES: I don't like the look of them.

MR JONES: Oh, they're quite harmless.

MRS JONES: They look like savages. Orientals. I thought we were absolutely the last people.

MR JONES: I think they're Jews.

MRS JONES: WHAT? What presumption. I mean, really! This is going too far. We mustn't lower ourselves.

MR JONES: Oh they're quite civilized, if you treat them kindly. They're rather quaint. Let's all go into the sea together.

MRS JONES: I never thought I'd have to share judgment day with Jews.

MR JONES: I admit he does look rather greasy but I'm sure he has some nice points. There are good and bad in all races, so I believe. I admire her. She has a biblical face. Fat, hmm, plenty of meat on her, forget her face. But that boy is the sort who gets them all a bad name, but we must be tolerant.

MRS JONES: Get them away from my house.

MR JONES: You let them in. I knew a Jew chap once. Rather nice, despite his obviously unattractive personality.

MRS JONES: Get rid of them—get rid of them. They may be dangerous.

MR JONES: Oh, I fancy a bit of—company this evening. You can't pick and choose all your life.

MRS JONES: Shush—they're whispering. I don't like it.

MRS LEMMING: Harry, let's get out of here.

MR LEMMING: I like a bit of company. He's a lovely feller, he's not even an anti-semite. He's well educated.

MRS LEMMING: Two sorts of people in this world. Jews and Jew haters; scratch a stone and you'll find an anti-semite. I hate them. [*She finishes the hair-cut and sees* MRS JONES *looking over. They wave at each other.*]

MRS JONES: Here's a nice hot cup of tea.

MRS LEMMING: You're very kind—but we've got— [*They rejoin* THE JONESES.]

MR LEMMING: Six lumps please.

MRS LEMMING: No sugar, just lemon. It's getting very dark.

MR JONES: Biscuit?

MRS JONES: It's very close.

MRS LEMMING: Yes, there's no escape. I didn't bargain for the night.

MRS JONES: It's getting rather chilly.

MRS LEMMING: Yes the nights are drawing in.

MR JONES: Tell me, you're of the Jewish persuasion, aren't you.

MR LEMMING: Believe me, we weren't persuaded.

MR JONES: Some of my best friends are Jews.

MR LEMMING: So are mine. At least they was.

MRS LEMMING: I'm all shivery. It's dark. Suddenly. I didn't bargain for the night. Let's go.

MR JONES: Do you play cards? Bridge?

MR LEMMING: Solo. Let's play solo. Look Sarah, if it's too dark we'll have to wait till tomorrow.

MRS LEMMING: I won't. I'm not going to.

MR LEMMING: Do you want to walk into the sea in the pitch black? No. Well face facts then. So all right; tomorrow's another day. What's so marvellous about today? We'll do it at dawn, first thing. It will be more romantic. Give us a kiss. Oooh, she's lovely, I could bite lumps out of her.

MRS LEMMING: I'm not going to wait. Soon as the moon comes out I'm going out and if you're not going with me— I'll go alone with Norman.

MR LEMMING: Darling, as if I'd let you. After all the years together. All right, give us ten minutes, time for a few hands.

MRS JONES: Don't upset yourself Mrs—er—?

MRS LEMMING: Lemming, Sarah Lemming. And we're as good as anyone else.

MRS JONES: Have a cigarette?

MRS LEMMING: WHAT? AND DIE OF LUNG CANCER? We're better than anyone else.

MR LEMMING: I'll try abundance. Sarah come away from the open sky.

MRS LEMMING: Where has he gone then? Why does he do this to me? Never seen the sky as black. Just my luck, everything happens to me.

MRS JONES: THAT DOG! How thoughtless of it. PRINCE!
[*She calls for the dog out in the open.*]
PRINCE! PRINCE! [*She returns inside.*]
[*The seagulls shriek again and the waves boom again.
It gets darker.* MR LEMMING *and* MR JONES *settle
down for a card game and the two women for a natter.*
MRS JONES *shivers and whispers to her husband. He
reluctantly gets up and closes the flap of their tent. Now
we can hardly see them.*]
[IRIS *wanders on again. Holding a shell to her ear. She
stops near the pram and then* NORMAN *comes on. He
shines a torch with one hand while he throws stones into
the sea with the other hand.*]

IRIS: You're a strange boy.
NORMAN: Did you see that one bounce five times?
IRIS: You can switch it off now. The moon's coming out.
You can switch—
[*It gets a little lighter and he switches the torch off.*]
NORMAN: I was going into advertising; going into the sea
is better.
IRIS: So you said before.
NORMAN: Why are you so pleased to be going in there?
IRIS: Who said I was? They always nagged. 'What are
you going to do?' 'You're too good for them' ... 'You can't
play with her ...'
NORMAN: Well now they've solved it all for us. Now we
don't have to worry about settling down. The sea solves
our problems. I shouldn't be speaking to you.
IRIS: Let's walk on the shore.
NORMAN: I'm Jewish. Hundred per cent.
IRIS: So what? What are Jews?
NORMAN: Who knows?
IRIS: Who cares?
NORMAN: We're proud. We love life. We cover mirrors
and sit on low chairs.
IRIS: Why?
NORMAN: I forget.
IRIS: Are Jews better than other people?
NORMAN: Yes.

IRIS: Are they worse?

NORMAN: Yes! What other people? We got lost. We strayed in the fog. I ought to go back to my Mother now.

IRIS: No, stay a while longer. Sit over here. The sea's so calm and beautiful now.

NORMAN: It looks like ink. [*Sings.*] If all the world was paper and all the sea was ink, and all the trees were bread and cheese, what would we have to drink?

IRIS: I never cared about life. When my parents said 'let's leave' I came. I didn't particularly want to die.

NORMAN: They know best.

IRIS: I thought like you, only this morning, but I'd like to live now, here, on this beach. I'd like to have a home here, just here, on the edge of the earth and sea and sky.

NORMAN: Jerusalem's our home. That's why we say 'Next year in Jerusalem.'

IRIS: What a lovely word. JERUSALEM! Where is it?

NORMAN: It's nowhere. It's next year. It's just a dream, I suppose. We're not connected to anything. We don't belong anywhere.

IRIS: Isn't this your country?

NORMAN: No, but that's our sea.

IRIS: Why don't you go to another place then? Instead of into the sea?

NORMAN: WHY! WHERE TO? WHAT FOR? We had everything. Except happiness but then you can't buy that.

IRIS: Don't you have relations? Anywhere?

NORMAN: No. None! Nowhere!

IRIS: Would you like to kiss me?

NORMAN: No thank you! I promised my Mother not to talk to you.

IRIS: Don't talk then. Kiss me. Don't you know how? I won't eat you. Do I have to tell you what to do with your hands? Push me backwards. No, not like that. Kiss me properly. Open your mouth.

[*He obeys her instructions, awkwardly.*]

NORMAN: What? Like the kiss of life? I never touched a gi ... [*They kiss.*]

VOICES [MRS JONES *and* MR LEMMING *open the*

flap and shout]: PRINCE! NORMAN! PRINCE! NORMAN! NORMAN! PRINCE!

NORMAN: OH CHRIST! God that was wonderful. It's the kiss of life. The kiss of death to my mother! MY MOTHER! Listen!

MRS LEMMING: NORMAN! WHERE ARE YOU?

IRIS: Don't let them find us. [*They crouch down.*]

MRS LEMMING: NORMAN. I'M WAITING.

NORMAN: Can I put my hands into your dress?

IRIS: No one ever touched me. Well they have. Yes do! I mean no one ever touched me deep down, touched me properly . . . nothing ever touched me.

MRS LEMMING: NORMAN. [*Now she ventures outside.*]

NORMAN: She has to spoil everything. I'll kill her if she comes nearer.

IRIS: FORGET HER. WE HAVEN'T GOT TIME. I WANT TO LIE DOWN FOR YOU. WE HAVEN'T GOT TIME. I WANT YOU TO HAVE ME. [MRS LEMMING *finds them.*]

MRS LEMMING: NORMAN! WHAT ARE YOU DOING LYING DOWN? WHAT? AM I DREAMING? STAND UP, YOU DISGUST-ING MONSTER.

NORMAN: YOU COME ONE STEP NEARER AND I'LL SMASH YOUR SKULL.

MRS LEMMING: AM I DREAMING? TELL ME I'M DREAM-ING. I'M FINISHED!

NORMAN: I MEAN IT YOU LOUSY, FILTHY COW! GET BACK. Mother I'm sorry. I don't know what I'm doing! Get away! GET AWAY! MY HANDS ARE SHAKING!

[*She moves away, backwards.*]

MRS LEMMING: Yes! NORMAN, YES. I'm going now. Look, I'm walking backwards! You hungry? I've got food in the pram. We'll have a snack. Don't upset me. We must all stick together. I'm your mother; you know I am. I'm a human being. I've got feeling. We'll put up the tent for ten minutes and I'll sing you a lullaby! Come with me now and I promise I'll sing to you.

IRIS: Please leave us alone. Just for a little while.

NORMAN: I'll come soon, I promise. You can rely on me . . . BUT GET OUT OF MY SIGHT! Just a little while, then

I'm yours. I'll do anything you say. Go On. Get Away. I'll Throw This Rock If You Don't Get Away From Here. I Mean It.

MRS LEMMING: I can see you do. Don't do anything dirty. Come into the sea pure. I know you will. You're my Norm . . . I'll make some soup. I've got a packet and I'll sing you a song . . . Lullah-Lullah-Lullah . . . Lullah . . . Bye-byes . . . Does You Want The Moon To Play With . . .

[*Confused, she goes to the pram and starts making soup.* MRS JONES *comes out and joins her.*]

MRS JONES: There you are! I meant to ask . . . Are you a member of the Women's Voluntary Services?

MRS LEMMING: Don't go over there! We're being related over there! Your daughter and my son . . .

MRS JONES: Don't upset yourself. Take no notice. They're very forward these days. They're only playing. Besides my child is discriminating. I'll handle this. It's rather chilly again. [*She wanders over to the young couple.*]

MRS LEMMING: Norman! Don't forget your promise! You've got to hold the candlesticks! I'll call you when the soup's hot!

[*She starts putting up a small collapsible tent that was rolled up in the pram.*]

MRS JONES: Oh darling! I've been looking everywhere for you! What are you doing on the ground? You're not very strong you know. Get up young man. Do you know who my husband is? Iris, do up your dress, there's a good girl. It's very draughty. He's a Jew! How could you do this to me?

IRIS: Take no notice of her. She always goes on like this. Let's go over there.

NORMAN: No, I promised my Mother. Oh, what the hell! Why not? Why shouldn't I be free for ten minutes?

MRS JONES: They drink blood. They're dirty. Look at his hands! How can you let them touch your body . . .?

IRIS: It's a pleasure. A pleasure, but anything would be a pleasure after you [*To* NORMAN.] I didn't mean that. I do want you. Ignore her. I want just one night with you.

MRS JONES: They're not even rich!

NORMAN: One night can't hurt. Why shouldn't I?
  [*They embrace again.*]

MRS JONES: I'LL SCREAM FOR YOUR FATHER! I'LL CALL
  THE MEN! [*She is about to dash back to the trailer.*]

IRIS: Shut her up. Kill her!

NORMAN: No. I couldn't kill a stranger but leave it to me.
  [*He goes after her.*] Mrs Jones, you haven't seen your dog
  all evening have you?

MRS JONES: No! WHY? PRINCE! PRINCE!

NORMAN: I know where he is.

MRS JONES: Do you? Oh, I'm so pleased.

NORMAN: I'll tell you.

MRS JONES: How sweet of you.

NORMAN: In the morning. Now don't worry. He's quite
  safe. Safe in a cave.

MRS JONES: Take me there. Please, take me there this
  instant. I'll be ever so grateful.

NORMAN: In the morning. I'll have your daughter tonight
  and in the morning I'll give you your little dog. That O.K.
  with you?

MRS JONES: Why of course. I think it's absolutely delightful. I thought I'd lost him forever. You promise me he's
  safe? He won't suffocate in there? He must be famished.

NORMAN: Don't worry. I put some food with him. I knew
  that I needed him for bargaining power later. [*They
  laugh.*]

MRS JONES: You naughty boy. I'm so relieved.

NORMAN: There's just one thing more. You must persuade
  my Mother and Father to stay the night.

MRS JONES: NOT IN MY PLACE?

NORMAN: No, no. On the shore!

MRS JONES: Leave it to me. Don't worry. Have a lovely
  time together. You're only young once. Toodleloo.
  [*She returns to the trailer happy and goes inside.*]

IRIS: Will you marry me?
  [*They lie together. We see* MRS LEMMING *very busy
  with the tent and the others laughing and playing cards.*]

NORMAN: Yes, I'm marrying you now, as I do this!

IRIS: But what's the use of one night?

NORMAN: Oh, well, we mustn't expect too much.

IRIS: I want to turn my back on the sea.

NORMAN: We have to do what our parents tell us, eventually.

IRIS: I expect so. Anyway, a whole night is enough if you love someone.

NORMAN: Exactly.

IRIS: If only we could kill them.

NORMAN: Shush! Let tomorrow morning take care of them.

IRIS: Tomorrow morning takes care of all of us. But now, now—kill me.

[*The sea booms. It gets dark where the children are. We cannot see them anymore.* MRS LEMMING *is having trouble with the tent.*]

MRS LEMMING: HARRY! HARRY! Will I give that man when I see him. Harry!

[MRS JONES *comes out from the trailer again, this time she leaves the flap open.* HARRY *hears but ignores his wife.* MRS JONES *leaves the men and goes to* MRS LEMMMING. *She sings as she goes. She has a contralto voice, of rather bad quality which she believes, modestly, is rather good.*]

MRS JONES [*sings*]: ROSE OF ENGLAND THOU SHALT FADE NOT HERE. Mrs Lemming I'm glad you're putting up your tent. That's very sensible.

MRS LEMMING: HARRY! Harry! Never known him like this. Harry, help me with the tent. Harry! Call yourself a man.

[*She gives up for the moment and inspects the objects around her.*]

MRS LEMMING: Now the candlestick is tarnishing.

MRS JONES: Do you suffer from bronchitis? No? Neither do I.

MRS LEMMING: That man. My whole world's crumbling. What did the children say? Did you show them the folly of their ways?

MRS JONES: They say they're in love.

MRS LEMMING: Disgusting. Send Harry to me. I must get this tent up and the soup on.

MRS JONES [*to herself as she walks*]: Quite a well-built lad. The lucky little bitch. [*She returns to the men.*]

MR JONES: Jews are the loveliest people in the world.

MR LEMMING: The Belgians are quite nice. Do you play any other games?

MR JONES: I play nothing else except the organ. No, really, Jews are my favourite sort of people. It would be absolutely lovely to walk into the sea with God's chosen.

MR LEMMING: I'll have to go now, really. [*He walks towards his wife.*]

MR JONES: Our Lord was of the Jewish persuasion.

MR LEMMING: Lord who?

[MR LEMMING *goes to his wife, who by now has the tent up.*]

MR LEMMING [*looking inside*]: Hello, darling.

MRS LEMMING [*hitting him with a broom*]: Don't talk to me. [*She goes back into the tent and every time he approaches she throws something at him.*]

MRS LEMMING: Don't you come near me.

MR LEMMING: All right—I'm going.

MRS LEMMING: What? And leave me all alone.

MR LEMMING: I don't want to, darling—I want to be near you—

MRS LEMMING: That's better.

[*More happy he approaches again but as he gets close to the tent she hits him again with the broom. Now he just sits on the sand, brooding, not knowing what to do.*]

MRS JONES: Charles, we've got to keep them until the morning. Don't stand there gawping, do as you're told.

MR JONES: That's what I've been saying all along. But how?

MRS JONES: Get him drunk.

MRS LEMMING [*from inside her tent*]: Harry! I'm going in without you!

MR LEMMING: But we've always shared everything. I'm ready.

[M R J O N E S *goes to* M R L E M M I N G *and pulls him away.*]

M R J O N E S: What about one for the road?

M R L E M M I N G: Thanks. No, I never drink.

[M R S J O N E S *comes and* M R L E M M I N G *is between them.*]

M R S J O N E S: Warm yourself up. The sea's very cold.

M R J O N E S: Wet the old whistle. Come on, be a sport.

M R L E M M I N G: All right, just a drop. Thanks . . .

[*Outside their trailer*—J O N E S *gets the cocktail shaker going.*]

M R J O N E S: Cheers!

M R L E M M I N G: Not used to drink. Cheers! Blimey! No no, not another . . . I really . . . Le Chaim! To life! Mustn't let the old defences down . . .

M R S J O N E S: Cheers, come on, you're a strong man, what muscular arms you've got.

[*They start feeling each other's arms.*]

M R L E M M I N G: You're a bit scraggy aren't you? No more, no more! I can hear her . . . I'm all mixed up . . . You see we're not a drinking race. Mrs Jones!

M R J O N E S: We're all pals together! Live and let live, that's my motto. Share and share alike. How old is your wife?

M R L E M M I N G: I've lost count. Cheers! This is wonderful . . . I'm hot now . . .

M R J O N E S: Sit down Harry . . . come on. [*He throws* M R L E M M I N G *into a deck chair.*]

M R L E M M I N G: Mustn't let the defences . . . I've got nothing to lose but am I scared of losing it. Cheers . . . no thanks, no more! Cheers . . . my darlings . . . let me kiss both of you. We're surrounded. Le Chaim! Give me that bottle. On the brink of death we are in life.

M R S J O N E S: He's well away. Turn him out now Charles. He'll not be able to walk anywhere tonight.

[M R L E M M I N G *staggers and falls on his face.*]

M R L E M M I N G: Let's roll on the sand. Come on Charlie.

M R J O N E S: Come on then, I'll take you home, to your lovely, plump, biblical wife.

M R S J O N E S: You stay here with me.

MR JONES: Oh shut up.

MR LEMMING: That's too bad. Too bad. We're all the same, flesh and blood and bone, walking into the sea. Come on, skinny Liz, walk into the sea with me . . . [*He rolls over and over away from them.*]

MR JONES: Where's Iris?

MRS JONES: That Jew boy is having her.

MR JONES: I'll kill him.

MRS JONES: You? You little coward. Leave her alone.

MR JONES: Once she wanted to marry me, when she was five or six. My little Iris! I'll kill him.

[*He is about to rush over but* MR LEMMING *grabs his ankles.*]

MR LEMMING: Come on Charlie, come and meet my wife!

MR JONES: Leave me alone, you lousy Jewish bastard.

MR LEMMING: I'll cut your throat and hang you upside down and all your blood will run out of you.

MR JONES: Stop it! Stop tickling me . . . Ohohohohoh [*he laughs hysterically*]; I'l bash your brains in . . .

MR LEMMING: I'll rip your stomach open; [*They continue laughing.*]

MR JONES: I'll smash this ice pick into your eyes. [*He reveals one that he carries in his inside pocket.*]

MR LEMMING [*rolls over and away from* MR JONES]: You can't catch me! Yooohooo!

MR JONES: Oh yes I can. You rotten, stinking, disgusting, filthy . . . dirty . . . slimy . . . ohohoh . . . I've caught you.

[MR JONES *catches* MR LEMMING *and now they both roll over and over.*]

MR LEMMING: Stop cuddling me. This is wonderful. Best day of my life.

MR JONES [*hooting with laughter*]: Stop tickling. That's my funny bone. You've no right. Oh, I'm so miserable. Forgive me for crying.

MR LEMMING: Let me brush you off. There! There, wipe your eyes.

MR JONES [*sobbing*]: It's . . . just that . . . you're the best friend I've ever had . . . When she was five she walked around the house in a bridal gown, saying over and over again 'I'm going to marry daddy today'. And now your son is turning her into a woman.

MR LEMMING: Don't upset yourself. The gilt's soon off the ginger-bread. They'll come to their senses by the morning.

[MRS LEMMING *comes out.*]

MR JONES: There's your lovely lady wife!

MRS LEMMING: Rolling over the sand, with a man, at your age? I always said you had a screw loose. Help me take the tent down . . . We'll have to go without soup or lullabyes. I've had enough. Get Norman.

MR LEMMING: You can go in without me. I'm staying here tonight!

MRS LEMMING: Let me smell your breath. [*Sniffs.*] Drink? Has there been a wedding or something? This is unforgivable. This is it! I'm pulling my hair out. [*She prepares herself.*]

MR LEMMING: If that's your way of protesting, go ahead. [*She does pull her hair out.*]

MRS LEMMING: There! There! Satisfied? If you don't follow me into the sea I'll scream. I'll divorce you. I'm spitting blood, look . . .

MR LEMMING: Do me a favour Sarah. Let's all go to sleep or dance. Stay here tonight and we'll make a fresh start early in the morning.

[*He staggers as he tries to embrace her.*]

MRS LEMMING: Look, he can't even walk a crooked line. My whole family's gone to pieces. How can I ever face the sea with you in this state? [*Weeps.*] I'm ashamed. Thank God my Mother isn't alive. It would kill her. Promise you'll be ready first thing in the morning. I feel ashamed, I feel uneasy. I feel lost . . . That I should have lived to see this day. I'm crying, he doesn't even care. I'm alone! Pulling my hair out, alone. Promise me for tomorrow or I'll go in without you.

MR LEMMING: Go without me.

MRS LEMMING: Promise!

MR LEMMING: I promise.

MRS LEMMING: Help me then with this tent.

MR LEMMING: Up or down.

MRS LEMMING: I don't know now. I'm all confused.

MR LEMMING: I'm just lying here, looking up.

MR JONES: I'll help you Mrs Lemming. There we are. [*The tent is up.*] He doesn't appreciate you. You've a beautiful biblical beauty, you know. Your husband doesn't deserve such primitive bliss.

MRS LEMMING: Thank you very much, Mr Jones. Now you must help me get my boy away from your girl. Give them an inch and they'll take a mile. We'll have to watch them or they might grow out of us. [*She is making beds on the sand.*]

MR JONES: That's a good idea. We'll go over in a party and watch them. Keep our eye on them. We've got a lot of time to kill before dawn. I'll get my wife and the brandy flask. Come on, Harry boy, oops a daisy. Up you get. Put your arm . . . that's it . . . around your strong biblical wife.

MR LEMMING [*sings drunkenly*]: Bring me my bow . . . of burning gold . . .

MRS LEMMING: Let's all stick together now, this is lovely, so lovely, I'm really enjoying myself tonight. The tent's up, the beds are all made. It's just like Passover. Hold on, I'll snatch a bit of bread for Norman, he must be getting hungry.

MR JONES & MR LEMMING: Bring me my spear oh clouds unfold, bring me my chariot of fire . . . [*They all go towards the trailer.*]

MR LEMMING: I thought we were going to look at the kids.

MR JONES: The night's long—and they're young and they're not going to go to sleep just yet. What do you bet? We've got bags of booze, come on, let's have a party . . . Darling, put on your evening dress, we've got company.

MRS JONES: Oh, how nice. Come here Mr Lemming, I'll teach you to dance . . . properly.

[*They dance together for a moment.*]

MR LEMMING: Don't turn sideways or you'll vanish.

MRS JONES: As long as you vanish with me. [*They laugh.*]

MR JONES: Come on my biblical beauty, don't slip away.

MRS LEMMING: I'm only going to get a chicken. We'll have a beano.

[*They drink and dance and all go into the trailer where they have a party.*]

[IRIS *gets up, straightens her clothes. They walk around, see the people inside the trailer and walk away.*]

IRIS: Let's look for a cave.

NORMAN: No. The night's nearly gone. I must keep in sight of my parents.

IRIS: Let's refuse to go with them. Let's survive and build a house here.

NORMAN: Isn't one night long enough for you.

IRIS: If you loved me you couldn't say that.

NORMAN: If you've had one day you've had them all. They're just more of the same thing. One must be thankful for small mercies. My Mother would never let me. She knows best anyway.

IRIS: I want to live now.

NORMAN: I never wanted to live up till now and now I don't know. I don't think so. Three times I tried to kill myself, this year. I stuck my fingers in the light socket. I tried hanging myself in the garden and the third time I pulled a bread knife across my throat.

IRIS: Horrible.

NORMAN: No, the horrible part was in-between. Plucking up courage for the next attempt. As my Mother always said, the only thing you should worry about in life is to make sure you can fall into your coffin without debt . . . My parents have solved all my problems now. And I've really lived, now that I've had you.

IRIS: You're stamped with your past. Don't you want to live? Making love and having kids?

NORMAN: I'm a coward. Besides, we're not the same religion.

IRIS: Religion! Who cares? If being a Jew is being you, I love every Jew on the earth.

NORMAN: If being a non-Jew is being you, I love every non-Jew in the world.

IRIS: Do you also hate your parents as much as I do?

NORMAN: Yes, but I hate your parents more.

IRIS: Then let's build a house and live on the shore.

NORMAN: No. Sorry, that's out of the question.

IRIS: That's too bad. All right then. Pretend. Let's build a pretend house.

NORMAN: That I don't mind doing.

IRIS: We'll pretend that we're going to live; pretend that life is worth living.

[*They start getting sticks and branches and are utterly engrossed in building a small shelter. The others silently come out of the trailer. Their mood has changed—however—they crawl along the ground.*]

MRS JONES: Mr Lemming. Stop tickling my toes.

MRS LEMMING: Shush. We don't want them to know.

MR JONES: You're going to find it hard to camouflage yourself.

MRS LEMMING: You're very naughty and I don't like them remarks, even from you. What are they doing?

MR LEMMING: Crawl on your belly. Keep your bottom down.

MRS JONES: They're building a sort of . . . shelter.

MRS LEMMING: I don't like this at all.

MR LEMMING: Shush! If we're very quiet, we might see them making love. Well don't be shocked. It's only human, everybody does. It's lovely to see young people enjoying the fruits.

[*They all by now are quite close to the young people.*]

MR JONES: She's nicely made, isn't she?

MRS LEMMING: We must break them up. Shush!

MRS JONES: Charles, take your shoes off and stop breathing heavily.

IRIS: A house of leaves. It's going to be beautiful.

NORMAN: Break off those myrtle branches. We'll use them as a ceiling. We'll festoon the walls with lemons and tangerines and palm leaves. My mother always said I should provide a house for a nice girl. She always said

that was the purpose in life, before we came here. That
branch there, that evergreen. I'll build it beautifully.

IRIS: Can you remember before you came here? How you
came here?

NORMAN: Yes, but I have a feeling I'm sinning, if I speak.

IRIS: I can remember but they can't. As you get old you
forget. We don't grow up—we cover up.

NORMAN: How's this coming? You rest. I'll finish it. I
remember that day well. I think it was yesterday.

MRS LEMMING: Mr Jones? Did you ever see the Royal
family close up?

MR JONES: Shush! Please, this is most interesting . . .
Give your husband a shove. His snoring makes me feel
sick.

[MRS LEMMING *keeps on throwing scraps of bread
which* NORMAN *keeps on eating automatically.*]

NORMAN: I was doing my homework when my mother
dragged me out of the house. Then she brought out cans
of paraffin and me and Dad threw it all over the house.
Then my Dad got an axe and smashed his car. Meanwhile my mother was praying in the garden and made me
pray. I don't know any prayers so I pretended to. Then
she lit a match and prayed some more as the house
cracked and burnt down . . . Then we pushed off. I pretended to know a short cut. We got here late but at least
we got here. There! Our house is finished. I never built
anything with my own hands before. Someone keeps on
throwing bread.

MR JONES: Stop it Mrs Lemming or you'll give the game
away.

MRS LEMMING: I know my boy. He's growing, he needs
it.

IRIS: Don't eat it, it may be poisoned. Chuck it away.

NORMAN: For you I'd even do that.

MRS LEMMING: Look, he threw it away without kissing
it. How could he treat me this way?

MRS JONES: I wish they'd get down to something. I'm
bored. We were having such a nice party . . . Mr Lemming!
Harry . . . Cootcheycooooooo . . .!

IRIS: So now we're going to live here for ever.

MRS LEMMING: Over my dead body.

NORMAN: The sea doesn't impress me any more. Your eyes are deeper . . .

MR JONES: That's better.

NORMAN: I'm happy with what I've got but I want more.

IRIS: We'll get it, we'll have kids.

MRS JONES: That's rich. They want to survive and have kids. What can you do with them?

MRS LEMMING: Some mothers do have them. Let's stop them now! They must be under the water and safe.

IRIS: You're the first and the last. It was so painful but worth it. You are the morning star.

NORMAN: Nearly morning. We deserve a bloody miracle now that we're here. If I could grow in time before I throw myself away I might be able to save myself.

IRIS: Oh, it's just as well. No child of mine will be born blind in both its heads. What am I talking about? I keep on thinking we're not going to survive.

MRS JONES: Are they going to follow us or aren't they going to follow us?

MRS LEMMING: They'll do as they're told.

NORMAN: It's rotten that we weren't born some other time, on some other planet, where people have already found the secret of love and the secret of how to live forever. I feel cheated.

IRIS: Make love to me again.

MR JONES: Wake up Harry! Wake up!

MR LEMMING: I'm awake, don't worry. He's a block off the old chip.

MRS JONES: No, that's going too far. Stop it! Get out of there you dirty little cow. Pull your dress down.

MR LEMMING: Adjust your dress all ye who enter here. [*Confusion as the adults all stand up.*]

NORMAN: Keep away from us. Listen all of you . . . if you all want to walk into the sea, that's your affair. We've changed our minds.

MRS LEMMING: I knew it! I told you so. You ungrateful boy, after all I did for you. Give them an education. I

slave to bring him up well and all he wants to do is
survive.

MR JONES: I pride myself on being modern but this is
going too far.

MRS LEMMING: Come on quickly everyone . . . I smell
daylight . . .

IRIS: We're not going with you. We mean it.

NORMAN: You can stick the sea up your . . .

MRS LEMMING: Give them ten minutes they want all
night. Give them all night and they want eternity. You
little bitch enticing my boy.

IRIS: We're not coming out. The sea will have to come in
and get us.

MRS JONES: I didn't mind them making love even, but
now they expect to survive and that's the last straw.

MRS LEMMING: They're only human so they're bound
to succumb, Mrs Jones. Come on Norman, smarten yourself
up and no more nonsense.

IRIS: This is where we belong, on this beach, in this house
of leaves.

NORMAN: I hate you all. I'm beginning to see straight at
last.

MR JONES: Up till this moment she did what she was told.
Your boy has turned her head.

MR LEMMING: Up till this moment he was content with
water. She's turned him against us.

MR JONES: Your offspring.

MRS JONES: Out of your Jewish loins.

MRS LEMMING: Your daughter's fault. Now they're contaminated with life and love. Comb your hair Norman and
come away from her.

MRS JONES: Give these bloody foreigners an inch. Let
them into your home to shelter from the rain and your
own daughter turns bad. Come and have a nice cup of
tea and sort things out.

MRS LEMMING: You got us into enough trouble. I told
you Harry to stay away from them.

MRS JONES: Hit him Charles! Kill him!

MRS LEMMING: Swipe him one!

MR LEMMING: I like you Mr Jones.

MR JONES: And I think you're a jolly nice sort.

MR LEMMING: So take that then! [*Hits him.*]

MR JONES: And that! [*They hit each other mercilessly.*]

MR LEMMING: And that!

MRS JONES: In the guts! In the guts!

MRS LEMMING: Kick him in the teeth!

MR LEMMING: You're the nicest feller I ever met. Oooooh.

MR JONES: You're a white man, a jolly decent . . . ooooh.

MR LEMMING: Sorry Charlie but I want to dislocate your shoulder!

MR JONES: Do forgive me, I have knocked three of your teeth out.

MRS LEMMING: Cut him up.

MRS JONES: Pulverize him! Emasculate him!

NORMAN: Stop it! Stop it! Call yourself grown men! Now come!

> [*He tries to get between them, and he succeeds in separating them.*]

MR LEMMING: Stop interfering.

MR JONES: Stay out of this.

NORMAN: Stop it all of you. Listen to us! Make up your minds! Loving, hating . . . keep away from him! You keep on changing your minds. Be consistent so we know where we are.

MR LEMMING: Let's do him up, Charlie!

MR JONES: That's a jolly good idea Harry!

> [*They both kick* NORMAN.]

NORMAN: Help! Help!

IRIS: Leave him alone. How can you let them do this to your son?

MRS LEMMING: He's no son of mine if he won't listen to me.

MR JONES: Take that!

> [*They kick him over and over again.*]

MR LEMMING: And that! And that! Right! Had enough yet!

NORMAN: Yes!

MR LEMMING: Right . . . have some more.

[*It is getting quite light now.*]

MR JONES: I've got some rather nice scones we can have with cream. Come on Mrs Lemming, let's prepare it for the menfolk.

MRS LEMMING: It's almost dawn all right. All right Harry, if that doesn't bring him to his senses he's not worth troubling about.

[*They stop punishing* NORMAN.]

MR JONES: I think we can call it a day now!

MR LEMMING: Yes, it is almost light.

[NORMAN *and* IRIS *scamper away from the others and cower near the ground together.*]

NORMAN: I can see straight at last. I'm free of you! Before I was kidding but now I'm determined. You brought us here but this is as far as we go.

MR LEMMING: I'm sorry you take that attitude son.

IRIS: Leave us alone, just leave us alone.

MRS LEMMING: I have a feeling about them. Let them try and stand on their own feet. They'll learn. I'm so ashamed. Come on Mr Jones.

MR LEMMING: Consistent! He wants us to be consistent! [*They all laugh.*] We're human, what do you expect? Miracles?

MRS LEMMING: We must have nothing more to do with them.

MR JONES: They must be put into isolation. Come over here, Harry, I have some interesting Negro poses to show you.

MRS JONES: They'll drag us down.

MR LEMMING: It may be contagious.

MRS LEMMING: It may be. You mad! It is. Come away quickly, they're contaminated with love and life. Kissing his wounds eh? You'll learn! Love flies out of the window . . . Do you know Harry, she looks like a Jewish girl. At least we must be thankful for that! Norman, straighten your tie! And wash the blood off your face.

[IRIS *concerned with* NORMAN *is bathing him.*]

MR LEMMING: Care for a cigar? Charlie?

MR JONES: You bet!

MRS JONES: Come on folks. Back to our place. We just have time for early breakfast . . .

[*They all go into the trailer singing 'We do like to be beside the seaside'.*]

IRIS: You mean it. I can see you do.

NORMAN: We'll build a bigger house, here. I've got the urge to Build.

IRIS: Not too big! This house of leaves is so beautiful.

NORMAN: I'll do great things. There's nothing to hold me back. I let them beat me up. I could have licked them hollow if I wanted.

IRIS: You'll be stronger when you realize how weak . . . we . . .

NORMAN: So pleased they've gone. How could we be their children? We've got nothing in common.

IRIS: They are us.

NORMAN: We're free.

IRIS: We must know where we are, exactly, if we hope to have a chance.

NORMAN: I've done it; I'm free! The cow has released me! The lousy, rotten, filthy, stinking cow of my mother!

IRIS: Stop cursing! We'll manage.

NORMAN: We'll show them. I want you more than the sea.

IRIS: All we need is here, please stay here with me.

NORMAN: Shall we try to save them?

IRIS: No.

[*Seagulls scream.*]

NORMAN: I want you more than the sea! I want you more than the sea.

IRIS: Please don't keep on saying it.

NORMAN: I want you more than the sea.

IRIS: Let's explore, try and find a sheltered place to build.

NORMAN: Oh, but I must say goodbye to them.

IRIS: We'll return. Let's just go for a moment. It looks beautiful over there. Come on, are you terribly hurt?

NORMAN: I'm all right.

IRIS: Lean on me.

NORMAN: I can manage.

[They go off.]
[MRS LEMMING *comes out and watches them go off. The others come out.* MR JONES *lays up a table and puts on breakfast things.]*

MRS LEMMING: They've gone for a little walk, that's nice.

MRS JONES: We'll have breakfast in the open air.

MRS LEMMING: That's nice. Yes, I'm confident in my boy.

[They all sit down to breakfast.]

I know which way he'll turn. You'll see. Well thank God I can see some light in the sky. *[Takes a tea-cup.]* Thank you Mrs Jones, no, we needn't worry about them.

MRS JONES: Toast? I think we should tempt them, show them how easy it is to imagine you're in love. I'll do them both a favour. He's a very sexy boy so he won't be able to resist me. We'll have one last shot. I'll walk naked into the sea. He'll follow, you'll see. What do you think of that?

MRS LEMMING: I'm not sure of that one.

MR JONES: Those of us with kids know how thin the layer of civilisation is, how quick the beast breaks out. *[He and* MR LEMMING *start laughing and howling and making wolf yells.]* So, before I do you a favour Harry, tell me what you Jews have contributed to the world.

MR LEMMING: Eddie Cantor and cheesecake . . .

MRS LEMMING: And Jerusalem and smoked salmon . . .

MR LEMMING: Moses! Einstein! Spinoza and Shakespeare! And what have you contributed?

MR JONES: Land of Hope Assurance . . . Tottenham Hotspurs . . .

MRS JONES: The Women's Voluntary Services and William Blake . . .

MR JONES: Toasted teacakes, crumpets and marmalade. Anyway, I'm asking the questions.

MR LEMMING: Why?

MR JONES: Would you like to seduce my daughter? Now don't turn your nose up.

MR LEMMING: I was twitching with excitement . . .

MR JONES: I made her myself. I mean I helped to create her . . . Incidentally, tell me, as a Jew, as a dispassionate man, is incest all that bad? Do your people allow it? She's worth saving you know—worth saving for the sea. Please do this for me . . .

MR LEMMING: You don't have to sell her to me.

MR JONES: They must be led into temptation . . .

MR LEMMING: Too late for that; there's the first real streak of daylight. Come on Harry, outside.

MRS JONES: Dawn! What a lovely name; come on Charles! [*She kisses him.*]

MR JONES: All right you skinny cow, I'm coming and stop biting my ear.

[*She starts breaking crockery and chairs. The others join in and they get more and more excited breaking things. MR JONES and MR LEMMING push the trailer right to the back of the stage, then he brings out two huge cans of paraffin.*]

MR LEMMING: Want a hand?

[*MR JONES nods and they both splash it all over the trailer.*]

MRS JONES: Spread it all over. Oh you are hopeless. Over there! That's right. That's better.

MR JONES: Stand back everyone. [*He lights a match and sets the trailer alight.*] There she blows.

[*The fire consumes the trailer.*]

ALL [*sing*]: Keep the home fire burning, while our hearts are yearning.

MRS JONES: That's that. It burnt so nicely.

MR JONES: Good British workmanship. Well made. Well, I'm ready.

MRS LEMMING: Morning at last. I didn't think we'd survive long enough to die decently . . . so where's the sea?

MR LEMMING: The tide's miles out, can't even see it.

MRS JONES: Oh this is too bad.

MRS LEMMING: There's only one thing you can be sure of, that is you can't be sure of anything. I feel funny. I'm going to faint.

MR LEMMING: We'll have to go out and search for it?

MRS LEMMING: With my bunions.

MR JONES: I've got a marvellous idea, folks. Let's kill ourselves.

MRS LEMMING: You mad? It's against the law.

MRS JONES: What law?

MRS LEMMING: The law's the law.

MR JONES: We could stick our head in our gas oven. Take it it turns . . . Oh, I forgot, there's our gas oven gone up in flames.

MR LEMMING: There's nothing to stop us killing each other, Sarah, please.

MRS LEMMING: How could you all be so terrible?

MR LEMMING: The men could kill the ladies and then cut each other's throats at the same time . . .

MRS LEMMING: That sounds ceremonial . . . What am I going on about? Are we all going mad?

MR JONES: Or we could all stand in a ring and strangle each other . . . one minute . . . I remembered to bring my cyanide pills . . .

MRS LEMMING: Harry! You know as well as I do it's a sin to even talk this way. The sea can't let us down. Meanwhile, I'm going over to the tent. I've got some washing to do to pass the time.

MR LEMMING: What are you going to use for water?

MRS LEMMING: Oh ye of little faith.

[MR JONES *has stooped to pick up a bird.*]

MRS JONES: How can we pass the time? I'm so bored. What's that Charles?

MR JONES: What a pretty little thing. It must have fallen out of its nest. How silky, how furry.

MR LEMMING: Let's look for its nest and return it.

MRS JONES: Charles, stop strangling it.

MR JONES: It won't feel a thing.

MRS JONES: Anything that moves he must destroy. Stop it!

MR JONES: There! That's put it out of it's misery.

MRS JONES: But it wasn't in misery.

MR JONES: Had it lived it would have been.

MR LEMMING: Let me hold it now!

MRS JONES: No, please let me. Thanks.

MR LEMMING: Come over to the tent. We have a little Palestine wine . . . Sarah, we've got company . . . give me my opera glasses . . . [*She gives them to him.*]

MRS LEMMING: Racing glasses you mean . . . What is it? What do you see?

MR LEMMING: There it is! I told you not to worry. The sea! What a sight for sore eyes.

[*They all fight to look.*]

MRS LEMMING: I feel better now. I had such heartburn. Let's burn the tent—I'm glad I waited for the morning. It seems more proper than the dark.

MR LEMMING: Hold your white horses! It'll take a few minutes yet!

[MRS JONES *rummaging in* MRS LEMMING'S *things comes across something to interest her.*]

MRS JONES: A gramophone! How quaint. Shall we dance? [*A record of Victor Silvester 'Au Revoir but not good-bye'.*]

Mr. Lemming, do you dance? You Eastern Asiatics are very loose. You should dance beautifully.

[*The two couples are dancing with opposite partners now.*]

MR LEMMING: You're very proud, aren't you? I like proud, scraggy women. You're high class too, way above my station. I'd like to pull you down a peg.

MRS JONES: Pull me down? Mr. Lemming! How thrilling! I feel so happy because I'll soon be re-united with my beautiful Prince.

MRS LEMMING: Don't look so sad Charlie. The sea's coming in thick and fast.

MR JONES: I love your biblical shape. There's something of you to hold. When I touch her she disappears.

[*We hear the others laughing.*]

She shrinks and disappears.

MRS LEMMING: I never knew another man. We should get to know each other more. All the troubles of this world are caused by people being strangers.

MR LEMMING: Sarah! You know how they say in Arabic, I divorce you three times? Well shake hands with a Yiddisher Arab for I divorce thee! I divorce thee! I divorce thee!

MRS LEMMING: He was such a lovely husband. Harry, I'm throwing your ring into the sand. Where are you taking me Mr Jones? Please Mr Jones, we're not married.

MR JONES: I now pronounce us husband and wife.

MRS LEMMING: Ooh Mr Jones. Oooo Charlie.

MR JONES: I want to get close to your people.

MR LEMMING: Oh, Mr Jones, quickly before the sea comes. I can see it reflecting on top of your beautiful bald head.

[*They all lie on the ground.*]

MR JONES: Oh Sarah Lemming. I've been missing something all my life. I never knew it could be like this. [*He pulls her into the tent.*]

MR LEMMING: I marry you, my dear, twitching wife. Let me warm up your blue blood.

MRS JONES: Oh Harry boy, beg now! Come on. That's a boy. Dirty paws! Down! Down! Up! Turn over! Oh my Harry—Prince. I've been missing something all my life. I never knew it could be like this.

[MR LEMMING *acts like a dog to her command and is about to make love to her when* MR JONES *and* MRS LEMMING *come out from the tent.*]

MRS LEMMING: For the sake of decency go inside.

[MR LEMMING *pulls* MRS JONES *into the tent.* MRS LEMMING *and* MR JONES *cuddle. She meanwhile keeps on popping pieces of bread into his open mouth. The sea booms again and the gulls shriek.*]

MRS LEMMING: Harry! Hurry! The sea's back. Hurry Harry, Hurrah!

[MR LEMMING *followed by* MRS JONES *comes out of the tent, they are beaming.*]

MRS JONES: The sea! The sea! Hip! Hip! Hip!

ALL: Hooray!

[IRIS *and* NORMAN *return, arm round each other.*]

MRS JONES: Look at the lovebirds.

IRIS: Go on, tell them . . .

MRS LEMMING: Oh Norman, isn't love lovely. We all know each other a little better now. Sea water! Now I can get on with the laundry . . .

NORMAN: I hope you're going into the sea . . .

MR LEMMING: Of course we are. You changed your mind?

NORMAN: No, I want you all to know that we are going to carry on the good work.

IRIS: No, no, not the good work. Get it right.

MRS LEMMING: So they still want to live after a night together. Gluttons! To live on this dirty old shore.

MRS JONES: And have dirty old kids . . .

MRS LEMMING: Who'll treat you the way you treated us. I hope not.

MRS JONES: There's no bringing them to their senses. No accounting for taste.

IRIS: Get on with it, Norman.

[NORMAN *clears his throat, as if he had rehearsed it.*]

NORMAN: I have seen sense during the night . . . you're driven . . . by . . .?

IRIS: Yourselves.

NORMAN: Yourselves. There's nothing out there . . . but death . . . You all want to die. Have you asked yourselves . . . Why?

MR JONES: Why? What's that?

MRS LEMMING: He should have been an inventor. Suddenly he invents a new word— Why!

NORMAN: We want you to know that we mean to survive— to profit from your experience. To change course . . . to start again . . . start loving each other. Here on the edge of death we want . . . to resolve . . . I forget.

[*They all cheer.*]

MRS LEMMING: He should have been a barrister. Isn't he a lovely boy?

MRS JONES: I love his twisted simplicity. Can I have a word with you . . . Norman.

IRIS: Let's leave them now.

MRS JONES: What about my dog?

NORMAN: I cut its throat . . . I cut its head off. It's dead . . . all its blood turned the sea red.

MRS JONES: I want you to look after it. It's a lovely little fellow.

NORMAN: I killed it.

MRS JONES: Thank you. Thank you for watching over it and keeping it safe. Please have it and keep it as a present, for you and Iris. My wedding present to both of you.

NORMAN: I cut its head off. It's rotting in the sea.

MRS JONES: You see, I don't want it to go into the water. He's so full of life.

NORMAN: I killed it. It's no more.

MRS JONES: Thank you. Thank you so much. Bring it up well. Thank you. I want him to live, with you.

IRIS: Let's go back to our house of leaves.

NORMAN: No, let's watch them until their heads are all covered.

MRS JONES: How charming the sea looks, Mr Lemming. Let's coagulate together.

MR LEMMING: Sarah, I'm marrying you again. [*He cuddles his wife. She is still busy washing clothes.*]

MRS LEMMING: Good, I promise to be a dutiful wife.

MRS JONES: Charles darling, till death do us part.

MR JONES: Dear heart. The trouble with my wife is she understands me. And I need her understanding.

MR LEMMING: So stop the washing. You were in such a hurry. We owe the sea a debt. Ourselves.

MRS LEMMING: I always kept a clean house and I'm not going to change now.

MRS JONES: You ready darling? Right! Stand to attention. Remember the flag . . .

MR JONES: My country right or wrong!

NORMAN [*shouts*]: You say it all wrong. Always remember the question mark. My country right or wrong?

IRIS: Leave them alone now, let's get on with our lives.

NORMAN: Shush!

MRS JONES [*sings*]: Britannia rules the waves.

MR LEMMING: So finish with the laundry already.

Stop covering the rocks with shirts; gather it in.

MRS LEMMING: Help me then! You gather it in. I'll set the tent alight, I want lots of smoke, so that people . . . there we are . . . so that anyone on the other side of space knew we lived here and didn't live in vain . . .

[*They burn the tent.*]

ALL: Keep the home fires burning!

MRS LEMMING: We were the Lemmings. We live in hope. Where there's life there's hope.

MRS JONES: Behind each cloud there's a silver lining.

MR LEMMING: The sun will set without our help.

MR JONES: Every good turn deserves another.

MRS LEMMING: You always have time for your own death.

MRS JONES: People are nice.

MR JONES: Everything turns out all right in the end.

MRS LEMMING: If you're destined to drown you will in a spoon of water . . .

MRS JONES: The good die young.

MR JONES: It's all for the best.

MR LEMMING: God has given; God has taken. Blessed be the name of the Lord.

MRS LEMMING: God has his reasons. Now wash your hands for God's sake. Wash them quickly. Harry!

[MR *and* MRS LEMMING *wash furiously.*]

MRS JONES: Charles, share my shampoo.

[*The* JONES' *shampoo their hair.*]

MR JONES: Harry. You were right, I have to admit. Unfortunately it's true and damn it. We are all the same. All bloody well the same. Skin and blood and bone walking into the sea.

MRS LEMMING: Norman, you'll miss me. You'll see. Try and survive! Wash your hands, Norman, and your neck. Wash, don't forget. The last sight I want to see is my boy washing himself . . . That's the least you can do. That's right! Norman, I'm leaving the candlestick. Hold it high, don't catch cold. Hold it high and when you walk into the sea make sure it's the last thing to be seen.

MR LEMMING: She was quite a passionate woman until she got this obsession with candlesticks ...

NORMAN: Leave me alone. Leave me alone. Just go into the sea and leave me alone ...

MRS LEMMING: The sooner you start washing the sooner I'll go. [NORMAN *washes himself.*] Thank you! Thank you, yes. Now I'm ready ... Come on Harry ...

MRS JONES: Oh no. Don't try stealing a march on us, Mrs Lemming.

MRS LEMMING: I wouldn't dream of such a thing. Take my arm. What a lovely day ...

MRS JONES: Isn't it glorious? Those men, they do dawdle. [*At the back of the stage, the ocean begins.*]

MRS LEMMING: What a beautiful lot of sea. We're one big happy family at last. Don't worry Mrs Jones, don't worry about the men. They're bound to follow us. [*The men are chatting. The women go arm in arm.*]

MRS JONES: They live in a world of their own ...

MRS LEMMING: Let's sing. [*They sing.*] 'The more we are together, together—' [*They splash through the water.*]

MR LEMMING: Shall we join the ladies? The more we are together, together ... [MR JONES *joins in and now the four of them are all singing.*]

ALL: For your friend is my friend, and my friend is your friend ... [*A great splash and they vanish.*] [*Silence. Seagulls.*]

NORMAN: Goodbye, you lousy stinking bitch. You'll never get me! You rotten, grabbing, pulling ...

IRIS: Don't let's waste time or breath.

NORMAN: Let's go.

IRIS: No, let's stay! You promised you wanted to stay here.

NORMAN: Anywhere but here. Here we need a miracle to survive.

IRIS: If we expect a miracle, we're finished. Come into our home. [*She points to their house of leaves.*]

NORMAN: We need a larger one. Doesn't the sea look beautiful.

IRIS: All right, I agree. Let's push off. Let's go inland.

NORMAN: I won! I beat her. Now perhaps I can get some time.

IRIS: We can start growing things. We can live off the land.

NORMAN: I want a simple life. I never had time, you know. They never left me in peace. I'm really ambitious now. There's nothing I can't do.

IRIS: Come down to earth. If we live in dreams we're sunk.

NORMAN: I want to build jet planes with my own brain. I can do it . . . I can de-salinate the sea. [*Seagulls.*] Shush! Did you hear my Mother calling me?

IRIS: It was seagulls.

NORMAN: Yes, you're right! There it goes again. Are you sure it's seagulls?

IRIS: Let's go inland.

NORMAN: I'm on very good terms with my parents. I want you to know.

IRIS: But they're dead.

NORMAN: That's what I mean.

IRIS: I'm going to catch a fish and cook it for you. [*She sits on a rock.*]

NORMAN: Lovely idea. Do you know, I don't think the sea's all that deep. Let's paddle. [*They do.*] Able to live my own life, thanks to you. [*They laugh and play and splash around.*] She's calling me again, calling me in. You'll never get me!

IRIS: Come over here. Sit here! I'm afraid we may not survive.

NORMAN: Oh come on misery. Give me one word of hope. You give me one word of hope and I'll give you one.

IRIS: Sorry!

NORMAN: That's too bad. [*He, bending over the water, grasps a fish and holds it up.*] I've got one! A beautiful fish with my own hands. I'll cook it for you . . . [*He takes it to the pram and cooks it.*] My mother was an optimist you know.

IRIS: Optimists make me sick.

NORMAN: I'm different. For instance, if I went into the sea I'd be going in for reasons, different reasons, because I have a plan.

IRIS: Make love to me in our house of leaves. The house we built.

NORMAN: All roads lead to the sea and the sea leads to opportunity. I want a better life for our children.

IRIS: We won't have any if you don't come over here. Darling, don't look towards the sea. There's nothing out there.

NORMAN: There's marvellous land out there, better than here. Richer land.

IRIS: Your dead mother's out there. Nothing more. Come inland.

NORMAN: I want to build. I have the urge.

IRIS: Build here then. A bigger house if you need. That would be lovely, I agree.

[*He gives her the fish—she tries to eat it but can't and throws it back into the sea.*]

NORMAN: The sea's so attractive. I want to go into her, to cross over; I can hear her calling me again . . . I've won. I'm free at last. The sea's calling me, there's a land out there, a happy land. I'll build a great skyscraper . . . with my own hands, brick by brick. I'll stick it up. I'll stand up and be proud and erect a tall monument in memory of my . . . future . . . The sea is so calm, I want to go into her.

IRIS: Please be happy with me?

NORMAN: I am but I can see the land. It's not far. We can wade across. It's all glistening gold. I want it for you.

IRIS: We'll die in the sea.

NORMAN: We'll emigrate like refugees. Listen, if I say walk into the sea, you'll walk into the sea.

IRIS: Unfortunately I don't want to be left alone.

NORMAN: We'll survive. I'll leave the candlestick on the rock. Why should I do exactly what my Mother wanted. That's all there is on this shore. A candlestick on the rocks, a battered pram and a house of leaves.

[*He gets the candlestick and is about to smash the house with it.*]

IRIS: Don't destroy it . . . please! [*He does.*]

NORMAN: I had to. Don't worry. I'll give you everything you want on the other side. I'm an optimist.

IRIS: Then there's definitely no hope left.

NORMAN: Can you swim?

IRIS: No!

NORMAN: Neither can I.

[*He unzips and reveals that he has a swimming costume on. She laughs.*]

IRIS: Now a surprise.

[*She unzips. She too has one on.*]

NORMAN: Oh, you look stunning in that. [*They laugh.*] Let's go swimming then.

IRIS: Hold me tight. Dance me along the silver waves. Lift me up. [*He does.*] I can't be left alone. Dance me not into the sea but along it.

[*The seagulls cry and they both dance round and around.*]

NORMAN: The sea looks like glass. Hard and still and beautiful. Look, the morning star. Two of them. One in the sky and the other in the sea.

IRIS: You were the first and the last. [*They stand on the brink.*] Why are we drawn to the edge?

NORMAN: No more questions.

IRIS: If we can't swim, we'll probably drown. But there might be a miracle.

NORMAN [*laughs*]: Who didn't believe in miracles? Yes, there might be a miracle.

IRIS: Otherwise we're bound to drown.

NORMAN: Yes, we're bound to drown unless we can walk on the water. Who knows . . . we might be able to walk on the surface of the water.

[*They laugh and the sea booms and they dance into the water. A big splash. We can't see them anymore. We hear only the seagulls and the sea.*]